CRICKET'S GREATEST RIVALRY

CRICKET'S GREATEST RIVALRY

A HISTORY OF THE ASHES IN 10 MATCHES

SIMON HUGHES

CASSELL
ILLUSTRATED

TO MUM, DAD AND BETTANY
FOR THEIR PERPETUAL LOVE AND SUPPORT

An Hachette UK Company
www.hachette.co.uk

First published in Great Britain in 2013 by Cassell Illustrated,
a division of Octopus Publishing Group Ltd
Endeavour House, London, WC2H 8JY
www.octopusbooks.co.uk

ISBN 978-1-844-03743-8

A CIP catalogue record for this book is available from the British Library

Printed and bound by CPI Group (UK) Ltd, Croydon, CR0 4YY

10 9 8 7 6 5 4 3 2 1

Editorial Director Trevor Davies
Editor Jo Wilson
Art Director Jonathan Christie
Design and Typesetting Grade Design
Production Manager Peter Hunt
Copy Editor Caroline Taggart
Proofreader Jane Birch
Indexer Pam Scholefield

Statistics and records by Andrew Hignell (Secretary of the Association of Cricket Statisticians and
Historians) with the kind assistance of www.cricketarchive.com

CONTENTS

LOVE IS...

It has been called a perfume pot, a useless artifact, a silly little eggcup. It is barely 6 inches high and sits in a glass case at Lord's Cricket Ground. It looks like something your grandmother has at the back of her kitchen cabinet that was handed down to her by Great Uncle Harry. Inside it is, well, something. A thin layer of debris. Could be ashes. Could be dust. It doesn't really matter. That little urn means everything to the people of England and Australia. It has captured their imagination for a hundred years and counting. Sweat, blood and tears have been shed, jubilation and despair felt and lives radically altered in the constant quest for its reclamation.

The Ashes urn is, of course, just a symbol of something of much greater significance. England against Australia at cricket transcends sport. It is Old World against New, northern hemisphere versus southern, Conquerors against Colonials. Australia was claimed on behalf of Britain by Captain James Cook in 1770. Ever since, Australia has strived to establish its own identity. Its success against the Mother Country at cricket remains a barometer of the state of both nations.

At a more basic level this enduring rivalry is about intransigent fathers and impudent sons. The majority of Australians (55 per cent) are, after all, British descendants. Or were, anyway. Don Bradman's grandfather was born in Suffolk. Ray Lindwall was of Irish stock. So is Glenn McGrath. Michael Slater's parents are from Durham. Could you get more English names than Keith Miller, Mark Taylor, Steve Waugh or Michael Clarke? England versus Australia, the oldest surviving international sporting contest in the world – dating from 1877 – is essentially an age-old family feud. The Ashes is a 135-year battle for bragging rights.

Here are two quotes from totally different eras and opposite sides that emphasise the idea:

'The Australians are uneducated and an unruly mob,' Douglas Jardine, 1928.

'I couldn't wait to have a crack at 'em. I thought, "Stuff that stiff-upper-lip crap. Let's see how stiff it is when it's split." Jeff Thomson, 1974.

If that translates as brain v brawn it's a gross misrepresentation. There are just as many intellects and thickos in both countries. But the *intensity* of this rivalry has its roots in the idea of the English as upper-class snobs and the Australians as low-life convicts. Australia has shed its inferiority complex but the legacy lingers.

Mike Brearley, the Ashes-winning England captain, describes playing against Australia thus:

> 'You are carrying all the prejudices of England. You are representing deep and paranoid urges, jingoistic sentiments you may prefer to distance yourself from. But it is unavoidable.' And this is Australia's greatest bowler, Shane Warne: 'It's been drummed into you since the age of about five that if you're Australian you have just got to beat the Poms.'

Even if the players try to submerge these emotions, the public from each side will keep them afloat.

This book is the story of the Ashes. How the rivalry began, the way it ebbed and flowed, the crafty, brilliant, appalling, mystifying characters it has featured, the heroes and villains it has unearthed. England and Australia have so far played 326 Test Matches against each other (Australia are 31 wins ahead). Even though 91 of these games have been drawn, there has rarely been a dull moment. While reflecting on many of these encounters, the book focuses on 10 great matches, chosen not just because they were epics in themselves, but also because they defined an era, a style of play and had a major impact on the two countries. They captured the essence of the Ashes.

The narrative starts in the 1870s when life expectancy was 45, people travelled about in horse-drawn cabs, the average annual wage was £200 and Britain was champion of the world in most sports, mainly because it was the only nation that played them. Australia, at the time, had a population of just two million, many caught up in the Gold Rush. It didn't prevent them producing a series of magnificent cricketers who regularly beat England at the game they invented.

The story unravels the way both nations twice emerged from the ravages of war both to captivate, and to infuriate, their traumatised people. It takes a fresh and revealing look at the bodyline controversy, assesses Bradman's 'Invincibles' of 1948, chronicles England's re-emergence until they were terrorised by Lillee and Thomson, the fastest, nastiest pair of bowlers ever seen, and analyses the extraordinary prowess of Australia from 1990 onwards.

There is a rich cast. The famous names are portrayed in a variety of fascinating duels: Grace v Spofforth, Hobbs v Armstrong, Bradman against Hammond as much as Larwood, Hutton v Lindwall, Greig v Lillee, then Botham dominating one decade and Warne the next. These are the legends you'll know. But there are many you may not be so familiar with.

There's George Bonner, Australia's 'Hercules', described as 'a man without guile', who could throw a ball 120 yards and hit it further, and his English equivalent Gilbert Jessop, who regularly made a century in under an hour (OK, the fielding was pretty lame in 1900). There is Eric Hollies, the wicked English spinner who not only bowled Bradman for a duck but predicted it first. And Sid Barnes, the maverick Australian batsman who once offered an apparently short-sighted English umpire a dog and a white stick.

The wonderful thing about England v Australia is that we are mainly from the same stock. But the players on either side are so different. The gimlet-eyed, gum-chewing, gabbling Ricky Ponting is the archetypal Aussie. Andrew Strauss, his opposing captain in the 2010–11 Ashes – decent, diplomatic, self-deprecating – is the epitome of an Englishman. Australian batsmen usually pulverise the ball. English batsmen tend to persuade it. Muscular Australian bowlers traditionally run in and hit the deck hard. Sinewy Englishmen pitch it up and swing it. There are many players on both sides who haven't conformed to the stereotype. But exceptions generally prove the rule.

These differences stem from our contrasting environments. England, the green and pleasant land; Australia, a vast inhospitable country full of sand and flies. It possesses all 10 of the world's most venomous snakes, and numerous other animals that can kill or maim. The most dangerous thing in England is a wasp (or a Friday-night drunk). Historically English pitches have been soft and mottled, Australia's hard and abrasive, though the contrasts are less stark than they were.

The jargon is different too. An Englishman's bat is a 'stick' in Australia; the ball is a 'seed' or a 'pill'; Down Under an extra (e.g. a no-ball) is known as a 'sundry' and for reverse swing they say, 'It's going Irish.' Hitting a ball to the fence is 'into the pickets'. Like the bathwater going down the plug hole differently, the Australians even put the score round the opposite way: 2-10 is not an ignominious collapse – in England that would be 10 (runs) for two (wickets.)

My own first encounter with the Ashes was in 1968. As an eight-year-old my hero was Colin Cowdrey, and I saw him on a black and white TV celebrate his 100th Test by making a century against the Australians at Edgbaston. I liked the way he gracefully eased the abrasive Australian bowlers to the cover boundary, almost apologising for doing so. At the end of that series I also watched a posse of spectators dry up The Oval pitch with mops and blankets to allow time for another of my favourites, Derek Underwood, to bowl England to a dramatic victory. It planted in my mind how important it was for an Englishman to beat the Aussies (and to play them on a wet pitch).

I never earned the chance to attempt it myself, but I aided the cause by bowling every prominent English batsman of my generation into form during the county season (unfortunately I did the same for a few Australians in Sydney and Perth club cricket). I was also on hand as a sort of 13th man when Mike

Gatting's side won the Ashes in Australia in 1986–7, ferrying drinks and food to the team. With that captain it was a harder job than playing. I have seen all or part of nearly 100 Ashes Tests through six decades.

And that's the best and most unique thing about England v Australia. It is a never-ending contest. At the finish of one series you are already starting to think about the beginning of the next. Apart from during the two world wars, there has never been more than two years between encounters. It is an interminable vie for supremacy, as perpetual as employees versus the taxman. The myth of the Ashes urn provides that continuum. No one can keep it or own it or even touch it. It is the Holy Grail of sport, always tantalisingly out of reach.

In the end England v Australia is about mutual affection. There is a common bond of language, of culture, of heritage, of values. We may be 12,000 miles apart but we are really joined together as one big family. The English actually love the Australians, though they rarely admit it. The feelings are reciprocated. But we love beating each other at cricket even more.

1

THE OVAL, 1882

'The lanky Spofforth lopes in from the Gasworks End, past umpire Thoms, bowls, W G Grace goes for the drive and is bowled!…Goodness me! There is an audible gasp in the ground… W G is looking back at his broken stumps, now he's looking at the umpire, he's thinking about appealing, for what I can't imagine!… But Spofforth is having none of it and nodding towards the pavilion and that's where the Doctor better go… It's 13-1 in reply to the Colonials 63 all out…that's put the cat amongst the pigeons… and there are some dastardly pigeons alighting on the Oval square…'

England and 'the Colonists' had already played each other eight times before the Ashes were created (should that be cremated?) after that match in 1882. England had won two, Australia four and there had been two draws. Even from the start England were playing catch-up. All but one of these test matches took place in Australia, which is why the 1882 one in England (above) was so momentous.

The first few tours between the countries were largely money-making enterprises, with slightly random itineraries and lots of disputes about players' fees. The standard of play – and opponents – was very variable, and so was the size of the crowds. The occasional game between a chosen 'England XI' and the Australians was only labelled as a Test Match some years later. What was to become the great Anglo–Australian rivalry had very convoluted beginnings, but bear with me…

And They're Off…

The first ever 'Test' took place in 1877. Played at the Richmond Police Paddock – now the Melbourne Cricket Ground – it was the culmination of a two-month tour of New Zealand and Australia by James Lillywhite's (professional) England XI and was the fourth such tour of Australia. The original one had been initiated indirectly by Charles Dickens, who, after a successful speaking trip round the United States in 1860, was invited to do the same thing in Australia. He declined claiming exhaustion, a polite way of saying he didn't fancy hauling himself around an inhospitable land full of spiders and ex-convicts. A substitute attraction was sought – and found: an English cricket team, offered £150 a man (a considerable increase on their usual fee of £3 a match). Captained by Surrey's Heathfield Harman Stephenson, they drew 15,000 spectators to their first match against 18 of Melbourne. Yes, 18 – the Aussies were trying it on from the start!

That 1862 tour was a financial success and, by the time of Lillywhite's visit, Australian cricket had evolved considerably: they now felt obliged to field only 15 players at a time. They were enhanced by English professionals like Surrey's William Caffyn, who remained behind after tours and coached them in the art of staying in, bowling overarm and not walking when they nicked the cover off it. Further strengthened by some excellent English players lured Down Under by the Gold Rush, the Australians were becoming rather good. (A Melbourne club side – Castlemaine

— had actually beaten the 1862 Englishmen, though they had 22 players, and a report of the time suggested that 'just possibly the abundance of lobsters and champagne was a contributing factor'.)

By the 1870s club cricket in Sydney and Melbourne was becoming strong (the Melbourne Cricket Club — Australia's MCC — which was founded in 1838, invited and funded the first international touring teams.) So strong, in fact, that at the end of the 1877 tour Lillywhite's men were challenged to a 'grand combination match' against XI — yes, 11 — of Victoria and New South Wales. This was the game at the Richmond Police Paddock. It was hurriedly arranged and most of the Englishmen were suffering from seasickness or fatigue following the New Zealand leg of the trip. They had only 11 fit players. It wouldn't be the last time that happened to an England team in Australia.

Beginning on 15 March 1877, the match lasted four days and the Australians won it by 45 runs, thanks largely to an extraordinary knock of 165 not out (out of the Combined Australian XI's first innings total of 247) by Charles Bannerman, who had been born in Woolwich, Kent. Left-arm spinner Tom Kendall took 7-55 in England's second innings. He was from Bedford. In fact six of that first 'Australian' team had been born abroad — four in England, one in Ireland and one in India.

Subsequently this game was labelled the first ever Test Match, because it was regarded as a proper and equal 'test' of the cricketing strengths of the two countries. It was a moot point. Not only were the Aussie team of mixed origins, but also England had left all their amateurs at home after ructions with the professionals on a previous tour. The amateurs were the country's leading batsmen (they tended to leave the professionals to do the bowling, which the 'Gentlemen' thought was rather below them).

The absentees included W G Grace, who had already become the first player to make 2000 runs in an English season, but had stayed at home to finish his medical degree. Also missing was England's first-choice wicketkeeper Ted Pooley, who was stuck in jail in New Zealand for 'affray' – that's fighting to you and me – while for the Aussies 'the Demon' Frederick Spofforth, soon to become a legendary fast bowler, had refused to play as he didn't approve of the wicketkeeper chosen, the unorthodox but brilliant Jack Blackham. Added to that the Englishmen perpetually overdid the amber nectar at lunchtimes during the game. So this first Test wasn't quite the definitive encounter it could have been.

The English *Morning Post* did not superimpose James Lillywhite's head on top of a turnip after this humbling defeat, or threaten to send his team to the moon. Well, rockets hadn't been invented then. Anyway, the news didn't reach Blighty for several days and when it did *The Times* announced that the match 'began and ended in good temper and Lillywhite's pecuniary success must have consoled him for his defeat'. In other words, as long as the organiser made money, no one gave a monkey's about the result. Frankly, in early March people in England were more interested in the preparations for the University Boat Race in, as the *Morning Post* put it, 'the most trying weather'. (On page five of the paper, below a report of the crews on the river, is an advert for Rossetter's Hair Restorer. Even then sport and receding hairlines were inextricably linked, more than 70 years before Graham Gooch was born.)

A re-match between England and the two Australian states was organised at the same ground 16 days later. The English won by four wickets, chasing 122 for victory. The bowling figures of Nottinghamshire's medium pacer Alfred Shaw deserve a mention. In the match he sent down 74 overs, 46 of which were maidens, and conceded just 57 runs without, however, taking a wicket. A stout, niggardly slow-medium pacer, Shaw was the archetypal Victorian – the type who believed that children, and batsmen, should be seen and not heard. His bowling was like a gag (not the amusing type); relentlessly accurate, he never delivered a wide and conceded fewer runs than he bowled overs. Admittedly at this time there were only four balls in an over, but even so... It was the cricketing version of Mogadon. But he did take over 2000 wickets at an astonishing average of 12 in a professional career spanning 33 years, including an amazing 19-150 in one innings against 22 of Newcastle (Australia).

So England v Australia was 1-1 after two. Even Stevens. England were not worried, reasoning that they were missing W G, their best player, and were tired after a long tour in harsh surroundings, so one loss was excusable. In hindsight it was a wake-up call which the English didn't heed. Despite England's 150-year head start in the development of the game, the Australians now knew they had their measure and were capable of beating them. It was the beginning of a long and tortuous struggle...

Demonised

The Australians were invited to England the following year (1878) in a tour arranged by Lillywhite. They were led by David Gregory – whose moderate batting is reflected in his progress down the batting order (2, 4, 9, 10, 11) – and they were a huge draw. More than 30,000 people turned out to watch them play Surrey at The Oval, compared to just 4000 who had watched the FA Cup final at the same venue. The feature of the tour was an extraordinary performance by 'the Demon' Spofforth in a match against the MCC at Lord's, scheduled for three days but completed in just one.

Including W G, the MCC team was ostensibly an England XI (England were still called the MCC on tour until the late 1980s), but they were routed for 33 all out in the first innings (Spofforth 6-4) and a pathetic 19 in the second (Spofforth 4-16, including W G bowled second ball), enabling Australia to win by nine wickets a match which lasted less than five hours. It wasn't regarded as a Test Match – well, it was more like Kwik Cricket. This was the game that awoke the English cricketing establishment to the potential threat of what the papers often liked to call 'the Colonists'.

Spofforth was tall (6ft 3in) and spindly and described as 'all arms, legs and nose'. He was depicted as a sort of nasty insect in *Punch* (see the picture in plate section). His bowling was decidedly slippery, though it is interesting to note that two of his victims in the Lord's match were stumped. In those days wicketkeepers, especially Australia's Jack Blackham, were masochists who stood up to almost everything, but if Spofforth was that fast batsmen would have been edging back onto their stumps rather than stumbling out of their crease.

In fact the Demon deserved his moniker for crafty variations of pace and cut – he tended to bowl more slowly on damp English pitches – and a peerless appreciation, and exploitation, of batsmen's weaknesses. His duels with W G were described as 'like forked lightning threatening the great oak'. Facing him on a bouncy wicket, often without batting gloves, was described by one player as like standing 'on the brink of the tomb'. He tormented England for a decade. He was like a 19th-century Glenn McGrath with Dennis Lillee's moustache. Not a pleasant proposition.

That Australian touring team of 1878 played 37 matches in England, losing just seven (there were no 'Tests'). The English public were surprised by their success, taken aback that the alleged 'mysteries' of the game were not, as *The Times* put it, 'the exclusive privilege of a small island in the northern hemisphere'. The paper went on, with quite cringing pomposity, to say that the Australians had 'given us no opportunity to indulge in a pleasing sense of compassionate superiority. They have produced an eleven very hard to beat and quite impossible to despise,' despite 'Australia not being so naturally as favourable a home for the game as England'. Given the choice of a biting wind slicing through your bones in Chester-le-Street or a baking sun in Sydney which soon banishes any residual stiffness, I know which I'd prefer.

Australia hosted England again in 1879. Lord Harris (of Kent) recruited the England team, which this time did include some amateurs, though again not W G Grace. There was one Test, again in Melbourne, in which Spofforth was the decisive influence. He took 13 wickets in the match, including the first hat trick in Test history, and twice obliterated England's middle order, creating the first of many of England's one-Test wonders. In this case they were the Reverend Vernon Royle and Francis MacKinnon, the 35th MacKinnon of MacKinnon. Being picked for England had suddenly become the preserve of the titled and privileged. It didn't do them any good: they were hammered by 10 wickets.

In a subsequent game against New South Wales in Sydney there was a dispute surrounding the running out of Australia's Billy Murdoch. The crowd invaded the field and Lord Harris was assaulted. Inevitably this caused outrage in the English press – they seemed more interested in the assault than in the result. Already you could feel a conflict between the old masters and the new pretenders stirring.

For the first Test between the teams in England – at The Oval in 1880 – Spofforth was absent. There had been some adverse comment about his bowling action in a previous match against Yorkshire and he developed a mysterious finger injury before the Oval game. Making his Test debut, W G Grace took full toll to make 152 in England's first innings and lay the foundations for a five-wicket win. So now we are at two Tests all.

Alfred 'Mogadon' Shaw – the Notts bowler who once recorded innings figures of 41 overs, 34 maidens, 7 runs and 7 wickets against MCC – captained England on tour to Australia in

1881–2. Again the tour was financially successful (they obviously hadn't used Shaw's bowling statistics in the marketing), but of the four Tests played Australia won two and the others were drawn. Overall, then, it was England 2, Australia 4, draws 2.

Runners and Riders

So that is the prologue to the most important match in cricketing history, England v Australia at The Oval in August 1882. Britain was booming at the time. Almost a third of Africa was now pink, manufacturing trade was flourishing and bank holidays had been introduced. Football, 'lawn' tennis and rugby had been codified, offering the Victorians plenty of leisure pursuits. The spirit of adventure was evident, with newspapers full of adverts for train rides to the coast and voyages to far-off destinations – it was £4 to sail to America and about £15 to Australia.

London, the leading city in the world with a population of 2.3 million, was buzzing with activity, invention and, apparently, 80,000 hookers. There were all sorts of unusual attractions on offer including, that August, an audience with the 'Famous Royal American Midgets' at the Imperial Theatre, attended by Her Majesty Queen Victoria. A sort of early version of the Royal Variety Show, it was hosted by General Mite (who weighed 9lb) and Millie Edwards (7lb) – the 1880s equivalents of Ant and Dec.

The sport of the day – racing and cricket (not a mention of football, even though by mid-August the transfer window was well and truly open) – was contained in two columns in the paper, where a sort of fledgling County Championship featuring 11 teams was in full swing. The county matches vied for space with Harrow Wanderers v Gentlemen of Yorkshire, but at least they got some coverage.

Lancashire and Notts were the two strongest sides in a random County Championship in which some teams played 16 games and others only four. It was left to the press to decide who were the champions, usually based on fewest defeats rather than most wins. Thus the county sides, a mixture of amateurs and professionals, were littered with blockers.

England had a decent batch of players to choose from. The selection panel included Vyell Walker, a former Middlesex captain and president of MCC who took bags of wickets in the 1860s with slow underarms, and the Lord Harris mentioned earlier. Harris was a vast influence on cricket in this era, both as a player and administrator – reflected by the presence of the Harris Garden at Lord's and a huge portrait in the Long Room.

The team they chose was as good as England had ever fielded. The captain was Albert 'Monkey' Hornby, a feisty Lancastrian opening batsman who also captained England at rugby. He was joined by his regular Lancashire opening partner Dick Barlow, a renowned stonewaller and bowler of useful left-arm spin. Hornby, who looked the spit of Thompson and Thompson in *Tintin*, was an amateur and Barlow a professional; because they therefore had different changing rooms and came onto the field through different gates, they often only met in mid-pitch.

The rest of the batting consisted of W G Grace, the solid amateur 'Bunny' Lucas and the spectacular professional George Ulyett, a clean-hitting Bothamesque all-rounder known as 'Happy Jack' for his constant whistling. Charles Studd (one of three brothers who all played for Middlesex), who topped the national batting averages that year and had just become the second man after Grace to perform the season's double of 1000 first-class runs and 100 wickets, completed the top six.

Also handy with the willow was Notts' Billy Barnes, who was rather fond of his beer. Staggering to the wicket the worse for wear in one county game he made a match-saving hundred, was reprimanded by the committee and retorted, 'How many of you could make a hundred drunk or sober?' It brings to mind a classic retort after Bob Willis bowled a succession of no-balls for Warwickshire at Edgbaston one day. 'Come on, Willis, keep your foot behind the line,' shouted one irate spectator in best Brummy after yet another transgression. 'Fuck off and build a Maestro!' a colleague yelled back.

The Hon. Alfred Lyttelton was the England wicketkeeper. A superb all-round sportsman, he also played football for England and excelled at tennis. In one later Test Match against the Australians he was put on to bowl his slow lobs and, still wearing his keeping pads, winkled them out, taking 4-19. The England bowling was in the hands of Ted Peate – first in the line of superb Yorkshire left-arm spinners – Ulyett, Grace and Allan Steel, almost the equal of Grace as an all-rounder, who bowled slow-medium. In today's parlance he'd be known as a 'phantom'. The team was made up of six amateurs – including four Cambridge University blues – and five professionals, who were all from the northern counties. The era of Central Contracts was a fair way off. 119 years, to be exact.

After a seven-week voyage the Australians had arrived in England in May with the best team they had yet fielded. Back home, interstate cricket had been underway for 20 years (the first match between Victoria and New South Wales – who initially played in socks or bare feet – was in 1856, though the official competition, the Sheffield Shield, didn't begin until 1892) and some considerable talents had emerged. The captain was Billy Murdoch, a prolific batsman who two years later would score the first ever Test-match double century. There were Spofforth and Blackham, a fine opening pair in Hugh Massie and Alick Bannerman, brother of the first Test-Match centurion Charles, and frugal medium pacer and fearless close fielder Harry Boyle, a sort of Brian Close of the 1880s.

There was also the colossal George Bonner, a 6ft 6in bear of a man often referred to as 'the Australian Hercules' for his gigantic hitting. From rural New South Wales and described as 'a man without guile', he had caused a stir on a previous tour during a dinner at the Johnson Club in Fleet Street. Having confessed that he had never heard of the great author Dr Samuel Johnson, after whom the club was named, he was subjected to mocking laughter. Unabashed, he rose from his seat and pronounced, 'What is more, I come from a place where you can ride a horse sixty miles a day for three months and never meet a soul who has heard of Dr Johnson either.'

As soon as he had stepped off the SS *Assam* at Plymouth, Bonner won a £100 bet with a fellow passenger who had challenged him to throw a cricket ball 110 yards without a warm-up. On a nearby parade ground he hurled it 119 yards from a standing position and made off with the money, worth five figures in today's currency. The Australians then embarked on an arduous itinerary of 28 matches against an assortment of teams – counties, universities, clubs – and won 24 of them. This served as an enticing build-up to the one-off Test Match. There was inevitably huge public interest.

Oh, for Peate's Sake!

The one-off Test was assigned three days, beginning on Monday 28 August. The *Morning Post* declared it 'lamentable' that there was only one match organised between Australia and the full strength of England and 'at a late period in the season when the weather is uncertain and the light so bad that play cannot be prolonged after six o'clock'. Administrators never can get it quite right, can they?

The Australians stayed in the Tavistock Hotel in Covent Garden, which at the time was a poor area regarded as 'noisy and smelly'. It was a large place with 200 rooms where the team stayed regularly, not necessarily because it was a former bordello with a woman in every room. The players were transported to the ground at 10.30 by horse-drawn carriage.

There had been a lot of rain in the run-up to the match, and of course there were no covers or super-soppers in those days: the pitch was left open to the elements. A drawing of the event suggests it was indistinguishable from the outfield. England, with their deep batting strength and lots of players in form, were favourites to beat 'the Colonialists'.

Some 20,000 spectators crammed into the ground, paying a total of £1000. The captains – England's Hornby and Australia's Murdoch – tossed up, in the pavilion, at 12 o'clock. The Australian won, but there was no time allotted for the captains' interviews, for Geoff Boycott to stick his key in the pitch (he would probably have lost it if he had) or the five pre-match commercial breaks. Ten minutes later the England team emerged, the six amateurs first, followed by the professionals, and then the Australian opening pair of Charles Bannerman and Hugh Massie.

Not long afterwards Massie was walking back, bowled by a yorker from Ulyett. In fact Ulyett might very well have invented the delivery and given rise to its name, since he was from Yorkshire and 'to put Yorkshire on someone' meant, in 19th-century parlance, to hoodwink or deceive them. The damp in the well-used pitch was making the ball jump and 14 successive maiden overs – bowled by the spinners Barlow and Peate – followed as Bannerman and Murdoch literally dug in. But on the hour Murdoch played on to Peate, and Bonner, having nearly been clean bowled first ball, was yorked for 1. The score was 22-3. The crowd went wild – well, there was 'a tumult of applause' – when Grace dived and caught Bannerman left-handed at point. 26-4. It was like the first morning at Lord's in the epic 2005 series when the pace quartet Harmison, Flintoff, Hoggard and Jones ran amok. Except that this was death by stealth...

At lunch, taken at 2pm, the Colonials were 48-6. The England spinners had shared five wickets. Soon after 3pm the Australians were all out for 63, their lowest total of the tour. Dick Barlow had taken 5-19 from 31 overs and Ted Peate 4-31. Eighty overs, 52 of them maidens, had been bowled in the two and a quarter hours' play. That's about 35 overs an hour! But before anyone gets on their high horse comparing that with the sluggish over rates today, it should be remembered that these were four-ball overs, that 'run-ups' were a couple of paces and that there were no endless huddles at the fall of a wicket (everyone pretty much stayed where they were) or batsmen interminably marking their guard or punching gloves between balls. Not many of them even wore gloves.

The exultant crowd in their top hats and waistcoats waited expectantly for the England openers to emerge. Twenty minutes later Grace strode out, accompanied by Barlow. They were confronted by the Demon Spofforth from the Gasworks (now Vauxhall) End, though his field setting of a slip, a short leg and everyone else in a ring did not exactly give them palpitations.

Still, Grace fell for it, being bowled by Spofforth for 4 to a collective gasp from the spectators. Grace looked back aghast at his disturbed stumps, contemplating whether to give it the 'Strong wind today, umpire!' ruse, but soon realised there wasn't and made his way off. Some umpires were prepared to stand up to him anyway. When he tried that on one occasion the official replied, 'Very strong wind, Doctor! Mind it doesn't blow your cap off on the way back to the pavilion!' When Barlow was caught at 'forward point' (silly mid-off) it was 18-2.

In their contrasting ways Lucas and Ulyett stabilised the situation and with a third-wicket partnership of 39 took England to within six of the Colonials' score. But confidence got the better of Ulyett and 'rushing out wildly to drive Spofforth' he missed and was easily stumped by Blackham for 26. This rash move was a turning point in the match, as the innings now went into decline. Lucas and Lyttelton were caught behind and Studd was bowled third ball by Spofforth. A couple of lusty blows from Steel got England past 100, but only just. Bizarrely, Hornby, who opened for Lancashire, kept himself back until number 10 and lasted only nine balls against the rampant Spofforth. The Demon ended with figures of 7-46, having bowled 36.3 overs out of the innings total of 71, not only unchanged throughout, but also with two overs in succession (the 27th and 28th). This was allowed back then if the bowler wanted to change ends. Spofforth's spell was an exceptional feat of stamina, because although they were only four-ball overs, he got only four balls rest between each one.

So England had a narrow but precious lead of 38. The *Morning Post* assessed it thus:

> *It was incredible looking at the previous performance of the Australians and the remarkable batting strength of England that in the course of five hours actual cricket both sides should be dismissed – Australia for 63 and England for 101. For this failure three good reasons can be assigned – the very difficult condition of the wicket, the extraordinarily good bowling and the general over-anxiety.*

The interest in the match had intensified overnight and even more people scrabbled to get into the ground for the second day. The crowd was 'mainly of the middle class,' said the *Daily Chronicle*, 'but there was a number of the rougher element about.' Play was scheduled to begin at 11.30 but heavy rain in the morning forced a delay.

When it eventually did begin after midday the pitch was still a quagmire and there was a feeling among the England players that Hornby's agreement to take the field had been misjudged. So it proved, as the bowlers struggled to keep their feet and a spade had to be used to dig out the footholds and fill them with sawdust. The ball was described as 'like a bar of soap'. Briefly, conditions were in the batsmen's favour and, seizing his opportunity, Massie, something of a dasher, played a brilliant innings.

Favouring the offside and not afraid to hit the ball in the air, he plundered the bowling, hitting nine fours, some of which cleared the boundary on the full (until 1910 a six was awarded only if the ball was hit out of the ground), and totally dominating the opening partnership with Bannerman. Dropped once on the long-off boundary when he had made 37, he brought up his own 50 – the only one in the match – in under an hour.

Eventually he took one liberty too many and was bowled by Steel. Thereafter the innings slowly subsided as the pitch dried out and became unpredictable. In the circumstances Billy Murdoch's 29 was a gem, as he artfully eked out runs with the ball popping and scooting and wickets falling at the other end. Lunch was taken with the Australians 99-5, leading by 61.

At 113-6 there was controversy. In partnership with Sammy Jones, Murdoch turned the slow-medium Steel for a run on the leg side. The throw was wayward and wicketkeeper Lyttelton had to move away from the stumps to collect it. He lobbed the ball to W G Grace, standing beside the wicket. Jones, who had easily made his ground, now wandered out of it to pat down a divot on the pitch, thinking the ball was dead. Grace, who had a intricate knowledge of the laws of the game, whipped off the bails and appealed.

Umpire Bob Thoms had no option but to give Jones out. Well, he could have said, 'Is that a warning, Doctor?' or 'Isn't that appeal a bit hasty?' but, clearly not being from the school of authority, he said, 'If you claim it, sir, then out!' He denied being this deferential afterwards. People usually do. But out Jones was. This was a good

94 years before Tony Greig threw out the West Indian Alvin Kallicharran for wandering out of his ground at the end of the day. W G was a century ahead of his time.

This was the first in a fruity list of diplomatic incidents that have spiced up the Ashes contests. The Australian captain Murdoch stood at the crease, steaming. But there was nothing he could do. There was no Decision Review System. And anyway Grace was an enormous, imposing and hugely respected personality. Practically deified. No one was going to challenge him. So the decision stood.

Soon afterwards Murdoch ran himself out. When Spofforth was bowled Australia were all out for 122. England needed 85 to win. Time was not a factor. It was 3.15 on the second day, so there was still a possible day and a half left for play, weather permitting.

The teams gathered in their dressing rooms. Hornby, the England captain, made a significant change to the batting order, promoting himself to open with Grace, dropping Barlow to number 3 and moving everyone else down one position. In the Australian room, Spofforth resembled Devon Malcolm. His remarks didn't quite have the bluntness of Malcolm's 'You guys are history!' (his prognosis to the South Africans after being hit on the head by a bouncer) but, encountering Grace before the resumption of play, he said, 'This will lose you the match.' Knowing the spiciness of the pitch and his own exceptional ability, he told his team, 'This thing can be done.'

Spofforth was quite some adversary. He was an intimidating sight (see the picture in plate section) and knew exactly how to exploit these specific conditions (after 30 previous matches on tour, during which he had taken 140 wickets). He was also amazingly versatile. Variation, he said, 'was only any use if you learn to hide it. The sole object in variation is to make the batsman think the ball is faster or slower than it really is.' He experimented with different grips and understood that if you held part of the ball in your hand (rather than the whole) you could bring your arm over at the same speed and the delivery would be slower. Such variations of pace are de rigueur today. But as a master of disguise, Spofforth was a pioneer.

The England run chase was delayed slightly because W G, in doctorly mode, had to attend to a spectator who had suffered a heart attack. It was a portent of things to come. When the innings began Spofforth bowled his fastest, with wicketkeeper Blackham standing an unusually long way back. Grace survived the first over but confessed later that Spofforth's bowling was 'intensely difficult and most disconcerting'. The score progressed mainly in quick singles. It's hard to believe the colossal Grace was nifty between the wickets, though worth remembering that aged 18 he scored 224 in a county match, then went off to Crystal Palace and won the 440-yards hurdles championship. But with the score at 15 Hornby was bowled by Spofforth. In the same over, Barlow, one of the safest batsmen in England, was bowled for nought by a sharp off-cutter.

Grace was now joined by Ulyett. The situation eased, a few runs were collected and Grace drove a ball towards the onside boundary. Here it was intercepted by what was described as 'an urchin' who had strayed onto the field and potentially earned England an extra run (it might have been fielded if he hadn't been there). The culprit, who had apparently been trying to help, was ejected from the ground. He wasn't dressed as a bride or a nun. Maybe if he had been they would have let him stay.

Spofforth changed from the Gasworks to the Pavilion End, again bowling two consecutive overs. (Imagine if Shane Warne had been able to do that on a last-day pitch!) But Grace was handling him comfortably and Ulyett was looking positive. Grace brought up the 50 in the 22nd over with a meaty hit to leg. There were only 35 to win and 8 wickets in hand. Victory looked secure.

At last, in his 13th consecutive over, Spofforth whistled one past Ulyett's bat, just grazing the edge, and he was out caught behind for 11. Calamity struck England in the next over from the accurate Boyle, as Grace went to drive over the top but found the hands of Bannerman at mid-off. A yard either side and it would have been four. The Australians were delirious. Grace was out for 32; England were now 53–4 and looking decidedly jittery.

Bunny Lucas was at the wicket with Alfred Lyttelton. Mostly through Lyttelton they added 10 runs in five overs, meaning England now needed 20. But a sort of mesmerised inertia set in and a succession of 12 maidens ensued. The pitch was 'drying and bumpy' and the Australians were fielding like 'terriers'. Lucas was resolutely blocking out Spofforth, to such an extent that the Demon suggested a misfield might be worthwhile to get Lyttelton down his end. He had his wish: a single to Lyttelton off Boyle materialised, from a misfield. But a further four maidens were the result. The batsmen seemed hypnotised. The crowd were equally spellbound.

In his 26th over Spofforth, firing rapidly from out of the dark background of the pavilion, a gloom further enhanced by thick wafts of tobacco smoke from the members' area, found a way through Lyttelton's defence, bowling him middle stump. It was 66–5. Still 19 to win. Steel, a reputable batsman, came in and immediately looked like a novice. He was clearly as nervous as Hornby, the England captain, who was pacing up and down in the dressing room and fiddling with the batting order, mysteriously holding back Charles Studd, the leading batsman in the country that year.

Lucas, who had not scored a run between the 26th and 51st overs, edged a boundary to ecstatic cheering. Fifteen to win. But Steel was suckered by Spofforth's slower ball and poked a return catch. 70-6 soon became 70-7 as Maurice Read was clean bowled second ball by a vicious Spofforth breakback. The Demon had taken six of the seven wickets to fall. The crowd stood in disbelief.

Now Billy Barnes walked to the middle. There was still no Studd, who was apparently strutting about in the dressing room with a blanket over his head. Barnes shuffled past Australia's Tommy Horan on his way to the wicket. 'By Jove, Barnes, this is an exciting match!' Horan chirped. 'Yes, but you'll win,' Barnes replied, barely able to get the resigned words out because his throat was so dry.

It was still 15 to win. One spectator was so nervous he chewed pieces out of his umbrella handle. In the members' stand people were heard declaring that the suspense would 'surely spoil their appetite for dinner'. One man said, 'If only they would play with straight bats, they would surely get the runs.' His female companion replied, 'Really? Couldn't you get them some?'

Barnes, certainly no tailender, pushed Spofforth for two and then a fumble by wicketkeeper Blackham allowed three byes. Ten to win. If you happened to be at Edgbaston in 2005, or watching on TV as the Aussies' ninth-wicket pair of Warne and Lee edged ever closer to their unlikely target, you'll have some idea what the atmosphere was like. It was what the modern player likes to call an arse-twitcher.

More drama. Lucas dragged the next ball from Spofforth – the first he had faced from the Demon for 10 overs – into his stumps. His vigil was over. It had not been a productive one. From 55 balls faced he had managed just one single and a streaky edged four (that's a 'strike rate' of 9.5). In a harsher era, the finger would have been pointed at him afterwards for his limp, inert performance, allowing the Australian bowlers to build intolerable pressure – I mean, 12 maidens in a row, it sounds more like a Jane Austen novel than a Test Match. But in the 1880s papers, the innings of

'Mr' Lucas (the 'Mr' in deference to his amateur status) was complimented for his 'exhibition of superb defence'.

Now, with the score 75–8 and still 10 to win, in came Charles Studd, the man who had already done the double that season. Surely he would be able to shepherd England home? Unfortunately for him and England Lucas had been out to the last ball of the 54th over, so Studd was the non-striker. He watched helplessly as Barnes was caught off his glove from Boyle's nagging medium pace.

The left-arm spinner Ted Peate was England's last man. He had no great pretensions as a batsman. A bit of a Monty Panesar, if truth be told, with a touch of Phil Tufnell-maverick thrown in. His orders were to survive the rest of the over – just three balls – to allow Studd the strike.

He squirted his first ball for two past square leg. Spectators tossed their top hats in the air. Eight to win. Questions might have been asked afterwards as to why Studd agreed to the second run: presumably he thought Peate had a better chance of holding out at the same end against the medium-paced Boyle rather than the Demon Spofforth. Peate played and missed at the next ball. There were relieved gasps in the crowd, seven or eight deep cramming round the boundary. He had one more ball to negotiate. He flailed at it. He missed it. It bowled him.

Many years later the Poet Laureate John Masefield summed the moment up beautifully:

> *Boyle took the ball; he turned; he ran; he bowled.*
> *All England's watching heart was stricken cold.*
> *Peate's whirling bat met nothing in its sweep.*
> *The ball put all his wickets in a heap…*

Australia had won by seven runs. It was, of course, England's first defeat at home. They had lost their last eight wickets for 26 and

Spofforth had taken 7-44 from 28 successive overs with not so much as a drink or pee break, to give him an extraordinary 14-90 (from 64 overs) in the match. It must be considered one of the finest bowling performances in the history of the game, and stood as the best Australian match figures for 90 years. The England batsmen had played out 28 maidens of the 55 overs bowled and Charles Studd hadn't faced a single ball. No wonder he deserted cricket soon after and became a missionary.

There was a fairly disorderly invasion of the field, and Spofforth was chaired off by, one assumes, a bunch of Englishmen. Earl's Court hadn't been taken over by Australians then. 'The victorious eleven were cheered as neither they nor anyone else had ever been cheered,' said the London *Standard*. 'Hats and umbrellas were waved in the air and the men were called for in front of the pavilion. Although Englishmen are naturally sorry that our eleven did not win, no one can grudge the Australians their victory.' The drama was too much for the heart-attack man, who fainted, was carted off into the pavilion with blood coming out of his mouth and was soon pronounced dead.

There was tentative conjecture in the England dressing room that Grace's action in running out Jones had galvanised Australia in general and Spofforth in particular. Grace himself remained unrepentant. 'Well, well,' he said, 'I left six men to get 30-odd runs and they couldn't do it.' As usual, he had a point.

It was an unambiguous reference to England's lack of gumption, of initiative, which is strange and uncharacteristic given the nation's pre-eminence in the world at the time. But even the toughest, hardiest individuals can sometimes be overcome by situations, and momentum shifts in sport are often imperceptible and therefore irresistible. There are so many occasions when a team thinks it's won the match, the players mentally relax and suddenly the tables are turned. Think Headingley '81, for instance.

RIP

The press reaction to this English defeat was mainly sympathetic. 'The victory reflects immense credit on Australian cricket as a whole,' said the *Morning Post*. 'We do not believe – and indeed very few Englishmen, and only a minority of colonialists will believe – that this match proves Australian cricketers to be better than our own.' Then it added the faintly smug rider, 'On a false and treacherous wicket, cricket quality has a strange tendency to level down.' With put-downs like that in the national press, how can we ever wonder that the Aussies want to give the Poms a good kicking?

The magazine *Punch* printed a poem entitled 'The Lesson of the Licking', of which the first, most damning verse was:

> *Well done Cornstalks! Whipt us,*
> *Fair and square!*
> *Was it luck that tript us?*
> *Was it 'scare'?*
> *Kangaroo Land's 'Demon', or our own*
> *Want of 'devil', coolness, nerve, backbone?*

The final line was clearly a rhetorical question. England lacked what the Australians would call a bit of 'mongrel'.

Death notices were a huge feature of Victorian newspapers. The front page was dominated by them (as well as births, marriages and times of trains from Fenchurch Street to Felixstowe). In keeping, the weekly magazine *Cricket* published a mock obituary on 31 August.

> *Sacred to the memory*
> *Of England's Supremacy in the*
> *Cricket-Field*
> *Which expired*

On the 29th day of August, at The Oval
'It's end was Peate.'

It must have been this notice that influenced Reginald Brooks, a young journalist on the *Sporting Times*, to write his now-infamous mock obituary the next day. He was the son of Shirley Brooks, editor of *Punch*, who was also a supporter of the Cremation Society. Cremation was very much a hot topic of the time, no pun intended, with much debate about the morality of the practice that was common in other parts of Europe but had yet to be legalised in Britain.

So, on page five of the *Sporting Times* of Saturday 2 September, wedged between the starting prices for the St Leger and whimsical comment on the milking of cows, was a small square panel, inside which read:

In Affectionate Remembrance
Of
ENGLISH CRICKET
Which died at The Oval
On
29th August 1882,
Deeply lamented by a large circle of sorrowing
friends and acquaintances
RIP

NB. The body will be cremated and the ashes taken to Australia.

It was clearly the kind of joke for which Brooks, a hard-drinking satirist who died at 34, was known. It would have gone more or less unnoticed but for the fact that only 12 days later – on 14 September – an England team captained by the Hon. Ivo Bligh was due to set sail for Australia. Because the tour was imminent and the Australians remained in England playing a few more festival matches, the idea that England were going to retrieve 'the ashes' gained popularity over those few days, among both the players and the public. On departure Bligh, christened 'St Ivo' by *Punch*, pledged to bring back 'the ashes' of English cricket, despite the fact that his team, with their baggy shirts and outlandish blazers and facial hair, looked more like the Traveling Wilburys.

Bligh, an old Etonian and a classic sort of amateur captain who batted at 9 and didn't bowl, was a confident chap and he kept the issue simmering on arrival in Australia. 'We have come to beard the kangaroo in his den and try to recover those ashes,' he said, making light of the team's lengthy voyage, during which their boat the SS *Peshawar* nearly sank in a storm. At a prominent Melbourne banquet given to honour the triumphant Australians, their captain Billy Murdoch proclaimed:

> *Our boys fairly won the Ashes, and we confidently rely on them to retain possession, at least for the present. When, as we hope we have shown our visitors that they cannot recover the Ashes, we can then place the sacred dust in a suitable urn in our Public Library…*

What always seems to grate for Australians is that, despite them having won more Tests against England than they have lost, and at one point winning eight Ashes series in a row (1989–2003), the famous urn itself has never resided in an Australian public library, or anywhere else apart from Lord's Cricket Ground, London NW8. In a way, it just adds to the mythical status of the contest.

There are conflicting stories about the origin and contents of the actual urn. One version suggests that at a country-house match at the home of the Australian aristocrat Sir William Clarke near Melbourne, during which the English players pummelled the ball everywhere, a miniature urn was presented to Bligh by Clarke's wife, who was known for her sense of humour. It was alleged to contain the ashes either of a bail, or of the leather casing of the match ball, which she and various friends, including Florence Murphy, whom Bligh later married, had burnt.

An equally credible story is that Lady Clarke presented a little terracotta urn – possibly a souvenir of her travels in Europe – containing the ashes of a bail to Bligh after England had won the third Test of the three-match series that had followed. Accompanied by a little velvet bag to put it in, the urn was inscribed with the words:

When Ivo goes back with the urn, the urn;
Studds, Steel, Read and Tylecote will return, return;
The Welkin will ring loud,
The great crowd will feel proud,
Seeing Barlow and Bates with the urn, the urn;
And the rest coming home with the urn.

We will never know for sure, as Bligh squirrelled the gift away without mentioning it again, and it remained on his Kent mantelpiece until after his death in 1927; his widow, Florence, then presented it to the MCC. This 6-inch high eggcup remains in a glass display cabinet in the MCC museum and has been let out only once (for a tour round Australia accompanying Andrew Flintoff's hapless team in 2006–7, when it was given its own business-class airline seat). The contents had been X-rayed a few years before, revealing some 'material' in the bottom, but also a number of worrying cracks in the urn itself, dissuading the MCC from further investigation. In truth they are happy to perpetuate the myth.

And why not? Too much information is dangerous.

2

FOURTH TEST, OLD TRAFFORD, 1902

*'Rhodes, left-arm round, tosses one up, and Trumper
with that great forward movement drives…over
mid-on's head…two bounces and into the crowd.
A grand shot! What daredevilry this Colonial
possesses! That takes him onto 62 in just an hour
and 10 minutes and brings up the Australian
hundred. What capital batting…'*

The concept of 'the Ashes' faded temporarily after that 1882–3
tour. Even though England and Australia played each other almost
every year through the 1880s, they weren't mentioned again until
the Australian sports journalist C P Moody referred to them in a
book about Australian cricket published in 1894. Perhaps the
oversight was deliberate because the Australians, riven by internal
disputes about money, lost every series between 1883 and 1890 to
a selection of highly professional English outfits. England won
eight series in a row and took a 19-10 overall lead in the Tests. The
phoenix had risen again.

W G Grace had missed the Ivo Bligh tour because, despite
being an 'amateur', he asked for too much money – £3000, about
five times what anyone else was getting. He remained the

dominant figure of the time, as famous as Queen Victoria herself. The price of admission to a match was doubled from sixpence (2½p) to a shilling (5p) if he was playing and he was the first sportsman to be identified with a product, appearing in large colour adverts for Colman's mustard. He deserved his fame, being utterly prolific with the bat (and very effective with his crafty round-arm leg breaks), transforming the art of batting, using his enormous physique to play both forward *and* back, and proving very adaptable to any conditions. 'He turned the one-stringed instrument into the many-chorded lyre,' wrote Prince Ranjitsinhji. Continuing the music theme, Grace was as ubiquitous to the English public then as Simon Cowell is now.

The stories of his gamesmanship are legion. Never mind being unbudgeable at the crease unless all three stumps were lying flat on the ground, running out batsmen he didn't like when they had wandered out of their crease to repair the pitch, or moving fielders behind a batsman's back, he also liked to try to distract them. Pointing to an imaginary flock of geese flying close to the sun, he would say, 'Look, did you see them? No? Pity – they've gone behind the trees,' and then, to the bowler, 'Quick, Fred, slip him a fast one on leg stump,' knowing the batsman was still squinting from looking into the sun. He persuaded one young opposing batsman to lob the ball back to the bowler, then appealed for handled ball and got him out.

Grace Expectations

Grace had power and influence because he was both huge (6ft 4in and 18 stone – that's 1.93m and 114kg) and incredibly successful. In mid-August one year, for instance, he made 344 for Gloucestershire against Kent, the first triple century ever recorded in first-class cricket. Then he travelled by train from Canterbury back to the West Country and made 177 against Notts. Two days later he went to Sheffield and compiled 318 not out against Yorkshire. That's the small matter of 839 runs in three innings. As a parting shot he then batted for 13 and a half hours against 'XXII' of Grimsby and, despite all 22 men fielding, made 400 not out (though apparently he should have been given out lbw when he was on six). I am not making this up.

He was also a canny bowler, who bustled up to the wicket, ball held in both hands, often behind his huge beard, and, frequently from round the wicket, tossed up inviting-looking leg breaks with meticulously set leg-side fields. Often he would jump towards the batsman after delivery, both to distract him and to block the view of the disorientated umpire. He suckered 2809 batsmen this way (the 10th-most first-class wickets in the history of the game) to add to his incredible 54,211 runs. He had an extraordinary zest for life, sustained by hearty lunches washed down with a large Irish whiskey, Angostura bitters and soda.

To Australians he was a metaphor for Englishness, representing both skill and ambition but also the arrogance and hypocrisy of the time (as an 'amateur' he earned over £120,000 from cricket – the equivalent of millions today, and a vast amount more than any professional). As captain he refused to let the Australians have a substitute for the injured Harry Moses in Sydney; he then precipitated a row about the umpires at Adelaide and he was regarded as a bad loser. His presence intensified the rivalry between the teams and a spoof letter was circulated on his departure, quoting him as saying that 'Australia is a fine country but wants steeping for 24 hours in the sea to rid it of the human vermin crawling all over it.' Imagine the lawyers' excitement if someone said that kind of thing now.

The Australians had never really forgiven him for the ruthless running out of Sammy Jones in that 1882 match and his presence heightened the intensity of the nations' rivalry. Yet, yet, they still granted him huge respect, for instance when their fearsome pace bowler Ernie Jones got a ball to rear up and apparently pass through W G's great beard.

'What…what…*what*??' exclaimed Grace in his strange falsetto.

'Sorry, Doctor, she slipped,' the bowler replied meekly.

W G made one big hundred – 170 against Australia at The Oval in 1886 – but in Tests his batting exploits were eclipsed by the Notts professional Arthur Shrewsbury, whose 164 on a dodgy Lord's track the same year is regarded as one of the great Test-Match innings. W G rated him the best player alive and always wanted him in the team. Small and prematurely balding, Shrewsbury was a masterly back-foot player whose scrupulous use of his pads made him very hard to dismiss. As he was passing the Trent Bridge gateman in the morning on the way out to the middle he was often heard to remark, 'Bring me a cup of tea at 4 o'clock,' and was frequently still batting when he received it. The tea interval hadn't yet been introduced.

Shrewsbury was a successful England captain (winning five Tests out of seven) but, shy and embarrassed about his baldness, he rarely socialised, invariably making a beeline for his Nottingham lodgings as soon as the match was over. He always wore a hat, even in bed. He was afflicted by depression and, in spite of his illustrious career, suffered acute anxiety. At the age of 46, while still making valuable runs for Notts, he bought a revolver and shot himself in his bedroom. He was the first of more than 20 former Test cricketers to have done such a thing. The fact is that Test cricket is an examination of character as much as of technique, especially for batsmen. It bores deep into your soul. Sometimes it leaves terrible scars. Just ask Marcus Trescothick.

Other names came to the fore in this decade, including George Giffen, known as the W G of Australia, a belligerent right-hand batsman and highly effective slow-medium bowler with a habit of conjuring caught and bowleds from gentle lobs. He topped the batting and bowling averages on every tour of England and, playing for South Australia at Adelaide, was the first man to take 17 wickets in a first-class match. One of the stands at the Adelaide Oval is named after him.

The Australians also unearthed their first great fast-bowling partnership: on their Test debut at Sydney, Charlie 'the Terror' Turner and left-arm J J Ferris shot England out for 45 – still their lowest Test score ever. Short, stocky and abrasive, Turner bowled brisk medium with an open-chested action. He found damp English pitches to his liking and in 1888 took an incredible 283 first-class wickets in the season, a figure only exceeded by two men. One of these was A P Freeman, the other Surrey and England's Tom Richardson (in 1895), a lanky fast bowler with a long run and amazing stamina who, when asked what he thought of an over being increased from four balls to five, said, 'Give me ten!'

If you are a cricket anorak or have listened to a lot of Geoffrey Boycott's commentary, you will know that there is one bowler who was a cut above the men from this era, or indeed from any other. Sitting proudly atop the list of best Test-Match strike rates for the last century is one G A Lohmann. In just 18 Tests (15 against Australia) George Lohmann took 112 wickets (average a ridiculous 10.75) at the quite extraordinary strike rate of a wicket every 34.1 balls. For comparison, the most devastating bowlers of modern times – Waqar Younis, Malcolm Marshall and latterly Dale Steyn – have taken their wickets at more than 40 balls each. Warne and Murali's strike rates are in the mid-50s.

Tall and strong, Lohmann, born in London, quickly rose to prominence for Surrey as a hard-hitting batsman, brilliant slip fielder and master of medium-paced cutters. His pace was deceptive from a beautifully fluid action and half his wickets were clean bowled (though only two were lbw, because until 1935 you couldn't get a leg before if the ball pitched outside the line of the off stump).

Like the great Spofforth, he could move the ball both ways, disguise his variations of pace and was always attacking, but his accuracy never wavered. In his third Test he demolished Australia for 68, taking 7-36, and, frequently bowling unchanged, took eight wickets in a Test innings four times, as well as 1700 wickets for Surrey. The Australians were spared his expertise only when he fell ill with tuberculosis and died prematurely at just 36. He left quite a legacy. No one, in 120 years, came near his incredible strike rate of a Test wicket every 5.4 overs until in 2012 he was briefly overtaken by South Africa's Vernon Philander, whose bowling style is probably quite similar.

Style and Substance

As W G declined in the late 1890s (he played his last Test in 1899, remarking that 'the ground was getting a bit too far away'), some other great names emerged for England. Two were from the same Yorkshire village of Kirkheaton, high up on the edge of the Pennines. George Hirst, a bustling, ultra-competitive left-arm in-swing bowler and hard-hitting batsman, is the only man ever to score 2000 runs and take 200 wickets in one county season. It was an amazing feat of endurance, never mind skill, underlined by his doctor, whom he had gone to see about his bad knee and sore feet. 'Don't you realise, Mr Hirst, you have given your legs more use than five ordinary men in a lifetime?' the doc said. GPs never did win prizes for sympathy.

Footsoreness must also have applied to Hirst's partner in crime Wilfred Rhodes, a left-arm spinner who got through more than 30,000 overs during a 32-year first-class career. Rhodes was a master of flight and guile – 'F and G', the proponents like to call it. The great cricket writer Neville Cardus wrote about him 'each over is in collusion with the others, part of a plot, every ball a decoy, a spy sent out to get the lie of the land, some balls simple, some complex, and one of them – ah! which? – the master ball.' If this is the definition of waxing lyrical, it was justified. Rhodes was the bowling machine that never broke, taking a mind-boggling 4204 wickets (still the most in first-class history). He was no mean batsman either, starting off at number 11 but finishing up opening for England with Jack Hobbs and batting at every place in between.

Generally the 1890s was a decade of better batting and more even contests between England and Australia. This included the extraordinary match at Sydney in 1894. Andrew Stoddart's England, having conceded a (then) record 586 in the first innings, were made to follow on, 261 behind. They occupied the crease for a further day and a half and set Australia 177 to win. The Aussies were coasting at 113-2 when an overnight storm saturated the pitch. Yorkshire's left-arm spinner Bobby Peel demanded the ball the following morning and bowled Australia out to give England a 10-run victory. It was the first and only time a team had won a Test after following on until the Headingley classic of 1981. Each time England went on to steal the series.

This was the beginning of cricket's so-called Golden Age and some more legendary figures emerged. For England there was the commanding Archie MacLaren, a product of Harrow School, who soon eclipsed W G Grace's record score with 424 for Lancashire and dominated a number of Ashes Tests; later came K S Ranjitsinhji, the Maharajah Jam Sahib of Nawanagar, who, though born in the Indian village of Sarodar, also went to Harrow.

Diminutive and nimble, Ranji brought deftness and deflection to the art of batting, making oodles of runs for Sussex with wristy flicks and glances. His batting was 'oriental magic', wrote the cricket historian H S Altham. Lord Harris, former England captain and chairman of selectors for the Lord's Test of 1896, blocked Ranji's selection, arguing that only 'native-born' players should be chosen, conveniently forgetting that he himself had been born in Trinidad. The Lancashire committee overruled this ludicrous hypocrisy for the Old Trafford Test, and Ranji made 62 and 154 not out in one of the great Test-Match debuts. 'Our Indian ally showed how the Australian bowling should be met,' declared the *Manchester Guardian*, though England actually lost the match. (They took the series 2-1, thanks again to Peel's left-arm spinners, dispatching the Aussies for 44 at The Oval.)

'Ranji moves as if he has no bones,' wrote his great friend C B Fry, the original *Boy's Own* figure. The two men embodied the spirit of the time. Their batting had flair and flamboyance, they cut a dash with their dress – both tending to bat in a cravat – and they both lived life to the full. Ranji once scored 285 for Sussex despite having been up all the previous night fishing, and Fry famously played cricket and football for England, rugby for the Barbarians and broke the world long-jump record, among other exceptional feats. Both were also prolific writers, co-authoring the *Jubilee Book of Cricket*, a definitive textbook produced to commemorate Queen Victoria's 60th year on the throne in 1897.

Outrageously gifted, scoring six centuries in successive innings in 1901 (a feat since emulated only by Don Bradman and Mike Procter), Fry brought an essence of Kevin Pietersen to batting – and to life in general. Possessed of a rebellious streak, he challenged the norm of playing forward and to the off side, stood back and tried to flick or pull the bowling to leg. He still managed to make it look stylish. 'He was the handsomest sight ever seen on a cricket field,' wrote Neville Cardus, who had an eye for such things. Nicknamed 'Almighty', Fry liked to draw attention to himself by wearing a large white sun hat, dressing eccentrically and making outrageous pronouncements. A fake Twitter account called CB Genius would have been utterly justified.

At about the same time the Australians unearthed a cavalier of their own in the form of Victor Trumper. The name is memorable enough. But the style too is indelibly imprinted in the memory of anyone who has seen a picture of him about to drive the ball (see the picture in plate section). The bat is swung back high as in baseball, the head is upright and poised, the expression animated, the legs, clad in 'skeleton' pads, wide apart, the left foot in mid-air. He looks as if he is intent on jumping on the ball to squash it. The whole position has so much energy and ambition, though because of it his name is sometimes taken in vain by pacemen versed in the history of the game. 'Who do you think you are, Victor Trumper?' was a common challenge from an aggrieved fast bowler to a batsman over-keen to get on the front foot (something quickies hate as a sort of slight to their manhood). The observation was often followed by a bouncer and a caustic, 'Try driving that!'

Trumper, wrote H S Altham, 'had the lissom and co-ordinated body of a natural athlete; like all great batsmen he seemed to sight the ball almost as soon as it left the bowler's hand, and he moved into his strokes with effortless and perfectly balanced ease...The better the bowling, the more difficult the wicket, the more likely was his genius to rise to the challenge.'

A graceful (and modest) precursor to Bradman, Trumper's name became synonymous with regal stroke play – as opposed to excessive flatulence – and he was a batting artiste, particularly brilliant on difficult pitches. Gifted with sublime timing, he shunned a rubber grip on his bat handle, believing it interfered with the sensitivity of his hands. He rubbed powdered resin into the string round the handle instead. He looked to attack any sort of bowling, but with graceful arcs of the blade rather than savage blows. His duels with one of the greatest bowlers in cricket history, Sydney Barnes, were as compelling as anything in the entire history of the Ashes.

Barnes was the antithesis of Trumper – a taciturn, blunt-speaking northerner who confronted authority and had a vicious temper. Perhaps the only player in history to be described as a 'swing and spin' bowler, he confounded the norm in seam-bowling circles by mainly moving the ball away rather than in. In essence he bowled fast leg breaks. Inspired by a total revulsion of batsmen (and county committees who paid their professionals a £3 a week pittance), he plied his trade in club cricket where he could earn £8 for a Saturday afternoon's work.

Barnes was recruited from the Lancashire League for the 1901–2 tour of Australia by Archie MacLaren after he had troubled England's captain in the nets. On his Test debut in Sydney Barnes immediately dismissed Trumper – the best batsman in the world – for two and got him twice in the second Test in the process of taking 13 wickets in the match. But, having bowled 64 overs in one innings, he was injured for the remainder of the series and Australia won it 4-1.

Alas, Poor Fred

The two sides encountered each other again in what should be regarded as the First Great Ashes Series, in the English summer of 1902. Though 'summer' was a misnomer: it was more like a monsoon. The first Test was abandoned on the third and final day after Australia had been knocked over for 36 (Rhodes 7-17) and the second was washed out after only 38 overs' play. The third – the only Test ever played at Bramall Lane, Sheffield – was won by Australia in spite of Barnes' 6-49 in their first innings. Bad light and pollution from Sheffield's steel furnaces were blamed for the defeat, setting the precedent for a century of lame excuses in Ashes contests.

There was a bit of a rumpus before the fourth Test at Old Trafford. The chairman of selectors was Lord Hawke, an autocratic dyed-in-the-wool Yorkshireman-actually-born-in-Lincolnshire, who was famous for saying, 'Pray God no professional may captain England' (and none did until 1952). He had had a few run-ins with his Lancastrian captain MacLaren, whom he found rather unpredictable. Intent on sending out the team he and the other selectors wanted, Hawke announced only 11 men for the match. Fry, Barnes and Gilbert Jessop – a ferocious-hitting, Bothamesque all-rounder – were controversially omitted, and Somerset's opener Lionel Palairet, the former Oxford University captain, renowned for his elegance, was called up for his Test debut.

As an afterthought a 12th man was added to the original 11 – 35-year-old Sussex stalwart Fred Tate, who had also never played for England. Furious at being dictated to, MacLaren left out George Hirst, England's most reliable all-rounder, on the morning of the match and included the Sussex man. The match has since been known as 'Tate's Test', though for all the wrong reasons.

The Australians, captained by the elegant and reliable batsman Joe Darling, had a solid batting line-up. It featured the dependable Reggie Duff as Trumper's opening partner and the sturdy left-hander Clem Hill – think Allan Border without the moustache and the chewing gum – at number 3. The all-rounder Monty Noble was in the middle order along with the future captain Warwick Armstrong, though the 'Big Ship' was a slightly slimmer vessel in those early days. The Australian bowling was in the hands of the medium-fast Noble and two fine spinners – Hugh Trumble, who bowled bouncy off spin, and the left-armer Jack Saunders.

The match began badly for England. After a two-day deluge the pitch was soaking and, having won the toss, Darling elected to bat, knowing the bowlers would have trouble keeping their feet. Acknowledging this, MacLaren opened the bowling with Rhodes' left-arm spin from one end. He suspected that the pitch would begin to play tricks as it dried out, so the order was to 'keep Victor quiet until lunch'. As Trumper proceeded to drive and cut the bowling with great elan to record a majestic hundred in the hour and 40 minutes of the morning's play (the first time it had ever been done in a Test Match), the plan could be said to have gone awry.

Trumper glided about the crease, stroking the spinners through the offside or deftly dabbing them wide of slip. When Tate was brought on for his first bowl in Test cricket, Trumper soon took 13 off an over, bringing up his 50 with a clip to leg. He lofted Rhodes over long on for four. The Yorkshire amateur the Hon. F S Jackson's first over of medium pace was struck for 10. Just before lunch MacLaren risked the Surrey fast bowler Bill Lockwood on the damp run-ups. Trumper pulled and hooked him for two fours to bring up his hundred at a run a minute. The innings evoked perhaps Greg Chappell at his finest. Australia were 173-1 at the interval.

A certain order was restored afterwards. Trumper was immediately out to Rhodes for 104 and, once the pacey Lockwood was able to keep his feet on the drying surface, wickets tumbled. Australia lost their last six men for 43 and totalled 299. But England were soon reeling at 30-4 with both MacLaren and Ranjitsinhji back in the pavilion, victims of the wily Trumble; they staggered to 70-5 by the close of the first day.

Bright sunshine greeted the teams on the second morning and the redoubtable Jackson held the England innings together with a stoic 128. They recovered to 262 all out, leaving the match nicely poised at the halfway stage, with Australia leading by 37.

The Old Trafford crowd, which had swelled to over 10,000, drew breath and ate their bread and dripping snacks. Australia batted again in mid-afternoon and Lockwood, a swing-and-cut bowler who had learnt much from George Lohmann and possessed a 'slower ball of almost sinful deceit', was brought on early. In a sensational opening spell, he removed Australia's top three, including Trumper, for just 10.

Beneath a thunderous sky Darling counterattacked. 'The defiant action of his bat was like a fist shaken at the unfriendly heavens,' wrote Neville Cardus. But on 17 he miscued a pull and sent a high catch towards deep square leg. The man under it? The debutant Fred Tate. Tate was a quiet, unassuming man lacking real fibre. He was at home wheeling away with his unobtrusive off breaks at Hove, followed by a few beers in the evening; he was not cut out for the titanic struggle of an Ashes Test. Unsteady under the spiralling catch, he stumbled and dropped it. In fact he had never looked like catching it. His face went white as a sheet.

Darling survived and, despite brilliant bowling from Lockwood and Rhodes on the treacherous pitch, added another 20 runs. It doesn't sound much, but his 37 represented almost half Australia's overnight score of 85-8. The lead at stumps on the second day was 122. The butter-fingered Tate consoled himself that worse things could have happened. He could have been clean bowled with England needing just four runs to win.

It rained for five hours in the night. Classic Mancunian weather. It is the reason Manchester is the most disorientating city in England: there are no landmarks and you can never see the sun. Play began late on the third morning and Australia quickly lost their last two wickets to the spinners Tate and Rhodes for the addition of just one run. Lockwood had taken 5-28 to give him 11 wickets in the match and England now needed 124 to win and square the series.

Promoting himself to open, MacLaren soothed nerves by seeing England to 36-0 at lunch in company with the debutant Lionel Palairet. But just after the resumption, as the sun again made the wicket more tricky, the left-arm spinner Jack Saunders, with his walrus moustache and weaving run-up directly behind the umpire, ripped one past Palairet's defence.

The diminutive Johnny Tyldesley was forthright in company with his captain and got the score to 68 before he was caught at slip off Saunders. Just 56 were wanted with eight wickets in hand and still Ranji, Jackson and Surrey's Bobby Abel to come. But four runs later MacLaren rashly attempted to loft Trumble's off spin over mid-on and was caught in the deep. Flinging his bat down in the dressing room, MacLaren declared, 'I've thrown away the match and the bloody rubber.'

Ranji joined Abel, but a shower interrupted play and Ranji looked a frail imitation of himself afterwards. He kept trying to step across his stumps and work Trumble's off spin to leg and was soon lbw for four. The score was 92-4. Abel, only 5ft 4in, bustled up and down the pitch, hitting out effectively but was then bowled through the gate. Just 27 were needed with five wickets in hand. 'It's quite all right,' said a parson in the half-crown (25p) stand, 'there's really no cause for anxiety. To doubt the ability of Braund, Lilley, Lockwood and Rhodes to get a paltry 27 runs would be scandalous. Besides, I do believe that fellow Tate is a batsman – he has an average of 16 for Sussex.' Actually he hadn't checked his facts. Tate's batting average was 9.5. Think Philip Tufnell. Or Glenn McGrath.

The words had barely left his mouth when Jackson, the first-innings century-maker, hit a full toss straight to mid-off, the belligerent all-rounder Len Braund was stumped and Lockwood bowled for a duck. The score was now 109-8. Fifteen to win. Two wickets left. It sounded like 1882 all over again.

Wicketkeeper Dick Lilley chanced his arm and hit one over the top. Rhodes followed suit. Eight to win. Lilley connected with another solid hit to leg which soared boundary-wards, but

Clem Hill pulled off an incredible one-handed catch at deep square leg, running at full tilt. So, still with eight to win, out walked number 11, Fred Tate. Cometh the hour, cometh the man. Or maybe not.

The batsmen had crossed when Lilley was caught and Rhodes was now on strike to Trumble. He carefully negotiated three balls and then, as if the plot needed any more twists, the heavens opened. The players were driven from the field and England's last pair hunkered down in the dressing room for an agonising 45 minutes.

Tate would be on strike when the match resumed. He rehearsed the stroke he would play to Saunders' brisk left-arm spin – low backlift, foot to the pitch, bat straight, prod the ball back down the pitch. Like any self-respecting tailender. All he had to do was hold an end up for Rhodes, who was a reliable batsman. He could get the runs.

At 4.54pm play resumed. Tate took guard. Australians clustered round the bat. Saunders prepared to bowl. Two hits would get England level in the series. One wicket would clinch Australia the Ashes. Nothing much at stake, then. The ball was a fast one. Tate saw a blur and thrust his bat hopefully at it. He heard a click. He glanced anxiously backwards but the wicket was still intact and the crowd were cheering as the ball scuttled towards the boundary off the inside edge.

Four to win. One more shot like that and England were home. Tate would be a hero. He would be chaired off the field, get all the headlines and receive the freedom of Burgess Hill. Darling rearranged the field and Saunders dried his hand in a small mound of sawdust. He bowled again. Tate blocked. The crowd gasped. This was a gripping climax.

Saunders bowled again. Tate poked optimistically at it. The ball gripped in the sticky soil, spun, slid past and under his blade and cannoned into the stumps. It was a delivery good enough not only for a number 11 but for numbers 1–10 as well. It was *the* ball of the century (until superseded by another at the same ground 91 years later). With it Australia had won by three runs and retained the Ashes.

Tate, of course, was inconsolable. After the match he hailed a hansom (horse-drawn) cab, pulled the blinds down and apparently wept. He later pulled himself together somewhat and said, 'I've got a little kid at home who will make up for this.' This was his seven-year-old son Maurice, who went on to become a highly successful fast bowler for England and helped them regain the Ashes in 1926. 'Poor' Fred, meanwhile, went back to Sussex and remained there for some years, happily floating down his off breaks and standing at slip. There are worse ways to earn your living.

The Original Beefy

The 1902 Ashes had been won, but the series was not finished. The fifth Test at The Oval was some finale. The feud between Lord Hawke and Archie MacLaren had been settled and both Gilbert Jessop and George Hirst were restored to the England team. Australia fielded the same side that had won at Old Trafford, batted first and made 324. England were caught on a tricky pitch and managed only 183, Hirst top-scoring with 43 after taking five wickets in the Australian innings. Hugh Trumble bowled 31 overs unchanged to take 8-65.

When Australia went in to bat for the second time with a lead of 141, the incomparable Trumper set off for a quick single, fell flat on his face and was run out. Australia collapsed and were bowled out for 121. It left England to make 263 for a morale-boosting victory, but at 10-3 and then 48-5, with the Aussie spin twins of Saunders and Trumble tying them in knots, all hope seemed lost. It was the stroke of lunchtime on the third and final day; many disgruntled members gathered up their belongings and headed home, unwilling to see England further humiliated.

Enter Jessop: 'the Croucher', as he was known for his wide, hunched stance. A big-hitting Bothamesque all-rounder who loved eating beef, he was described in Gloucestershire circles as 'a human catapult who wrecks the roofs of distant towns when set in his assault'. He was completely fearless, as evidenced by the fact that he never wore a box when he batted. Or maybe he was a masochist.

A man who once clubbed the Yorkshire bowling for 100 in 45 minutes, Jessop was a Twenty20 specialist a century before it came to prominence. He was not one for playing himself in. He scored off all the first six balls he faced and lofted Trumble into the pavilion. After surviving a stumping chance and a catch to long off, he sent a ball from Saunders skimming over cover point and another over the bowler's head. After lunch he cut Trumble for an all-run five and struck the nervy Saunders for five consecutive boundaries. He put on 109 in partnership with Jackson, who eventually hit a return catch into Trumble's gigantic hands.

Hirst joined Jessop with 106 still wanted. He survived a confident lbw shout and flayed the tiring Saunders. Jessop launched Trumble over the pavilion roof for six, pulled Saunders for four but had trouble with Armstrong's slow leg breaks. On 96 he hauled Armstrong to the fence to reach his hundred. It had taken him just 75 minutes and, in terms of time, is still the fastest hundred in Ashes history. (Adam Gilchrist's whirlwind effort in 2006 took 103 minutes.) A thousand straw boaters were flung in the air and the cheering of the crowd could be heard in Clapham.

The daredevilry of Jessop's innings can only be imagined, but it must have been not unlike Ian Botham's barnstorming knock at Headingley in 1981: a mixture of brilliance, bravado and outrageous luck. C B Fry later wrote that 'no man has ever driven the ball so hard, so high and so often in so many different directions.' But attempting a delicate sweep, Jessop brought his innings to a tame end on 104. It's what happens when swashbuckling hitters think they are real batsmen and try to play properly.

Now with 76 needed, Hirst took over, batting with great common sense and control. He lost Lockwood (the eighth wicket) at 214 and the busy wicketkeeper Lilley at 248. It was now 15 to win with one wicket left. In walked Wilfred Rhodes, Hirst's Kirkheaton and Yorkshire colleague. The story goes that Hirst greeted him with, 'We'll get 'em in singles, Wilfred!' It was refuted by Rhodes himself – well, anyway, no one could be *that* cool – and he opened his account with a lucky edged four. He was subsequently dropped at slip by Warwick Armstrong. But he remained calm and composed, while Hirst, twirling his bat furiously between balls and constantly patting down imperfections on the pitch, was focused and determined. The tension in the ground was unbearable. Every one of the 22,000 people in the ground was keeping score.

England's last pair inched closer, nudging singles on the leg side, in spite of Darling changing the field every ball. They crowded round Rhodes, but he was the best number 11 England ever had and held firm. With three to win, Hirst drove Noble's medium pace wide of mid-on. They thought about two but decided against it, so Rhodes played out the rest of the over. Hirst used his feet to the relentless Trumble, who had bowled unchanged through the innings, and the batsmen took another quick single. A huge roar went up in recognition of the scores now being level. A clergyman, who thought England had won, charged onto the field, pursued by a policeman (sounds more like a scene from Laurel and Hardy).

The field was moved again, with the sturdy batsman Reggie Duff posted at deep long on (a strange position to be in when the number 11 is on strike with one run to win). An Australian in the crowd shouted, 'Never mind, Duff, you've won the Ashes!' Then Rhodes hit Trumble in his direction and everyone ran – the batsmen for the winning single, the fielders for the ball and the spectators, who had been sitting in rapt attention for about six hours, onto the field. 'The noise and turmoil and prolonged cheering were the witness of the best finish,' wrote the *Manchester Guardian*. 'It surpassed the Manchester game in excitement, and it is difficult to say more.' In spite of that heroic last-wicket partnership, the game has gone down in folklore as 'Jessop's match'. The concept of 'Man of the Match' was not formalised until the founding of the Gillette Cup 61 years later (so no free shaving gear for Gilbert).

The euphoria was brief. England had lost the Ashes, after all, and the country was still recovering from the recently concluded Boer War, which had cost 22,000 lives. And there were more pressing concerns, like the appalling health of a nation which, according to the *Daily Telegraph*, was a 'raucous, grasping multitude, good enough at pushing through the turnstiles or bellowing at a footballer, but who have no notion of taking any decent exercise for themselves at any time.' *Plus ça change*, eh?

3

FIFTH TEST, THE OVAL, 1926

*'Richardson bowls, on the leg stump, Hobbs goes back
and nudges it into the leg side, Sutcliffe is quick to
respond, and he's up the wicket like a hare and
they've stolen another sharp single. That's the hundred
partnership – their third of the series, thanks Bill –
a splendid effort on such a sticky dog!'*

We are at 1903, and the Australians have now won four successive
Ashes series. It would have prompted them to demand permanent
relocation of the Ashes urn to the trophy cabinet of the Melbourne
Cricket Ground if anyone had known the whereabouts of the
blasted thing, or even its existence.

It was time for England to take exceptional steps to restore
colonial order. So it was announced that the MCC – the
Marylebone (not Melbourne) Cricket Club – would now take
responsibility for all England tours (which previously had been
funded by private enterprise) and the team would travel under
the MCC banner. Eureka! Everything was going to be all right
with the world. In fact it was impossible to see how this was a
panacea for an ailing nation – watching its cricketers being
regularly trounced as well as its empire ritually dismantled – but
that's cricket administrators and their ivory towers for you.

The MCC did come up with one inspired initiative, though. They chose Middlesex's Pelham Warner as captain and allowed him to take on tour England's new secret weapon: cricket's great conjuring trick, the googly. If I had a pound for every time someone has asked me either a) what a googly is or b) where the name came from, I would be a very rich man indeed.

Rights and Wrongs

Bernard Bosanquet was an Oxford undergraduate and also a multi-talented sportsman. Most significantly, he excelled at the game of 'twisty-twosty' – the back-handed spinning of tennis balls round obstacles. On the cricket pitch he had introduced his wristy sleight of hand into his bowling and bamboozled many county batsmen with it. Playing for Middlesex, he tried it against the 1902 Australians, with instant results. By propelling a leg break out of the back of his hand, making a ball that appeared to be spinning one way actually spin the other, he had turned a novelty into a wicket-taking phenomenon.

Having outwitted the great Trumper with this technique on a social tour of Australia, Bosanquet was unleashed on the Australians the following winter (1903–4). His aim was not always true (in fact sometimes his deliveries bounced twice), but he produced when it really counted: he took six vital wickets in an hour in the decisive fourth test in Sydney, many with googlies, and England regained the Ashes.

'Except when Rhodes and Arnold put Victoria out for 15 (!!), nothing more startling was done with the ball all tour,' Warner wrote in a best-selling book, *How We Recovered the Ashes*. 'The rubber was won, the "Ashes" were in my cricket bag, the hour of my Nunc Dimittis had arrived.' Like other spinners, Bosanquet's cause was helped by the extension of an over to six balls. It allowed for better planning, building up pressure on the batsman till his patience expired. Apoplectic with indignation over Bosanquet's emergence, the Australians christened his back-of-the-hand invention the 'wrong 'un' – normally a derisory term for a social misfit. Later it became known as the 'googly', an Australian word meaning a teasing or perplexing delivery, derived from the word 'goggle'. They also called it the 'Bosie'. And while the man himself subsequently disappeared back into relative obscurity, Australia began systematically unveiling leg spinners with better and more controlled googlies than Bosanquet had ever dreamt of.

County cricket was booming through the next decade, which saw the unearthing of several of the most prolific batsmen who ever lived. Jack Hobbs, a veritable run machine, first got the England call in 1908 – the same year, incidentally, that the 60-year-old W G Grace played his last first-class match (for the Gentlemen of England: once a hypocrite, always a hypocrite, eh?). Hobbs, who played against Grace in that match, was the first of 12 children of a Cambridge net bowler and groundsman, so he started with a useful advantage and soon lived with a team of willing fielders.

Practising for hours in a fives court with a stump and a tennis ball, he was a self-made batsman who had no coaching except one piece of advice: 'Don't back away from the ball.' He never did. Rejected by Essex as a teenager, he was signed by Surrey and filled his boots on the benign pitches at the Kennington Oval. Well, who wouldn't, to be honest? It is no coincidence that Surrey can boast more makers of a hundred hundreds (five) than anyone else.

Lightly built and nimble, Hobbs stylishly dissected bowling attacks and was in his element on a tricky pitch. During a 31-year career he made a remarkable 199 hundreds, 29 more than anyone else has ever managed. And it would have been many more if he hadn't had a habit, according to Wilfred Rhodes, of 'giving his wicket to one of his old pals if Surrey were going well'. He was the opposite of modern celebrities, marrying his teenage sweetheart (whom he took on tour to Australia – the first professional to do so) and preferring a quiet life of church-going, teetotalism and eating simple food in a Lyons Corner House. He certainly wouldn't have been the type to take to the floor with his partner Neva Toppelova to perform the Charleston, or require rescuing having fallen off a pedalo in an inebriated stupor.

About the same time, Frank Woolley, a tall, languid left-hander, made his debut for Kent. His batting exuded rhythm and panache and his incessant run-making (he finished with 58,959 of them) inspired the writers of the time to ever-increasing degrees of hyperbole. Like this from Neville Cardus: 'His cricket is compounded of soft airs and fresh flavours. The bloom of the year is on it, making for sweetness…' A contender for Pseuds Corner, don't you think?

The Australians weren't impressed with this new breed of superbats, and their own ringmaster, the gargantuan Warwick Armstrong – an all-rounder in more senses than one – made it his mission to undermine them. He subjected the benign Hobbs to a barrage of abuse at Headingley in 1909 after an appeal for caught behind had been turned down. Hobbs was so distressed he left a delivery two balls later and was bowled. The incident left a sour taste which lingered for some time.

Two matches later, on Woolley's test debut, Armstrong managed to make the batsman wait more than 15 minutes to receive his first ball as he sent down a series of deliberately wayward practice deliveries to another fielder. Woolley was promptly bowled and took a while to establish himself in the side.

Growing larger and more intimidating by the year, Armstrong was a tremendous batsman and canny spin bowler with a huge ego and a sharp temper. Umpires were terrified of him. Throwing his weight about came naturally. He was also inclined to deliberately bowl badly in some matches against English counties, gifting runs to ordinary batsmen he suspected would struggle if selected for a Test Match. He was more Machiavellian than Machiavelli. And he wasn't even captain at this stage.

These were the subplots to the Ashes encounters in the first decade of the 20th century, which gradually increased in pace and fervour. Unruly Australian crowds who tossed out insults like confetti added spice to the overall concoction. The culmination of the pre-war period was the 1911–12 series in Australia, when England fielded their first all-seam opening pair of Sydney Barnes and Frank Foster. Barnes was well known for his cantankerousness, as well as for his hatred of batsmen, but Foster was a dark horse. A skiddy left-armer, he fine-tuned a method of bowling short and into the body with catchers on the leg side. In effect he was the founder of bodyline, though at the time it was called leg theory. It was highly effective, too. Australia, distracted by wrangling (and occasional punch-ups) between captain and chairman of selectors, were a disorganised rabble and lost 4-1. Foster and Barnes shared 66 wickets in the series and celebrated with a glass of champagne at every interval.

The final Ashes series before the Great War was part of a one-off triangular tournament (also including South Africa) in England in 1912. The idea was a damp squib ruined by the weather and England were too strong for either visiting side. At that point hostilities on the field were suspended. England and Australia had played each other 93 times. England had won 39, Australia 35 and there had been 19 draws.

All-round Prowess

The war experience intensified the countries' rivalry. The battle of Gallipoli played a defining role. A thin, rocky peninsula on the edge of western Turkey, Gallipoli was regarded by the British as an important gateway to Russia and so a large Allied force was sent to invade it, including thousands of Australians and New Zealanders. It was a hopelessly botched campaign – one naval commander actually slept through the initial invasion – costing the Allies 43,000 men. More than 20,000 Australians were badly injured and 7500 were killed. The sacrifices made by Australian and New Zealand soldiers are commemorated annually on Anzac Day, 25 April, the anniversary of the Gallipoli landing.

This disaster increased Australia's desire to be independent from Britain. And to give them a good kicking on the cricket field. It is also the reason Australian touring teams of recent vintage tend to visit Gallipoli on the way to an Ashes series in England. Because if they don't hate the Poms already, they will after seeing the Anzac gravestones littering the barren landscape. (By the way, guess who came up with the idea of taking Gallipoli? That's right, Winston Churchill.)

Perhaps it was no surprise, then, that the Australians won the next Ashes encounter, in 1920–21, 5-0. Not only were they hugely motivated, under Warwick Armstrong, but there was a new robustness in Australian cricket born of better facilities and more first-class teams in the Sheffield Shield. Their domestic scene had not been as badly decimated by the war as England's. No fewer than 70 English county cricketers had been killed in those four brutal years, including the Kent and England left-arm spinner Charlie Blythe, who at that point (i.e. pre-Laker) held the best match figures ever recorded in county or Test cricket: 17-48 for Kent v Northants in 1907.

The advent of eight-ball overs in Australia also coincided with the arrival of several great batsmen and some astronomical scores as the poor beleaguered bowlers succumbed to the heat. It's bad enough having to bowl six balls in succession when it's 38°C, never mind eight. The English quicks must have felt like they needed defibrillators.

England had Hobbs, Rhodes and Woolley to get the runs (Walter Hammond came five years later), but Australia possessed the stylish left-hander Warren Bardsley, the dogged, dependable Herbie Collins and the already established Charles Macartney at the top of the order, augmented by the irrepressible Armstrong, an intimidating presence who was so big the bowler couldn't see the wicketkeeper, let alone the wicket.

The Aussies also had Jack Gregory, a wunderkind of a cricketer who bowled fast and abrasively, batted with gusto and fearlessness – left-handed and gloveless – and fielded brilliantly at slip. There have not been many born like him – someone who could harass the top batsmen with the new ball, knock over the lower order with fast bouncers and yorkers, and bat and field virtually anywhere. These men are priceless. They effectively mean you are taking the field with 12 players.

Gregory was one of very few – Sobers, Botham, Kallis, Miller, Greig, Imran, to name the most prominent others – whose batting average was higher than his bowling average, the mark of a genuine all-rounder (except if the figures in question are under 20). If these men have a slightly confident air, you know why. They are the definition of God's gift to cricket and they sort of know it (though Kallis, in particular, wears his prowess lightly, which is perhaps why he tends to sneak under the radar in discussions of the greatest cricketers of all time). Even in middle age they have the strut to go with the stats, are generally rather assertive and tend to wear their hair a bit too long (or get a transplant).

Gregory was definitely more Botham than Kallis. Tall and strong, he ran in fast, jumped high, unleashed rapidly, evoking perhaps the West Indian Wes Hall of more modern bowlers.

As Wally Hammond later commented he 'cultivated a fearsome stare and gave me the treatment'. He maimed a number of eminent batsmen with vicious bumpers. He also still holds the record for the fastest ever test hundred, time-wise – made in 70 minutes v South Africa. South Africa may have been the Bangladesh of the 1920s and the century may have taken Gregory 11 more balls than Viv Richards' 56-ball demolition of England in 1985–6, but it is still some effort for bloke who was principally a bowler.

Gregory routed England with 7-69 in the second Test in Melbourne, to give Australia an immediate 2-0 lead. By the third Test, he was partnered by Ted McDonald, a smooth, cool terminator to Gregory's explosive assassin. No wonder Armstrong walked round with a self-satisfied smile on his face and often drank whisky before striding out to thump the English pie-chuckers about, lunging onto the front foot with his great bulk, but then with an unerring eye and surprising style easing the ball around the ground. He averaged 74 in that 1920–1 series. 'The bat in his hand is like a hammer in the grip of a Vulcan,' wrote Neville Cardus. Perspiring profusely, he often left a small pool of sweat at the crease after a long innings, causing bowlers problems in their delivery stride. The kind of hidden extra impact that the sweatless Alastair Cook cannot provide.

Armstrong then let the leg-spin and googly bowler Arthur Mailey loose on the visitors. Mailey, a slight man, was not the most accurate of spinners, as his possession of the worst innings figures in the history of first-class cricket (4-362 for New South Wales v Victoria) illustrates. But he took it all in good humour ('I was just striking a length!' he said, when the last man was run out in that match); at heart he was a confidence trickster who loved bamboozling batsmen with considerable spin from his abnormally strong fingers. He snared 36 English scalps in the five-match series, then an Australian record.

Despite England fielding a strong side led by J W H T Douglas (an arch blocker appropriately nicknamed 'Johnny Won't Hit Today'), they could not cope with the skill and variety of Australia's attack and Armstrong's wily ruthlessness. There was no respite, either, as Tests in Australia were timeless, as opposed to the cushy three-day affairs that were played in England. Lengthy exposure to the harsh sun on huge Australian outfields was too much for the tourists. For the first time ever England were vanquished 5-0, a total eclipse not repeated until 2006–7.

Australia's dominance under Armstrong continued as England struggled to recover from the war and fielded 30 different players in the home series of 1921. It must have been like representing England at football in the 1990s, with five changes per match and players barely recognising each other. Quite apart from their varied bowling, Australia had a powerful batting line-up centred round the 'Governor General' Charlie Macartney, an instinctive genius who gorged himself on English bowling that summer and scored 100 before lunch at Trent Bridge.

By the end of the series, which Australia won 3-0, Armstrong had completely lost interest in the contest, posting himself on the boundary and allowing the English batsmen to help themselves to some cafeteria bowling as the match meandered to a draw. Soon afterwards he lost interest in cricket altogether, having set up a whisky-importing business with a man he had met in Glasgow. Unbeaten as Australian captain, he was, in retirement, a man of great wealth and happiness, evidenced by his enormous belly.

He left a considerable legacy. Under his command Australia intimidated the opposition with their aggressive fast bowlers, their deep-rooted batting and their cocksure attitude. They had the winning bit between their teeth and wouldn't let go. By the middle of the 1924–5 Ashes and despite the emergence of England's most famous opening pair of Jack Hobbs and Herbert

Sutcliffe, the Aussies had won 11 out of 13 post-war Tests, with the other two drawn. England had changed captain three times (chief qualification three initials or a large inheritance, ideally both) and did not know where to turn; they were then confronted by Clarrie Grimmett – originator of the back-spinning 'flipper' – who twisted them into even more complex knots. Australia won that series 4–1, though they still had nothing, other than pride, to show for it, as this rhyme in *The Cricketer's Annual*, pleading for English retribution, suggests:

> *So here's to Chapman, Hendren and Hobbs,*
> *Gilligan, Woolley and Hearne:*
> *May they bring back to the Motherland,*
> *The ashes which have no urn!*

Drawing Level

So we come to 1925. Jack Hobbs was the man of the moment. At Taunton in August he had equalled W G Grace's record tally of 126 first-class centuries (there was a special train laid on from Paddington for those who wanted to see him reach the landmark, though the film cameraman dispatched to capture the moment missed it and it had to be hammed up after play.) The next day he overtook it. He scored more than 3000 runs that season with 16 hundreds and, despite being now 43 years old, he was regarded as the best batsman in the world. He should have been made England captain. But oh no, he was that filthy word, a professional (paid £440 a year by Surrey), so it would never do. And he was too modest and magnanimous a man to complain.

So Hobbs remained part of the rank and file, although, in an unprecedented step, he was made an England selector. The *Old Etonian* and Notts captain Arthur Carr took charge of the England team for the Ashes series of 1926, which also included the diminutive Middlesex run thief Patsy Hendren, Frank Woolley and the future captain Percy Chapman. England's attack was led by Maurice Tate (son of Fred), by now the most feared fast bowler in the world – though that wasn't saying much, as Australia's pace attack was starting to age, South Africa's was non-existent and the West Indies weren't granted Test status until 1928. There were no other test-playing countries.

Suddenly Australia were a team in transition, with an average age of over 30. It's a status that creeps up on sports teams almost furtively, frequently after a run of unprecedented success. The cliché about sport, that it's harder staying at the top than actually getting there, is invariably true. Australia had a new captain, Herbie Collins (known as 'Horseshoe' for his luck with the toss), and new batsmen in Bill Woodfull and Bill Ponsford, new holder of the world-record score with 429 for Victoria.

But constant success makes a team vulnerable, as others try to knock you off your perch. That could be one explanation for the fact that Australia's victorious run finally came to an end. Or it could have been exhaustion. By the time of the summer's first Test (12 June 1926) they had already played 13 matches against the counties and other sides. When you factor in the inevitable social engagements they had to attend and the night-time train travel between games, it was quite an ordeal.

As it turned out they had time to recover, as only 17 overs' play was possible in the first test (at Trent Bridge). They could while away time eating egg and cress baps, sink decent pints in the Trent Bridge Tavern and meet the local Nottingham wenches.

The Lord's pitch for the second Test was a batting paradise. Only 18 wickets fell in the match, prompting calls for Test matches in England to be extended beyond three days. The clamour grew louder when Australia lost only three wickets on the first day of the third Test at Headingley and hung about batting for a day and a half, leading to an inevitable draw. It also led to much flak for Arthur Carr, who had not only put Australia in but dropped Macartney at slip in the first over and then watched him acquire 151. Halfway through the fourth Test at Old Trafford Carr contracted tonsillitis and Hobbs temporarily took over the captaincy, the first English professional ever to do so. This match was also ruined by the weather.

A Masterly Performance

All roads led to The Oval, then, for the final Test of the summer. It would decide the fate of the Ashes, which had been in Australia's possession for four successive series. With the first four Tests all having been drawn, Australia tenaciously held onto their prize, their ageing but sinewy fingers entwined round the still-mythical urn. The whole of England craved some good news, having endured a general strike in the summer, as well as the announcement from the Chancellor of the Exchequer Winston Churchill that all betting would now be taxed, and a splurge of road accidents brought on by numerous new car owners heading off along England's unmade roads without having taken a driving test.

The turnaround began with a decision from the Imperial Cricket Conference (forerunner of the ICC). In a departure from the norm, they had bowed to common sense and agreed to the fifth test's being played to a finish. Time was no object.

Carr was axed as England captain, to be replaced by Chapman; Wilfred Rhodes, who had played Tests before the new captain was born, was recalled at the age of 48. Well, he was a selector. The young fast bowler Harold Larwood, who had appeared with moderate success earlier in the series, was also called up. For Australia Herbie Collins, who had been ill for the previous two tests, reclaimed the captaincy from Warren Bardsley.

Newspaper stories of potential all-night vigils to get a ticket deterred many from turning up to The Oval on the first morning and the ground was not quite full when Chapman won the toss and decided to bat. A tall and flamboyant presence with a shock of curly blonde hair, he had had negligible captaincy experience, but 'radiated a debonair gaiety' and seemed quickly to capture the public's imagination. Although initially it seemed to have a rather ill-disciplined effect on the team.

Hobbs and Sutcliffe put on 53 for the first wicket in an hour until Hobbs uncharacteristically missed a full toss from Mailey. In common with most of his dismissals he did not look too distressed to be out – perhaps surprising for a man of such prolific achievement, although when you have already scored 50,000-plus runs you are entitled to the odd self-satisfied smirk. Frank Woolley was deceived by a Mailey googly and with Patsy Hendren miscuing a pull the score was 108-3 at lunch.

True to character, the left-handed Chapman batted with spirit and adventure to rattle up a brisk 49, but afterwards the Australian spin twins Grimmett and Mailey fiddled out the lower order. The last six wickets fell for 91 runs in an hour which, if you think about the numbers, suggests a bout of irresponsible slogging. With delicious understatement, reports of the time hinted at as much: 'In a match unlimited as to time, the lack of restraint shown by several of the batsmen was hard to understand.' Sutcliffe, at least, showed resilience, making 76 in three and a half hours. England were all out for a rather disappointing 280, but made amends by firing out four Australians for 60 by the close.

Sunday, as usual, was a rest day. On Monday The Oval gates were closed shortly after the start. People had camped out all night to get a seat. They weren't rewarded with shot-a-ball pyrotechnics, but with a gritty battle of attrition between Collins and Woodfull (known as 'the Worm-killer' for his determined forward prodding) and a disciplined England bowling attack featuring Tate, Larwood and Rhodes. Collins managed only two boundaries in nearly four hours at the crease. The crowd appreciated his dedicated commitment.

Woodfull was eventually bowled by Rhodes and the stalemate was alleviated by Gregory, who struck a breezy 73. Collins' vigil was ended by Larwood soon afterwards. But with 'capital batting' (can't you just hear the pinched vowels of that description?) from Grimmett and Bert Oldfield, a polite Australian keeper, the tourists stole a slender lead of 22. This was cautiously erased by Hobbs and Sutcliffe on the second evening, as England closed on 49-0.

A thunderstorm on Monday night saturated the pitch. Contrary to the perceived wisdom of drenched surfaces, and some nervous comment by the groundsman, Bosser Martin who said, 'Just our luck, now England are going to get the worst of the wicket – the rain has spoiled everything,' it played benignly when play resumed on Tuesday morning. The England openers proceeded carefully but without mishap.

The Australians employed an all-spin attack – presumably partly because the pacemen couldn't keep their feet. The miserly leg spinner Grimmett was at one end and the probing slow left arm of Macartney at the other. No risks were taken. There was a lot of prodding down of divots in the surface. (It was not unlike those scenes from village matches on sodden puddings – probably forbidden now by Health and Safety – when batsmen flattened out great holes in the pitch with the back of the bat, making a great smacking sound as willow whacked wet mud.) Sutcliffe resisted stoutly, not scoring for almost 40 minutes at the start, while, with excellent footwork, Hobbs smothered the potential spin and threaded the odd boundary off Grimmett. Macartney bowled nine overs for two runs. Every run was cheered joyously.

The more exploratory Mailey conceded a few runs and, when the off spin of Arthur Richardson was introduced, with five close fielders on the leg side, Hobbs provocatively flipped a few pull shots over their heads towards the boundary. He was trying to scatter the short legs. It didn't work, as Collins kept the men in. The pitch got trickier, so Hobbs went into defensive mode, dropping the ball dead at his feet as it reared up. At least it kept Richardson on, rather than exposing the batsmen to the even more dangerous pace of Gregory instead. The mischievous Pakistani Javed Miandad was notorious for this sort of tactic in the 1970s – deliberately edging the ball onto his pad to encourage the spinner, whom he was subtly milking for four an over, to stay on. Hobbs was decades ahead of his time.

He still looked to score when the ball was offered wide of the off stump and the England hundred came up to ecstatic cheering and hat-tossing. As the pitch dried and grew more spiteful, turning into a classic 'sticky dog', Richardson made the mistake of bowling exclusively round the wicket into the leg trap. Hobbs and Sutcliffe were judicious, leaving as many balls as possible and allowing others to lift and strike them on the body or step back onto the stumps and dead-bat them at their feet. With almost telepathic understanding, they stole quick singles – a silent nod was enough to initiate a run. It was batting of unprecedented commitment, courage and opportunism enjoyed by the Prince of Wales, who had just arrived. Hobbs and Sutcliffe played as if they sensed that their dedication was slowly but surely prising Australia's fingers from the coveted prize. Or maybe they sensed a possible knighthood.

Hobbs was brilliant. Knowing the result largely depended on him, he rose to the challenge. Nimble and resolute in defence, he was also quick to punish the wayward delivery, punching short balls between the cluster of close fielders towards the leg-side boundary, driving past mid-on and placing the ball with elegant precision wide of point. It was a flawless innings of controlled aggression, superb shot selection, meticulous defence, neat placement and great running. This was the Master at work.

His aplomb was remarkable. Despite the ball often jumping viciously from a length like an untrained dog, he managed surprising fluency, being principally responsible for England assembling 112 runs – for no wickets lost – in that treacherous first two-and-a-half-hour session. At lunch England were 162-0, with an already daunting lead of 140. Hobbs had 97.

He could retire to the England dressing room, a place wracked with nerves at the start of the day, and calmly light up a Players No. 6, as he liked to, aware that the tension had been defused. This is the psychological advantage a great opening pair can bestow on their colleagues. Whether they draw the sting of the fast bowlers armed with a new ball or, as in this case, absorb the pressure of a difficult pitch and a remorseless foe, not only soothing their own team's worries but also dampening the spirit of the opposition, they can effect a vital tilt in the balance of power. Momentum shifts in sport have the same properties as water: a practically undetectable leak can quickly become an unstoppable surge.

This is what clearly happened at The Oval on the morning of 17 August 1926. Perhaps realising it, the Prince of Wales, who was lunching with the captains and the chairman of selectors, walked over to the players' table and shook Hobbs by the hand before continuing with his 'roast guinea fowl luncheon' and conversation about the fantastic grouse-shooting at Balmoral.

On the resumption Hobbs soon completed his hundred, his 11th against Australia and the 137th of his life, with a scampered single. Pandemonium broke out in the crowd as the pent-up emotion and three hours of enthralled concentration were released. Play was held up for several minutes. The Australian captain shook the Master warmly by the hand. Hobbs waved his appreciation. Gregory, who had at last been risked on the damp ground, prepared to bowl, but still the crowd clapped. The fast bowler had to wait.

Eventually the game could continue. Hobbs settled into his stance, Gregory rumbled in. The crowd sat back down, elated but excited by what now lay in store. It was not what they expected. The ball nipped back from a perfect length, flicked Hobbs' back pad and trimmed his off bail. Briefly numb, the spectators slowly absorbed what had happened and a standing ovation ensued as the great Hobbs brandished his bat aloft, doffed his cap and exited the scene, having played one of the greatest innings anyone had ever seen. He was out for exactly 100, made in three hours and 40 minutes at the crease on a minefield. The score was 172-1.

Though the wicket gave Australia renewed hope, the damage had been done. A succession of England batsmen came in and played enterprisingly. Partnered by the resolute Sutcliffe, they all contributed usefully, sending the total past 300 as the Yorkshireman held up an end and picked off the odd boundary.

Always immaculately turned out, black hair scrupulously slicked down, Sutcliffe was not a pretty player. He stood open-chested at the wicket, bat picked up towards third man and on tricky pitches used every bit of his body to keep the ball out, as if his life depended on it. He was never flustered: playing and missing three balls in a row barely registered. He'd just steel himself for the next delivery. He loved a dog fight. His unbreakable resistance frustrated Australians to such an extent that it would incite abuse from the crowd. 'Send for Nurse Bland, she'll get the bastard out!' was typical from the notorious Sydney Hill. (Nurse Bland was an Australian midwife who had been in the news after an abortion scandal.) But barracking Sutcliffe was a waste of time. He had a countenance hewn from granite. It was this, as much as his superb judgement of length and efficient rather than elegant stroke-making – strong in the drive and the cut – that enabled him to be the only Englishman ever to finish his career with a Test average of over 60.

Despite the thunderstorm the previous night, which he knew would spice up the pitch, Sutcliffe said he had hardly heard the rain and slept peacefully. 'We shall be all right as long as Jack doesn't get out,' he had said in the morning. He had shared, with Hobbs, a seventh 100 partnership against Australia and in the five Tests that summer they had never been parted for fewer than 50. They were the perfect union of north and south, of style and substance, of panache and pragmatism. Averaging more than 80 together, they remain England's greatest ever batting partnership.

At well after 6 o'clock, Sutcliffe was still looking as impregnable as at the start. And then the unexpected happened. In the last over of the day from Mailey he sought a single to mid-on from a shorter ball. It skidded off the pitch faster than he expected, turned and bowled him off-stump for 161. It was the first mistake he had made. He too was afforded a standing ovation after a vigil that had lasted seven hours and wrested England an unassailable lead of 353. Hobbs observed his partner's return to the dressing room: 'There was Herbert, black and blue and not a hair out of place,' he said.

After returning home, Hobbs had dinner at the Trocadero restaurant (not as loud and tacky as it is now) and then went to the 'movies' – though, as this was mainly to see the *Movietone News*, it was a bit like watching the telly at home. There were some clips of his and Sutcliffe's partnership, but given that 1920s cameras had only very small amounts of film, it mainly featured the two men chatting in mid-pitch.

A throng gathered outside the gates the following morning to see the climax of the match. It was the first time a Test in England had been extended to a fourth day. They were joined by the Prime Minister Stanley Baldwin – the generous, pipe-smoking cousin of Rudyard Kipling – and Prince Arthur of Connaught, a cousin of King George V. (Typical of the VIPs to turn up just when the contest's getting interesting, isn't it? Through the earlier four drawn matches they hadn't been seen for dust.)

It had been dry overnight, but in the morning a shower delayed the scheduled 12 o'clock start by 15 minutes. England had four wickets in hand. It was soon only three as the all-rounder George Geary was caught behind off Gregory. Maurice Tate joined Rhodes and hit out enterprisingly, taking the total past 400. Two more wickets fell, and then at 1.15 there was another rain interruption. It was heavier this time.

About 3 o'clock the rain stopped and, impressively, play resumed only 15 minutes later. Despite the importance of the match, there was none of that poring over an imperceptible damp patch at long on and muttering about danger, obliging 22,000 people to stare at the grass for two hours. The England number 11 Herbert Strudwick was soon out, leaving Australia to make 415, more than any team had ever managed in the fourth innings to win a Test Match. And this was to win the Ashes.

The Aussies were soon in trouble, Larwood knocking over Woodfull for a duck and the dangerous Macartney for 16, both smartly caught by Geary at third slip. Chapman shrewdly brought on Rhodes' left-arm spin from the Pavilion End and, bowling teasingly and accurately with men round the bat, he reduced Australia to 35-4. There was a minor middle-order recovery terminated by Larwood and suddenly Australia were 87-8. Oldfield briefly delayed the inevitable before, at just on 6pm, Geary bowled Mailey. England had won by 289 runs and regained the Ashes for the first time in 14 years.

The scene at the finish was captured beautifully by a photographer from the *Daily Sketch* (see the picture in plate section). Men in dark or tweed suits and trilby hats are dashing across the field towards the pavilion. It looks almost like a stampede. Or, as the *Daily Telegraph* reporter Colonel Philip Trevor put it, 'Erstwhile grave parsons sacrificed their hats, men hugged each other and danced madly, and women grew hysterical. Retired (and usually retiring) military men leapt the barriers and scampered gaily for the pavilion, and the players, friend and foe alike, were mobbed.'

In the dressing room Larwood, who had given so much that final day, sat quietly sobbing, he was so overcome with the enormity of what had happened. Hobbs pressed a beer into his hand. 'This is the greatest day of my life,' Larwood said. 'There'll be more of them,' Hobbs replied.

Hobbs and Sutcliffe eventually emerged on the balcony and, like Rhodes afterwards, were greeted with tumultuous delight. Collins, the Australian captain, appeared and, according to the *Telegraph*, 'playfully shook his fist at Hobbs, an incident of merry-making which caused roars of laughter'. With a final wave, Hobbs, a private man, then retreated inside; soon afterwards he slipped out of a rear exit and went home for supper with his wife.

As news filtered through the London streets, passengers on open-top buses stood up, cheered and threw their handkerchiefs in the air. There was a real outpouring of emotion for a country still coming to terms with the loss of 750,000 men in the Great War. Other than time, only great sporting triumph can really help heal these terrible wounds.

Collins was magnanimous in defeat. 'It was the most enjoyable game I've ever played in,' he said. 'The better side won and it was played throughout in the finest spirit of sportsmanship. Particularly I want to congratulate Jack Hobbs on his century on Tuesday.

It was the finest piece of batting I have ever seen and England cannot show her gratitude too much. They owe nearly everything to him.' The Australian manager Sidney Smith was a little more tight-lipped. 'This will knock the bottom out of the three-day Test,' he said.

It didn't, in fact. Tests in England remained of three days' duration until an extension to four days was agreed for the Australians' visit in 1930. The English authorities were soon ruing that decision. Because the Aussies had the perfect person to exploit it. A bloke called Don...

4

THIRD TEST, ADELAIDE, 1933

'Bowes starts his run...now he stops...the applause for 'the Don' is continuing...people are still standing and cheering, 'Bradman! Bradman!'...Bowes is moving a fielder to deep square leg...now he's ready. In comes the big Yorkshireman, lumbering to the wicket, bowls...short and...he's bowled him! Bradman has pulled his first ball straight on to his stumps. Silence descends on the MCG!'

The year 1928 was quite a significant one on the world front. Alexander Fleming discovered penicillin at St Mary's Hospital, London (originally calling it 'mould juice'). He can thus be credited not only with saving more lives than any other human being, but also with inciting the phenomenon of man flu, enabling the sufferer to prove his infirmity to doubters by brandishing a bottle of Flucloxacillin. It was also the year of the first scheduled television programmes, aired by the General Electric Co. in New York, and the first machine-sliced loaf of bread, sold in Missouri. So began the age of the couch potato, as people increasingly spent their evenings slumped on the sofa watching TV and eating toast.

A Clash of Titans

On the sports field, 1928 was the tale of two Chapmans. Herbert, manager of Arsenal, introduced the first numbered football shirts, to the initial joy of spectators, who could now better identify their heroes – until they realised it consigned them to a lifetime of buying exorbitantly priced replica strips for their children (and, one might add, for themselves).

Meanwhile, Percy Chapman, dashing captain of the England cricket team, luxuriated in a 4-1 defeat of the Aussies Down Under. Like most successful captains, he had an enviable side, with a batting order featuring Hobbs and Sutcliffe, the prolific Phil Mead from Hampshire, the incomparable Walter Hammond, Patsy Hendren and the emerging Douglas Jardine, and a bowling attack centred on Larwood and Tate augmented by the steady left-arm spin of Jack White. With Jack Gregory succumbing to terminal injury, Australia's attack was headed by Ted a'Beckett and Stork Hendry (who? Yes, exactly) and their only bowler of note was Clarrie Grimmett. The captain, Jack Ryder, didn't have a prayer.

Hammond, arguably England's greatest ever batsman – well, Geoff Boycott says he was, so he must be – stole an early march on the 20-year-old Donald Bradman, playing in his first series. Batting at number 7, the Don managed just 18 and one in the first Test, his debut, after which he was dropped – for the only time in his career. Hammond compiled a dominant 251 in the second Test in Sydney and Bradman had a priceless view of it, since he was 12th man and had to field for the entire innings due to an injury to Ponsford.

It left a lasting impression. Recalled for the third Test in Melbourne, he made 112 in the second innings, batting at number 6 and becoming the youngest ever player to score a Test hundred. Trams in Melbourne ground to a temporary halt when the news was broadcast and there was delirium in Sydney. It was as if the Messiah had arrived. Not to be outdone, Hammond went on to score a monumental 905 runs in the 1928–9 series, then a world record and still today an English one.

The only cricket legend to have learnt the game first in China then in Malta, where his father was stationed in the army, Hammond came to first-class cricket late, owing initially to a ridiculous qualification period before he was allowed to play for Gloucestershire (he had been born in Kent) and then to a debilitating illness. He soon made up for lost time, winning over a legion of fans with his dashing stroke play – and a legion of females with his daring foreplay.

Statuesque and powerful, he took on the best bowlers with regal authority and audacious self-belief. Immaculately turned out, often with a blue handkerchief protruding from his hip pocket, he cut a dash at the crease and could annihilate bowling attacks with majestic shots mostly off the back foot. He specialised in a back-foot drive scorching straight past the bowler. Also typical were the hooked and pulled boundaries he unveiled from the first five balls of the day in a county game, delivered by the Australian quick Ted MacDonald, guesting for Lancashire. Hammond batted as a Roman Emperor might have done, sweeping aside his hapless subjects with a divine swish of his blade.

He would have been a shoo-in as the greatest batsman of any era but for the presence of one whose playing life coincided almost exactly with his own. Donald Bradman and Wally Hammond made their Ashes debut in the same match and after 20-year careers (interrupted by the Second World War) retired within a year of each other. In the interim they tortured bowlers' lives like no others as they went about their insatiable business. The Great Depression of 1929 might have been the title of the bowlers' lament. The subplot to the next six Ashes series was a personal duel between the two swordsmiths to see who could inflict the most misery. It was as if two gods had descended to earth for their own private game.

After Hammond's early lead, Bradman – who, as is well known, learnt to bat hitting a golf ball ricocheting back off a water tank with a stump (try it, at a safe distance from anything breakable, and you'll see how hard it is) – struck back with a vengeance. Arriving for his first trip to England in 1930, he warmed up with 236 against Worcestershire, then 185 not out against Leicestershire. Shortly after that he made an unbeaten 252 v Surrey and 191 v Hampshire.

That was just an appetite-whetter for the Test series that followed. The 131 on a difficult pitch at Trent Bridge in the first Test was just an hors d'oeuvre, to be followed by the Chateaubriand of 254 at Lord's. This was cited by the man himself as his greatest innings because 'I never hit the ball anywhere but in the middle of the bat, and I never lifted one off the ground until the stroke from which I was out.' That stroke was brilliantly caught, head high at short mid-off, by Percy Chapman, though why you would have a short mid-off when a bloke has just larruped you for 254 is another issue.

Then there was the Lobster Thermidor of 334 (including 309 in a day) at Headingley, the new record Test score. 'England bowlers flogged' yelled the *Daily Telegraph* headline. After that, 232 at The Oval was barely a Crème Caramel. In total Bradman made 974 runs in the Tests, overtaking Hammond's 1928–9 tally and setting a world record for a five-Test series which still stands. It was a veritable run feast. Hammond tried his best with a fine century in Leeds, but this was a Pot Noodle compared to Bradman's four-course banquet.

In the course of that 1930 series Bradman rewrote the blueprint for success in Test cricket, confounding the old adage that bowlers win matches. Australia won the rubber 2-1 with one of the worst attacks they have ever fielded (until the Kerry Packer-infected era, anyway). He proved that if you make enough runs, virtually anybody can take the wickets. In the final Test at The Oval, England made 405, but Australia replied with 695 and won by an innings, the deliciously named Percival Hornibrook taking 7-92 despite being a left-arm spinner who it was said 'bowled far too many bad balls'.

A fair bit of footage survives from that series, revealing that Bradman was a neat, compact player, just 5ft 7in tall, who moved smoothly and unhurriedly into position, often onto the back foot, and guided, levered, sometimes punched, occasionally flayed the ball into spaces. There was nothing especially provocative or outlandish in his shot-making, but a beautiful balance and complete certainty in everything he did. A sort of swivelling pull shot was probably his trademark as he pivoted on his back leg and pinged the shorter ball unerringly through mid-wicket. With great reflexes, superb judgement of length and total self-belief, he scored at a brisk rate – roughly a run a minute – and spinners were regularly assaulted from yards down the pitch. He rarely struck the ball in the air, hitting just two sixes in that 1930 orgy of run-making and only six in his entire Test career. He dissected a bowling attack with merciless deliberation and insatiable desire. 'Style?' he said. 'I know nothing about style. All I'm after is runs.'

Bradman had been born in Cootamundra, in the heartland of New South Wales. I played there once on a tour. It is hot and dusty (mind you, what town in Australia isn't?) with lots of scrubby fields and knobbly bushes. The sun bakes the skin the texture of tree bark. Someone could make a fortune selling anti-wrinkle cream. The bush flies – God's sick joke on such a sun-blessed land – drive you nuts.

The cricket is like the environment, buzzy and hostile. A guy known as Bushfire, an uncomplicated left-hander with an orange beard, thumps the ball over mid-wicket. (Australian nicknames, like their place names, are beauitfully straightforward – the Great Sandy Desert, the Great Barrier Reef, the Snowy Mountains, Tubby [Mark] Taylor.) His shorter, red-faced partner Blood Clot runs the fielders ragged. Later the team's wicketkeeper, Stumpy, greets you at the crease with, 'Mate, you're as welcome out here as a fuckin' turd in a swimming pool.' But there is humour and camaraderie beneath the aggression and afterwards we all gather round the back of a ute dispensing cold beers and laugh together about the match. And that, to most of us, is why we play the game. Making friends is intrinsic to a Pom's or an Aussie's approach to cricket.

But Bradman was different. He wasn't outgoing or friendly and he wasn't universally popular in the team. He rarely socialised after play or bought anyone a drink, preferring to retire to his room and listen to music or write letters home. The leg spinner Bill O'Reilly, later a revered newspaper columnist, said, 'Bradman was a chap who found it terribly hard to mix with the hoi polloi. He never made the slightest effort to be a real hundred per cent team man.' Bradman retorted, 'There were those who thought I was unsociable because at the end of the day I did not think it my duty to breast the bar and engage in a beer-drinking contest.' Some context is required here. Bradman was a Presbyterian and a Freemason. O'Reilly was a staunch Catholic. Enough said.

The observation is important, though, because, in spite of his great gifts, there was something essentially joyless about Bradman's batting. The English crowds marvelled at his amazing feats and flocked to see him bat, but there was an underlying resentment that he was a remorseless intruder who had invaded the old kingdom with a mission to obliterate everything in his path. He seemed to be murdering the English game in cold blood. 'Do you get nervous, Mr Bradman?' an interviewer asked him. 'No, never,' he replied coolly. 'A menace to English cricket,' the *Daily Mail* called him, though it seems to me that paper has always had a fearful dread that the aliens are coming.

With Britain in the depths of economic recession – and Australia too, for that matter – sport was a release, an escape from the anxiety and hardship of daily life. Bradman had eroded the beautiful unpredictability of their sport. Much as the Aussies loved hammering the Poms, and enjoyed the fact that Bradman had given them an identity in the world, even they were uneasy that it was becoming a bit one-sided. The Don was slaughtering the bowlers, toying with their existence, then killing them off. Bat versus ball had ceased to be a duel. Bradman had perpetrated a mass homicide. This could not continue. The bleeding must be stopped. Cricket itself was haemorrhaging to death.

Getting Under the Skin

England were due to tour Australia 18 months later. The planning began almost immediately. The MCC, self-styled protectors of the game, recruited Pelham Warner, who had led England to Ashes success before the First World War, to construct a new campaign to win back the urn (although this was by now in the MCC's possession). He in turn appointed Douglas Jardine as captain. Jardine, a taciturn Scot educated at Winchester and Oxford, had tasted Ashes success in 1928–9 but taken against the locals and their insulting ways. (Australian crowds had been provoked by his habit of wearing a striped Harlequin cap and silk cravat on the field; they yelled, 'Where's your butler to carry your bat?' and mocked him when he swatted at flies, bellowing, 'Don't kill them – they're the only friends you've got.') 'Australians are uneducated, an unruly mob,' Jardine declared. 'They don't seem to like you over here, Mr Jardine,' Patsy Hendren said. 'It's fucking mutual,' Jardine replied.

He didn't utter any of this at an elaborate press conference in front of the world's media, to be instantly used on the back page of the *Sun* to start a phoney war. But it was well known that he hadn't been to charm school and his acrimony towards Australians had hardened during the summer of 1930, in the field, suffering Bradman's ritual slaughter.★

Warner had suggested that England needed 'new bowlers, new ideas for Australia'. With Jardine he was preaching to the converted. Jardine had studied footage of that 1930 series and talked to a couple of influential former players, such as the left-arm quick Frank Foster, who had practised leg theory 20 years earlier. Jardine thought he'd spotted a weakness in Bradman's method. 'He's yellow,' he said.

One of the first people approached was Harold Larwood, the fastest bowler in England. He and his Notts opening partner Bill Voce were summoned to a secret meeting at the Piccadilly Hotel in August 1932, a month before leaving for Australia. Larwood liked Australians, enjoyed their wholehearted commitment and mateyness. (Have you ever noticed the number of different ways an Aussie says 'mate'? It can be a friendly 'mate!' or a quizzical 'mate?', a cautionary 'maaaate...' or a sympathetic 'mahayte...') But Bradman didn't impress him. He admired his ability but hated his attitude. He found him detached, disengaged with the

---

★It seems oddly poignant to be writing about Jardine a few days after the sudden death of another ex-England captain, Tony Greig, who in many ways was a similar character. He too had Scottish ancestry, despite being born in South Africa; he loved confrontation and could be astonishingly tactless. But he was a brave and innovative leader who never took a backward step and whose team were proud to stand behind him. It's hard to imagine a man of such presence and vitality suddenly dead. But his excited commentary and the unmistakable way he poked his finger at you in an animated discussion and said, 'Now I'll tell yooouuu!' in that strange Strine/Yarpy hybrid accent will live on in our minds.

opposition. It was almost as if the bowlers were there just for his pleasure, and he didn't even buy them a restorative drink afterwards. That really gets bowlers' backs up. 'He was cruel in the way he flogged you,' Larwood said. 'He made me very, very tired.' But also 'very, very angry'.

Larwood had dismissed Bradman only once in seven attempts – when he had already made 232. He felt a sense of injustice over an incident at the Headingley Test, when he thought he had Bradman caught behind before he had scored. Everyone else thought so too, except the umpire. Despite a 'snick you could hear all over the ground', Bradman remained at the crease and went on to make 334. Bowlers have long memories. Larwood wanted revenge.

At dinner at the Piccadilly Hotel, Jardine aired the idea of bowling short at Bradman's leg stump – effectively at his body. They had seen how he had flinched ever so slightly to the odd fast short ball when he first came in. Fast bowlers can pick up that sort of thing in an instant, like dogs sensing a nervous postman. They also believed they could control his scoring options that way, but accuracy was vital. Larwood was impressed with the idea, and believed he could accomplish it. He and Voce tried it out in the remaining county matches of the season – bowling at batsmen's bodies with predominantly leg-side fields – with mixed results.

But, accompanied by Voce's blunt assertion to the Australian opener Vic Richardson (grandfather of the Chappell brothers) that 'if we don't beat you, we'll knock your bloody heads off', the tactics worked as soon as England arrived in Australia. In some of the warm-up games against an Australian XI, Bradman looked shaky against the England fast bowlers and averaged just 17 in six innings. He had tried backing away to cut Larwood and been bowled, and then going across too far to pull Voce and losing his middle stump. More and more fielders had been moved to the leg side during these matches and Bradman complained to Australian officials about the tactics. Jardine remained undeterred, referring to Bradman as 'the little bastard' (which was a back-handed compliment) and preaching a sort of hate campaign to get under the Australians' skin.

Bradman was taken ill with flu before the first Test in Sydney and missed the match that England, despite a brilliant, fearless innings of 187 not out by Stan McCabe, won easily. With his beautiful, whirling action, sharp pace and skiddy bounce, Larwood took 10 wickets. Because he was relatively short for a quick bowler – just 5ft 9in – his bouncer didn't get up much and was hard to avoid. In that way he was slightly reminiscent of the brilliant West Indian speedster Malcolm Marshall.

Although England were now one up they were not entirely happy campers. The Nawab of Pataudi (Oxford Univ & Worcestershire) had refused to field in 'leg theory' positions, and despite making hundred in the first Test – his England debut – he was summarily dropped after the second. (He later played for India.) Also, the third member of the pace attack, Gubby Allen (Cambridge Univ & Middlesex), had refused to adopt the tactics of Larwood and Voce. When Jardine ordered him to comply he said, 'I've never bowled like that and I don't think its the way cricket should be played.' He also threatened to leak their conversation to the press.

Allen was a terrible snob who regarded Larwood and Voce as uneducated oiks (partly because they were from the north) and he loathed Jardine. He was revered at Lord's in later years for his administrative work, yet was always a law unto himself, with a house behind the ground (paid for and maintained by the MCC, whose groundstaff were expected to tend his roses), his own key in the pavilion and a special high-chair in the committee room to watch the game from. From here he would occasionally bang on the ceiling with his walking stick if Mike Gatting was making too much noise in the Middlesex dressing room above. He was not a man to be messed with, and Jardine gave up trying.

The second Test in Melbourne was three weeks later – none of that back-to-back Tests malarkey in those days – and Bradman returned. As was his custom, he ambled rather than strode to the middle, taking a slightly circular route – getting his eyes accustomed to the light – accompanied by unrelenting applause from a vast crowd. Bill Bowes, the bowler, stood at the end of his run, waiting for it to subside. Twice he had to abort his run-up. In the meantime he moved a couple more fielders over to the leg side. There were only two on the off.

Bowes, lanky-tall but only medium pace, moved into bowl. Expecting the ball to be short, Bradman shuffled across his stumps and shaped to pull. But he had moved too early and could only drag a very moderate ball into his stumps. It was the only first-ball duck of his Test career. 'Well, I'll be fucked!' said Bowes. At the jam-packed MCG you could hear a pin drop.

Helped by a foot injury to Larwood, Bradman re-established his prowess with a fluent, undefeated hundred in Australia's second innings, moving about the crease, making room to flay short balls through the off side, something he had worked hard on in practice. Wally Hammond admired the innings. 'He played golf shots and overhead lawn tennis shots and from one after another the ball went crashing into the pickets. That was sheer courage…' Australia won the match comfortably and levelled the series. But afterwards Bradman issued a formal complaint to the Australian Board of Control about 'bodyline bowling', which he warned would 'kill cricket'.

The Board did nothing. (The term, incidentally, arose from a journalist, Hugh Buggy, initially describing the bowling as 'on the line of the body' and then abbreviating it to 'body-line').

Drawing Blood

By the time of the third Test in Adelaide, the local mood was combustible. The England players were jeered by a large crowd at practice and Jardine had to order his team's net sessions to be closed to the public. That just incited the spectators' wrath further: their suspicions that the England captain had a low opinion of them were confirmed. Jardine, however, seemed to revel in being perceived as the villain.

The atmosphere was defused somewhat by Jardine winning the toss and electing to bat. He also promoted himself to open. But it didn't go according to plan. Both he and Wally Hammond were knocked over early by the combative Australian fast bowler Tim Wall and suddenly England were 30-4. They were rescued by those 'dreaded' northerners – the fine off-driving of Yorkshire's Maurice Leyland (83), Lancashire's pugnacious left-hander Eddie Paynter (77) and the leg-side biffery of Warwickshire's Bob Wyatt (78). England closed at 236-7 and the following day the last three wickets added a further 105 runs, thanks mainly to Hedley Verity's 45. By halfway through the second day they totalled a thoroughly respectable 341.

Then, after Gubby Allen had dismissed Australia's Jack Fingleton without scoring, came the duel that a packed Adelaide Oval had been waiting for. Larwood against Bradman. It was a typically warm South Australian afternoon, but there was a breeze and Larwood, bowling from the River Torrens End, had it at his back. The pitch, hard and bare, was also to his liking. He knew from previous experience that a ball banged in hard and short of a length would fly through, and at varying heights.

Taking a pinch of snuff, as he always did before bowling, claiming it focused his mind on the job in hand, Larwood hustled into bowl at the Australian captain, Bill Woodfull. The field was orthodox: one short leg, several slips, the rest saving one. It was very much not a leg theory field. The sixth ball of Larwood's second over (eight-ball overs still) was rammed in back of a length on a straightish line. It hustled onto Woodfull as he shuffled across and – to use modern parlance – got big on him. It slammed into his chest and immediately drew blood. Woodfull staggered across the crease as if he had been shot. The crowd roared its disapproval. Larwood, certain he had done nothing intentionally malicious, remained at his end, close to Bradman, the non-striker. Jardine, in inflammatory mood, called out, 'Well bowled, Harold,' deliberately in Bradman's earshot, and then, when Woodfull had recovered and was ready to face the next ball, stopped Larwood halfway through his run-up and elaborately moved a couple of fielders over onto the leg side in catching positions.

The next ball was also short and rose up, knocking the bat out of Woodfull's hands. This threatened to tip the crowd over the edge and there was a real fear that there would be a pitch invasion. A strong police presence dissuaded would-be rioters, and the mood passed, although at a drinks break one spectator yelled in the direction of Jardine, 'Don't give him a drink, let him die of thirst!'

Woodfull offered staunch if slightly passive resistance, but Bradman was obviously disturbed by events and was moving extravagantly across his crease or semi-crouching as the ball was delivered. A ball from Larwood at leg stump soon had him caught at short leg for eight, though if you watch the dismissal on Youtube, you can see that the ball wasn't especially short and rose only fractionally above waist high. Bradman just didn't play it very well. He was disorientated, evidenced by his weaving path back to the dressing room, initially going to the wrong gate. McCabe fell to Larwood soon after, and when Woodfull was bowled by Allen the Australians were 51-4. Profiting from a softer ball, the absence of Bill Voce with an ankle injury, and extra padding under his shirt, Ponsford, in company with Vic Richardson, took the score to 109-4 by the close.

Meanwhile Pelham Warner, England's manager and a diplomat at heart, had attempted to defuse a potentially volatile situation by knocking on the Australian dressing-room door. But, failing to see the hypocrisy of his actions, he only made matters worse. Before Warner was even halfway through his initial pleasantries, Woodfull, towelling himself down after a shower, famously said, 'Mr Warner. There are two teams out there on the field. One is playing cricket. The other is not. That is all I have to say. Good afternoon.'*

They are perhaps the most famous words ever spoken in cricket (alongside Tony Greig's 'Make them grovel' line and David Lloyd's 'We murdered 'em'). There is no concrete evidence confirming who leaked Woodfull's snubbing of Warner to the press, though the suspicion is it was Bradman, as he had various media contacts. By the following day – a rest day – it was all over the papers, stirring Monday's packed crowd to even greater degrees of hostility. The Australian Cricket Board approached Warner, requesting that England desist from posting leg-side orientated fields, but Warner argued, credibly, that he had no influence over Jardine on the field.

So began bloody Monday (16 January 1933), with Bill Ponsford spiritedly taking on the bouncers and hitting creamily through the off side in company first with Richardson and then with wicketkeeper Bert Oldfield. Ponsford was out for 85 at 194-6, soon after which England took the second new ball (available after 200 runs had been scored in an innings). On 41

---

*The Australian press conjured a humorous take on this after the Adelaide Test of 2010–11 which Andrew Strauss' England, after losing the toss, won handsomely with a peerless all-round performance. Over a large picture of Australia's departing number 11, Peter Siddle, the caption declared, 'There are two teams out there on the field. Only one is playing cricket. That team is England.' (See page 257).

Oldfield, attempting to hook Larwood, top-edged the new cherry into his forehead. It has been claimed Larwood wasn't bowling 'leg theory' at the time, though pictures of the incident – showing a leg slip and two short legs – do not support this.

Oldfield crumpled to the ground and for a horrible moment Larwood thought he was dead. He rushed towards the stricken batsman, mumbling, 'I'm sorry, Bertie,' to which the blood-stained but astonishingly forgiving Oldfield replied, 'It's not your fault, Harold, I was trying to hook you for four.' It sounds like a conversation on a village green in a P G Wodehouse novel rather than one between Ashes rivals with 50,000 Australians baying for Englishmen's heads. Luckily mounted police were on hand to keep control.

Woodfull strode out to the middle to aid his wounded player. Rather incongruously he was dressed in a dark suit. He obviously hadn't bothered to take part in the pre-match warm-ups. Or if he had, not very actively. (Mind you, some of the greatest Ashes heroes often didn't either – Denis Compton, Jeff Thomson, Ian Botham, Shane Warne.) He helped Oldfield, who had sustained a hairline fracture, from the field.

Bill O'Reilly replaced him and the crowd booed every time Larwood ran in to bowl. It didn't help O'Reilly, who soon missed a straight one. With Oldfield unable to return, the innings was over for 222 shortly afterwards. England had a lead of 119. Larwood's figures of 3-55 from 25 overs give no hint of the impact he had on the match, the series and international relations between the two countries, as well as on the life of British actor Hugo Weaving (Elrond in *Lord of the Rings*, Agent Smith in *The Matrix*), whose career took off after he was chosen to play Jardine in the successful TV mini-series *Bodyline* in 1984. Tea was taken, as it always is at these moments of high drama, and afterwards everything is all right again. Jardine marched out to open England's second innings and proceeded to block his way to a four-hour 50. In fact no one, not even Wally Hammond, was very fluent. England crawled to 296-6 over the next day and a half, ensuring that their lead would be over 400 and that any potential lynchers in the crowd would be asleep.

It was all kicking off in the boardrooms, though. Failing to conceal their sense of outrage, the Australians sent a cable to the MCC. It read:

> Bodyline bowling has assumed such proportions as to menace the best interests of the game, making protection of the body by the batsmen the main consideration. This is causing intensely bitter feeling between the players as well as injury. In our opinion it is unsportsmanlike. Unless stopped at once it is likely to upset the friendly relations existing between Australia and England.

In the history of the world, how often has a pompous letter actually exacerbated a situation? Probably about 99.9 per cent of the time. It wasn't helped in this case by being partly leaked to the press first, and also by being received by an MCC committee that included a Viscount, several other peers of the realm and the Speaker of the House of Commons, none of whom would take kindly to the 'unsportsmanlike' slur, even as they peeked at an opponent's cards at the bridge table. The English papers were understated as usual. 'Cheapest possible insult!' yelled the *Star*. 'Undignified snivelling' declared the *Daily Herald*.

In fact the English papers got it right. Australians like to refer to the English as 'whingeing Poms', but on this occasion it was the Aussies who were whingeing. Look at it this way. England's attack consisted of Larwood, obviously fast, but only 5ft 9in tall; Voce, incapacitated with an ankle injury; Allen, who refused to bowl leg theory; Hammond's brisk medium; and Hedley Verity's left-arm spin. It was hardly the fearsome foursome that the West

Indies fielded through the 1980s, from which a batsman's ribcage had no escape. In fact it was not even as potent an attack as Australia's Gregory and MacDonald a few years earlier, and they had meted out some bouncers. Only Larwood bowled short in Adelaide and then only intermittently. It was not a bumper barrage. And it was hardly life-threatening, as both Ponsford and Richardson proved in a fifth-wicket stand of 80.

What the Australians clearly did not approve of was the proliferation of short-leg fielders when Larwood was bowling. Writing in the *Daily Telegraph*, Surrey's Percy Fender, who had partly concocted the whole strategy, defended the ploy, saying it was a bowler's job to unearth a batsman's flaws 'and to play on them to his discomfiture'. That, after all, is the essence of cricket; all this 'jeopardising the spirit of the game' is balderdash. What, the 'spirit' of the game that allowed W G Grace to cheat or run out an Australian batsman who had left his crease to prod the pitch, or enabled Warwick Armstrong to bowl endless looseners to a teammate, making Frank Woolley wait 15 minutes for his first ball in Test cricket? Never mind a Hall of Fame, a Rogues' Gallery from the history of cricket could easily take up half of Madame Tussaud's. Interestingly, Australia's opening batsman Jack Fingleton said, some years later, 'I think, looking back, that the Australians perhaps made too much fuss about it.'

The MCC, with no real evidence to go on (the advent of Youtube was 80 years away), were piqued by the Australians' message and drafted a response. But, as typewriters had a habit of getting badly gummed up at the time, it took five days to complete. So the match continued. England, having finally been dismissed for 412 halfway through the fifth day, giving them a lead of 531, set about bowling Australia out.

Larwood soon had two early wickets – Fingleton and Ponsford – but Woodfull was defiant and Bradman adventurous. He raced to 50 in an hour and was particularly severe on the spin of Verity, saying afterwards, 'I wanted to hit one bowler before another hit me.' But after he had lofted the spinner for his first six in Test cricket, over-ambition got the better of him and he was caught and bowled. By the close Australia, 120-4 with Oldfield not fit to bat, were doomed.

Jardine called a team meeting after play and asked if a) leg theory should be continued and b) he should remain captain. Warner attempted to offer his views but was silenced by the players, who voted unanimously to carry on the mission in the same way. Some of the team may not have liked Jardine, but all admired his determination and ruthlessness.

On the sixth day, once the Woodfull–Richardson partnership was broken (Richardson caught at short leg hooking), the end was swift. The last four Australians were all clean bowled, three of them by Gubby Allen, leaving Woodfull to carry his bat courageously for 73 not out. Larwood had match figures of 7-126, Allen 8-121 and England won by 338 runs to take a 2-1 lead in the series.

After the match, Jardine made a speech. Well, not so much a speech as a remark. 'What I have to say is not worth listening to,' he said. 'Those of you who had seats got your money's worth, and then some. Thank you.' And after posing for a couple of pictures, he turned on his heel and left. He was the definition of actions speaking louder than words. It's a shame so few people abide by that.

England's triumph had left a bitter aftertaste. The players were irked by the charge of 'unsportsmanlike' play and Jardine sent a message to the MCC saying he would not carry on as captain unless pressure was exerted on the Australians to withdraw it. The local papers rather sided with England, the *Melbourne Age* labelling the Australian Board's suggestion that bodyline would sour relations between the two countries as 'hysterical', and in other papers the Australian players were just advised to butch up and get on with it. And that was the point. They could have retaliated, trying the same tactics on England, but they didn't really have the ammunition or, in the person of Woodfull, the desire. Rather uncharacteristically, they preferred to take it on the chin. Or should one say forehead?

Four days later, by which time England were playing up-country in Ballarat, the MCC's reply arrived. 'We deplore your cable,' it began, 'and we deprecate your opinion that there has been unsportsmanlike play.' It went on to support Jardine and the team, suggesting that they would not 'infringe the laws of cricket or the spirit of the game'. It finished with a veiled threat: 'If you consider it desirable to cancel the remainder of the programme, we would consent, but with great reluctance.' The MCC knew full well that the series was a box-office phenomenon and that for the Aussies to cancel it would be financial suicide. The *Melbourne Age* suggested that the MCC response was 'a snub, not wholly undeserved'.

Non, Je Ne Regrette Rien

Two weeks elapsed before the Australians finally withdrew their 'unsportsmanlike' slur. By now England were in Brisbane preparing for the fourth Test. Larwood still employed bodyline tactics in Australia's first innings, but searing heat and a flat pitch ensured they had negligible impact, in spite of Jardine trying to keep his bowlers going with regular swigs of champagne. (Don't you just love the completely original sound of this guy?) Australia finished the first day 251-3 (Bradman 71 not out) and the *Sydney Morning Herald* proclaimed 'Leg theory mastered'.

Larwood enjoyed the amber nectar – he invariably had a beer and a smoke during the lunch and tea intervals of a Test Match

– but Jardine, recognising the importance of the following morning's play, told Bill Voce, who was out injured, to ensure Larwood was in bed by 9 that night. He agreed, but later he, Larwood and two other players allowed themselves to be persuaded to go to a party, with inevitable results. They staggered back to the hotel plastered at 1am.

Despite the mother of all hangovers, Larwood cleaned up Bradman within three overs the next morning: he was bowled making room to cut, which tells you everything you need to know about Larwood's impact on his previously impenetrable method. Larwood also quickly accounted for Ponsford and Australia lost their last seven wickets for just 76 to be all out for 340. At lunch, Jardine made a special point of thanking Voce for looking after his spearhead, who had taken four more Australian wickets.

At 216-6 and with Eddie Paynter sick and unlikely to bat, England were in real danger of conceding a substantial first-innings lead. Enter Paynter who, with Voce's help, had discharged himself from hospital (suffering from acute tonsillitis rather than alcoholic poisoning) and, still in his hospital gown (hopefully not one of those that gapes open at the back), hailed a taxi to the ground. White as a sheet, he hung on till the close – helped both by his partner Larwood and by Woodfull who, according to Larwood was 'very considerate throughout his innings'. (Someone should check Bill Woodfull's birth certificate and find out if he was actually Australian.)

At the end of play Paynter booked straight back into hospital, but returned the following morning to make a defiant 83 and gain England a slender lead. His innings was described as 'one of the greatest examples of pluck and fortitude in the history of Test cricket'. He augmented the feat by agreeing to take the field (against doctor's orders) once Australia went back in.

It was one of those Brisbane days they like to call a 'bottler', which derives, I think, from the idea that it is so hot and clammy it feels like being cooped up in a bottle (another beautifully simple piece of Australian nomenclature). Larwood still glided smoothly into bowl, so light on his feet he was almost undetectable to the umpire as he ran in. He soon snared the big wicket of Bradman, caught at deep cover, which must have been galling for the Don as there was only one fielder in front of the wicket on the off side. Australia finished the day 108-4, with a lead of 92.

McCabe and the dashing left-hander Len Darling went on the attack the following morning in a last act of Australian defiance, but, after being softened up by Larwood, McCabe was dismissed by Verity; Larwood and Allen then polished off the tail. England needed 160 to regain the Ashes.

Sutcliffe was out early, but Jardine remained staunch and impassable, like a security guard who obstinately refuses to let you in. At one point he went 82 balls without scoring. This utterly uncompromising man had a countenance hewn from granite. He was out before the close, but England, 107-2, had eight fingers on the urn. The match was over just before lunch on the sixth day. Fittingly, Paynter sealed victory with a straight six.

The euphoria was kept in suspension, however, because news filtered through during the morning that Archie Jackson, a precocious young Australian batsman thought to be potentially as good as Bradman, had died of tuberculosis in a nearby hospital. He was 23. Flags were lowered to half-mast and players wore black armbands.

Nothing could completely scupper Jardine's triumphant moment, though. 'I am naturally delighted that we have regained the Ashes,' he said, 'but hope I can say with Kipling that cricketers can meet triumph and disaster and treat the imposters in just the same way.' Well intended as it may have been, he might have regretted using such pompous language when he reflected on it later. Not that Jardine ever regretted anything, or even knew the word existed.

After 28 hard-earned wickets in the four Tests, with the exertion sometimes causing him to vomit after play, Larwood was exhausted. With the Ashes regained, he asked Jardine if he could sit out the last Test in Sydney, which began only a week after Brisbane. Jardine considered his request for about a nanosecond, then refused. 'We've got the bastards down there, and we'll keep them there,' he said, with obvious reference to Bradman.

So, reluctantly, Larwood played. He ripped out three early wickets on the first morning, including Bradman (bowled for a quick-fire 48), before gradually tiring as Australia piled up 435. Then on the second evening the unforgiving Jardine sent him in as night watchman. Indignant, Larwood more or less tried to get out, but survived overnight and carved and hooked his way to 98 the following morning before the reality of a Test-Match hundred dawned and he poked a tame catch to mid-on. He left to a standing ovation.

Hammond made a commanding 101 and England took a 19-run lead. Larwood, complaining of a sore left foot in Australia's second innings, still whipped out Richardson for his second duck of the match and clocked Bradman a painful blow on the shoulder – the only time he was hit in the series. But the pain intensified and soon he could barely run in. He pleaded with Jardine to let him leave the field. Intransigent – OK, sadistic – to a fault and intent on giving Bradman the impression that he might whistle his spearhead up for another spell, Jardine said no.

Eventually Bradman was bowled for 71, cutting Verity. 'Right, Harold,' said Jardine. 'Now you can go.' What an extraordinary sight it must have been, the incomparable Bradman walking back to the green-roofed members' pavilion at the Sydney Cricket

Ground to fervent applause, with the limping Larwood following behind. Remarkably, he never took the field for England again.

England won the final Test by eight wickets, taking the series 4-1. Larwood finished with 33 wickets (average 19.5), including the wicket of Bradman four times. The Don still topped the Australian batting averages with 56.57, but, vitally, his output had been halved. Two days later, while the victorious party made their way to Melbourne for the last two matches of the Australian leg of the tour, the injured Larwood headed home.

The journey took six weeks. A crowd of 20,000 crammed round Nottingham station at close to midnight to welcome him back. He was showered with gratitude. Hundreds tried to touch or kiss him. Once back in England and freed from his tour contract, Larwood spoke out, giving an exclusive interview to the *Sunday Express*. He said, 'Bradman was frightened…yes, frightened is the word. He was scared by my bowling. I knew it, as everyone did.' A month later, his ghost-written account of the series, *Bodyline?*, was published. Quite apart from containing a defence of his bowling methods, it was somewhat uncomplimentary about Australia. A tour there, he wrote, 'would be a most delightful period if one were deaf' and he went on to denigrate the behaviour of the spectators. He was adamant that if he was asked to desist from bowling 'fast leg theory' he would quit.

In support, Jardine, in a one-off interview, also declared that the term bodyline was 'meaningless'. 'It was coined,' he added, 'by a sensational press to explain or excuse defeat and it would have died a natural and speedy death had it not been adopted by the Australian Board of Control in its lamentable wire to the MCC.' He was abiding by one of the golden rules of international sport: if in doubt, blame the press. Mind you, they're usually right.

In the corridors of power, however, support for Larwood and his methods had evaporated. Covering his back and anxious not to deter the Australians from visiting England in 1934, Pelham Warner wrote a series of articles distancing himself from Jardine (the man he had appointed as captain) and the tour. In September 1933, the MCC, responding to a request from the Australian Board, wrote, 'Your team can certainly take the field with the knowledge and assurance…that a direct attack by the bowler upon the batsman would be an offence against the spirit of the game…' (There's that ambiguous word 'spirit' again. In my book, spirit in sport equals trying to win. And surely a 'direct attack' on the batsman is what the game is all about. What is the bowler supposed to do – feed him half-volleys?)

In May 1934, having hardly played for Nottinghamshire the previous summer because of his injury, Larwood was approached by the county's rich benefactor, Sir Julian Cahn – clearly acting on behalf of the MCC and the British government – suggesting that he 'apologise'. Larwood didn't understand. 'What for?' he asked. 'For your bowling,' came the reply. Cahn handed Larwood a typed letter and asked him to sign it. Larwood was stunned. 'I've nothing to apologise for!' he retorted. 'You must, Harold,' Cahn urged. 'You must apologise to the MCC for your bowling and you must agree to bowl legitimately in the future. If you don't, you will not be picked in the Tests against Australia.'

Infuriated by this disloyalty and satisfied that he had done nothing illegitimate, but had merely followed his captain's instructions, Larwood stood his ground. 'I won't sign this,' he said. 'I am an Englishman. I will never apologise.' And through another 60 years of his life, he never did.

The MCC, in cahoots with the government, wouldn't budge either. It was all about money, of course. The MCC didn't want to jeopardise the 1934 Ashes series, and the government didn't want to damage trade relations with Australia. The Cabinet Minister and Dominions Secretary Jimmy Thomas made sure Larwood was never again considered for England selection. Duncan Hamilton sums it up superbly in his award-winning biography *Harold Larwood*: 'History embalmed Larwood in the bodyline series, as though he died bowling it,' he says. Which, to all intents and purposes, he did.

Guess what Bradman averaged in that 1934 series? Answer – 94.6. Guess who won the Ashes? Australia. Guess who was awarded a knighthood in 1937 for services to cricket? Pelham Warner. Guess who got nothing? Harold Larwood.

5

FOURTH TEST, HEADINGLEY, 1948

Bradman was a total phenomenon. There is no other word for him. Writers ran out of superlatives. He had everything a batsman required – a great eye, quick feet, superb balance, brilliant judgement, a shot for every delivery and situation and an utter hatred of bowlers.

In fact Harold Larwood got less than nothing. After 1934 he was ostracised by the Lord's mandarins, made a scapegoat for damaging Anglo–Australian relations and left out in the cold. He felt so alienated from the English game that eventually, in 1950, he sold his ailing sweetshop in Blackpool and emigrated to Australia with his wife and five daughters. They took the boat from Tilbury, Larwood using the same brown leather suitcase he had travelled to Australia with in 1932–3. The only person there to wave him off was a youngish John Arlott. A travesty.

In a further concession to Australia, the MCC, governors of the laws of the game, decreed that only two fielders could now be stationed behind the wicket on the leg side, killing off any lingering ideas about bodyline among the bowling fraternity (though it didn't stop a legion of 1970s pacemen from bowling at the batsman's head). As a result the remaining three Ashes series before the Second World War became a glorified run fest. In essence it was Bradman v Hammond.

Despite early sickness, Bradman won the first of these face-offs, scoring 758 runs in the 1934 series, which Australia won 2-1. He didn't have the uncompromising Jardine to contend with: he had resigned before the MCC pushed him, and covered the Tests as a journalist instead. Bradman began the series at a gallop, venting his pent-up frustration from the bodyline tour on the bowlers. But having being dismissed cheaply a couple of times, he became more calculating, taking almost sadistic pleasure in making the bowlers pay for their previous insolence: his last three scores in the series were 304, 244 and 77. The English public treated him like a deity. He wandered around trailing star-struck children (and adults) as if he were the Pied Piper. When he fell ill with appendicitis at the end of the tour and was unable to travel home, even King George V wanted health updates.

Hammond struggled in the series, with a top score of just 43, and suffering from a permanent sore throat, probably due to the amount he smoked (or swore). He was able to console himself that his arch-rival had failed to usurp his world-record score of 336 not out, made against a moderate New Zealand the previous year (many felt Hammond had made this score deliberately, just to knock Bradman's 334 off the top rung). Bradman stole a further advantage in the 1936–7 series by being made Australian captain. As a professional, Hammond was stumped.

The hierarchy were sticking to their absurd rules about amateur captains, so instead Gubby Allen, the man who had objected to bodyline, was selected to lead the MCC on that tour. A southern snob, he was influential in the non-selection of northerners such as Herbert Sutcliffe as well as a young Len Hutton, and the batting was over-dependent on Hammond. He had the satisfaction of making an imperious and unbeaten double hundred in the second Test in Sydney, driving England to an innings win and an unexpected 2-0 lead in the series. But on a gluepot in Melbourne, Bradman, underlining his ruthlessness, reversed the Australian batting order, allowing himself to come in when the pitch had eased and make 270. After tying up victory there, the Don notched up another match-winning double hundred in the third Test, at Adelaide, though he had to bat for almost seven and a half hours to get there because of the number of fielders England posted on the boundary. His batting was like a torrent, forever surging past, round or through any obstacle. Hammond could only look on forlornly, muttering, 'Bloody Bradman', and reassure himself with the knowledge that at least he was better at pulling *off* the field.

In the decisive fifth Test, also in Melbourne, Bradman won the toss, went in at number 3 and spanked 169 in 191 balls. That's 651 runs in three innings. OK, there was the minor aberration of 26 in between. But basically he scored runs at will. Who were these English pie chuckers, I hear you ask? Well, there were Bill Voce, Allen himself and Ken Farnes – a destructive 6ft 5in fast bowler from Essex – supported by Hammond's lively medium and the left-arm spin of Hedley Verity. It wasn't quite Botham, Willis, Old and Underwood, but it was a decent attack.

Australia won by an innings, of course, becoming the first team in Test history to win a Test series after being 2-0 down. This irked Hammond even more. He stormed home, gave up his day job (professional cricket) and became a director of a Gloucestershire tyre company. Now, as an amateur, he could be made captain of England – and he was, for the 1938 Ashes. Can you believe these absurd shenanigans?

It made negligible difference. After a drawn first Test at Trent Bridge in which Bradman defended stoutly on the last day for 144 not out, Hammond produced a commanding 240 at Lord's.

Pulling England round from 31–3, he batted with such mastery that the Australians could only stand back and admire. One scorching drive rebounded off the Lord's pavilion wall straight back to the bowler, who picked it up as if nothing had happened and ran in again. Hammond's double century took barely five hours. The legendary cricket writer C L R James claimed it was the greatest innings he had seen. But Bradman defied England again in the second innings with another undefeated hundred. This had become silly. Couldn't someone just run him out at the bowler's end or something?

After a third-Test washout, Headingley played host to the fourth. Here, on a difficult pitch, Hammond top-scored for England with a dextrous 76. In appalling light, Bradman trumped that with 103 and Australia had enough of a lead to eventually win by five wickets.

Unable now to win the series and generally unimpressed by the ruthless approach of Bradman's team, for the final Test at The Oval Hammond asked his batsmen for inexorable application, with no concessions to the Don. And that is what he got. Len Hutton's 364 was an epic performance, lasting over 13 hours – the longest and highest scoring Test innings that had ever been played – enabling England to post a colossal 903–7 declared. During it Hutton repelled 625 dot balls. That is more than a day of blocking. Can one man have ever put more effort into a completely lost cause? But it was all in vain. Australia had retained the Ashes again.

End of the Affair

War brought a halt to this personal duel. Hammond was recruited to the RAF but in an administrative role and spent much of the time in Cairo. Bradman enlisted with the Royal Australian Air Force, was transferred to the army, then contracted fibrositis and was discharged. He didn't play in the five Victory 'Tests' between England and the Australian Services in 1945 to commemorate the end of the war (the outcome was 2-2 – fair play to the Aussies, since they had only Lindsay Hassett and Keith Miller as recognisable Test players). Both Hammond and Bradman suffered further bouts of ill health so that when the Clashes for the Ashes resumed, with almost indecent haste, in 1946–7, neither man was match fit. Yet both were elected captain.

Their relationship was civil at best. Even as opposing captains they rarely spoke except at official moments. They never socialised together. Hutton observed that they didn't like each other very much and dwelt on their different approaches. Hammond's batting had more style, more soul – it had a human element to it. Bradman was an automaton, impervious to anything around him. 'I'd prefer to see an hour of Walter Hammond to eight hours of Don Bradman,' Hutton commented.

He didn't get his wish. The opposite happened. England lacked firepower and Bradman knew it. In the first Test in Brisbane, having struggled against Alec Bedser, he'd scratched his way to 28 when he drove at a wide yorker from Bill Voce and edged to slip. It was so obviously out that England barely appealed. Bradman stood there, one of only two men in the ground thinking it was a bump ball. The other was the umpire. To the visiting side's utter disbelief he remained to compile a vintage 187, his 18th century against England. All the talk before the Test of his impending retirement had gone up in a puff of Pommie smoke. Clearly he had been imbued with the W G Grace mantra that they've come to see me bat, not you bowl, and in his case it was true.

In Sydney, nursing a leg injury, the Don survived an appeal for lbw on the third evening and recovered the next day to help himself to 234. Fatigue claimed his wicket after six and a half hours. 'There's runs out there if only a man had legs,' he declared.

Australia, fuelled by the fastest pair of bowlers in the world – Ray Lindwall and Keith Miller, whom Bradman ordered to 'bowl faster, bowl faster…grind them into the dust' – went 2-0 up.

Bradman piled up more runs in the third Test. At last, in the fourth, England found the answer. The Don strode in at his adopted home, the Adelaide Oval, with a packed house expectant. Bedser, a master of in-swing, was experimenting with a new delivery, held across the seam so it went straight. He tried it to Bradman. It cut away and clean bowled him for a duck. It was, the great man said, the best ball he had ever received. He initiated a special net session after the match to replicate the delivery, but in six subsequent encounters Bedser dismissed him five times. His star was finally fading.

As for Hammond, his star was extinguished. He was 43, nursing a chronic back complaint and homesick. He managed not one 50, captained without enthusiasm and became more and more withdrawn, tending to travel separately from the rest of the team.

By the fifth Test, with the Ashes gone, he finally admitted defeat and left himself out. It was the end of the road for Walter, but with 7249 Test runs in 85 Tests, average 58, and 22 majestic hundreds – the most by an Englishman until Alastair Cook overtook it in 2012 – it had been one hell of a drive.

Bradman, five years younger, had more great deeds left in him; he received a knighthood in 1949 and remained revered wherever he went for the next 50 years, living until he was 92. Hammond, after one regrettable farewell match for Gloucestershire in 1951 in which he made a painful seven, retired to a life of relative obscurity in Durban with his South African second wife and, after being almost killed in a car crash, suffered a fatal heart attack aged just 62. He died plain Walter Reginald Hammond. But he left a magisterial legacy.

Alien Force

The Britain that the Australian team of 1948 arrived in was a dishevelled one. After the hardship of war and the bitter winter of 1947 people looked grey and haggard with crumpled, tatty clothes, bad teeth and greasy hair (you were allowed to fill a bath only to a depth of five inches). Rationing was almost more severe than during the war, with everyone restricted to a piece of meat the size of an iPod once a week, and limits on bread, potatoes and fruit. Shepherd's pie consisted of mash and gravy made out of an Oxo cube or, since horsemeat was sometimes available, a (dead) runner from the 2.35 at Uttoxeter (so that's where the ready-meal manufacturers got the idea from). It is perhaps not surprising that Denis Compton and Bill Edrich had had their remarkable run sprees for Middlesex in the summer of 1947 – Compton made 3816, Edrich 3539 – as the bowlers and fielders clearly had no energy. There were long queues outside surgeries and clinics created by the newly established NHS, not only because of illness but also because it was the one time in history when hospital food was better than what you got at home.

There was an atmosphere of great relief as well as unbridled joy at the arrival of the Australian cricketers. It was a throwback to the good old days, to the spirit of (a now ravaged) Empire. England v Australia was a rejuvenation of its lifeblood. Bradman's team were welcomed as if they had descended from another planet. And the way they played, it was clear they had. Five of their first six matches against the counties and Cambridge University they won by an innings. Against Essex at Southend they made 721 – in a day. Bradman scored buckets of runs, including 187 in two hours and four minutes in the Essex match. Just before lunch he hit four successive balls from one bowler to the mid-wicket boundary, despite a lot of tinkering with the field. 'Haven't you got any other shots?' asked Frank Rist, the Essex wicketkeeper. 'I'll show you those after lunch,' Bradman said. He then proceeded to hit the next to the same spot for another boundary, adding, 'I did say *after* lunch.'

The Australians, marshalled by Bradman, who had had a close involvement in assembling the squad, were on a mission to annihilate. 'Bradman,' reported the *News Chronicle*, 'remains the coolest and most ruthless strategist in cricket.' And by 'cool' they didn't mean trendy. The innings against Essex, it said, 'was all part of his deliberate, merciless, efficient plan, brilliant in its execution, to build up the biggest possible psychological advantage over the English bowlers.' And he clearly enjoyed letting loose his two fast and nasties – Lindwall and Miller – on county batsmen.

Not everyone in the Australian team approved of this approach. Miller, a fighter pilot in the war, had some sympathy with the Brits and what they had been through. Against Essex he walked in at 364-2, stood aside as Trevor Bailey bowled and calmly allowed the ball to hit his stumps. He was rumoured to have gone off to the races straight afterwards. He didn't feel comfortable terrorising moderate batsmen or bowling flat out on spicy pitches, either. Mind you, it didn't stop him pinging down five bouncers in eight balls at Len Hutton when the Tests began at Trent Bridge. Hutton resisted stoutly in England's second innings after the inevitable Bradman hundred, though he was more subdued than in the past.

Compton batted with great resolution for six continually interrupted hours – in generally appalling light – to make 184 and prevent an innings defeat, before treading on his wicket. But Australia ruthlessly exploited a new rule allowing a second new ball after just 55 overs (instead of after every 200 runs), rotating four seamers who took 19 of the 20 English wickets. With a storm brewing, Australia wrapped up the match by eight wickets. The domination continued at Lord's with victory by 409 runs, both the Australian openers – Sid Barnes and Arthur Morris – scoring a century. The fastest bowler England captain Norman Yardley had at his disposal was Bill Edrich, and he was only 5ft 6in.

The Australian steamroller met two hurdles at Old Trafford. One was Compton who, with the Dunkirk spirit still lingering, defied ferocious bowling from Lindwall and a cut head after top-edging a hook; he staggered back to the wicket to groggily hold the England innings together with an undefeated 145. The other was the famous Manchester weather, which consigned the match to a draw, though, on a wet wicket, Australia were obliged to block out the final afternoon, Bradman restricting himself to just two singles in the final hour.

The Aussies then travelled back to Lord's and thumped a decent Middlesex side by 10 wickets. They had now played 20 games on tour, won 17 (10 by an innings) and drawn three. What made them so good? Clearly attitude was the primary factor. Bradman had specified before the tour that he wanted disciplined types with a bulldog spirit and, almost to a man, he got them. The opener Sid Barnes epitomised the character of the team. A gutsy batsman, feisty and ultra-competitive, he was also a fearless short-leg fielder who stood perilously close to the bat during the 1948 Tests. At Old Trafford he took such a whack from a pull shot that, after trying to bat and collapsing at the crease, he spent 10 days in hospital. He also had a rather eccentric sense of humour, once during the tour capturing a dog which had run on the pitch shortly after a disallowed lbw decision, offering it to the offending umpire and suggesting that all he now needed was a white stick.

Barnes's opening partner, Arthur Morris, was an elegant left-hander with superb concentration, accomplished against all types of bowling but especially fluent against spin. He was the leading run-scorer in the 1948 series. Below Bradman came Lindsay Hassett, his vice-captain, an inch shorter (5ft 6in) than his captain but with a similar method and appetite for run-making. He was remorselessly consistent. So was the left-handed Neil Harvey, a dynamic batsman just starting out in 1948, who had grit, gumption and a real spirit of adventure. There was grace and style about him, too.

It's funny how people always say that about left-handers – that they look a touch more elegant (Gower, Lara and Sobers spring to mind). Is this extra style imagined? Well, yes, possibly. England's Paul Collingwood was jogging on a treadmill one day and noticed in the mirror a left-hander batting on the television behind him. He was impressed with the poise and grace of the strokes. When he turned round to look at the TV properly he realised it was a replay of one of his own innings. I saw the same innings on a video which had been deliberately reversed to show Collingwood as a left-hander. And he did look more stylish!

Further down the Australian order were Sam Loxton, a belligerent batsman who loved a scrap with fast bowlers and could give a bit back with the ball, and off-spinning all-rounder Ian Johnson. The other spin options were the leggie Colin McCool and the gangling Bill Johnston, a very dependable and persevering left-arm seamer who could turn to spin if necessary. Completing the bowling were another left-arm seamer, Ernie Toshack, who moved the ball in to the right-hander – relatively unusual at the time – and of course Ray Lindwall, known as 'Atomic' for his explosive bursts of pace. Inspired to bowl fast at the age of 12 by seeing Larwood in the bodyline series, he had a beautiful, smooth rhythm as if he were coming in on wheels, and an unusual, slingy action – not unlike Sri Lanka's Lasith Malinga. He mainly looked to pitch the ball up and swing it away, but his bouncer was lethal (like Larwood's, it didn't get up much and tended to skid at the batsman), his yorker was wicked and he also possessed a cleverly disguised slower ball and a superb appreciation of batsmen's weaknesses. Until the emergence of Michael 'Whispering Death' Holding, there was no finer sight in the game than Lindwall running in to bowl. Don Tallon, a gifted wicketkeeper with lightning reflexes, supported him excellently behind the stumps. These were the men who put Bradman's uncompromising tour plan into action.

Keith Miller was the exception. He was a cavalier in a team of roundheads. He didn't like to practise, enjoyed late nights, often didn't bother to mark out his run-up and was therefore liable to charge in from anywhere. Known as 'Nugget' because he had the golden touch, he was a fluid, dashing batsman who smashed 181 on his debut for Victoria, a slippery fast bowler who sometimes overdid the bouncer, often just to excite the crowd, and a brilliant fielder with the knack of taking inspirational catches. Bradman did not always approve of his attitude, and the feelings were mutual. In Bradman's farewell match in Sydney the following year, Miller bounced him out for four. Bradman subsequently ensured Miller never became Australian captain. But Miller had genuine style and charisma and the English crowds cherished him (except when he was dishing out the short stuff). The portrait of him in the Lord's Long Room – depicting an ageing, withered man in an ill-fitting suit – does him a total disservice.

A Worthy Pursuit

Australia arrived at Headingley for the fourth Test of 1948 the day before the game. It was their 21st match of the tour and perhaps they were tired. Certainly their attack seemed jaded as the recalled Len Hutton and his tough Lancastrian opening partner Cyril Washbrook put on 168 for the first wicket. The absence of Barnes at short leg – he was still suffering from the blow he had received at Old Trafford – gave them a sense of freedom and both batsmen prospered on either side of a number of rain breaks. Hutton, the local hero, was eventually bowled for 81 by a delicious out-swinger from Lindwall with the second new ball. Washbrook was dismissed just before the close for a polished, at times imperious, 143. Alec Bedser was sent in as nightwatchman.

He and Bill Edrich were not parted until after lunch on the second day. Bedser, after early sketchiness, hit out forcefully but Edrich laboured over his innings, not helped by Bradman's defensive field settings. He made an overcautious 111 and Bedser a jaunty 79, but after that England's innings declined. The last eight wickets fell for 73 and they totalled 496. Reporters of the time regarded it as disappointing, though it was a good deal better than England's previous first-innings efforts in the series.

Bedser snared Morris in the evening, bringing Bradman to the crease – though he could barely get there, such was the Emperor's welcome he received. Hero-worshippers clustered round the man who had previous Test scores on the ground of 334, 304 and 103. He didn't disappoint with a fluid 31 not out, leaving Australia 61-1 at the close. But a capacity Saturday crowd, relishing the sight of Bradman in full flow – a phenomenon they hadn't seen for 10 years, of course – were dismayed to see him bowled on the back foot by the Lancashire seamer Dick Pollard within 10 minutes on the third morning. Pollard, who had also just disposed of Lindsay Hassett, then disappeared into anonymity again. He'd had his 15 minutes.

Exuding class, Neil Harvey regained the initiative in partnership with the pugnacious Miller. They put on 121 in just over an hour and a half in a thrilling mix of panache and power. Loxton maintained the tempo, fearlessly striking five sixes in a vigorous 93, helping Harvey to his hundred. Still England glimpsed the chance of a healthy lead, but it was cut to just 38 after Lindwall's clean-hitting 77. Jim Laker was steady with his off spin, but England felt the lack of a leg spinner on such a flat track.

The brisk Kent leggie Doug Wright had been left out. Another century opening partnership from Hutton and Washbrook, weathering a ferocious early spell from Lindwall, then overcoming Bradman's defensive tactics, got England back on course on the fourth day. At 129 Washbrook, hooking hard and down, was brilliantly caught by Harvey running in from long leg. Hutton was out on the same score. Edrich and Compton – men who were clearly never bored with each other's company – consolidated the position, adding 113, and then, after a mini collapse, wicketkeeper Godfrey Evans supplied a jaunty riposte in partnership with the tail. Overnight, England led by 400 and it was assumed Norman Yardley would declare.

Surprisingly, he allowed the innings to continue for 10 minutes on the fifth morning. Thus Australia were set 403 to win – a big ask, as current players are fond of saying (don't they mean task?). In fact it was bigger than any previous (t)ask: 71 more than any team had ever made in the fourth innings to win a Test (that had been England with 332-7 in 1928 at the MCG).

The pitch was flat, the outfield like glass and England's opening bowlers ineffective. But spin was in short supply – especially spin away from the right-handers. So Denis Compton's occasional left-arm chinamen and googlies were employed and soon rewarded – Hassett was smartly caught and bowled for 13, bringing Bradman to the crease at 1pm. The Yorkshire public knew this would be his last innings at Headingley and he was applauded all the way to the wicket. He later said it was the greatest reception he had received from any ground in the world.

Perhaps the emotion of the day affected England more than Australia. Morris should have been stumped off Compton shortly afterwards, but the normally immaculate Evans fumbled the ball. On 22 Bradman also offered a sharp chance to Jack Crapp – believe it or not the safest close fielder in England.

But the chest-high catch was put down. Encouraged by the spin, Yardley brought on Hutton's occasional leg breaks. He didn't land many and was taken for five easy boundaries in two overs. In the half-hour before lunch the second-wicket partnership added 62. Australia had some momentum.

The weather was hot (for Yorkshire anyway), the pitch was dusty, there were no sightscreens. It was a perfect situation for a spinner, but Laker was inaccurate and the other slow bowlers were not up to scratch. Despite Bradman occasionally suffering from cramp, obliging Morris to take the majority of the strike at times, the runs flowed at 83 an hour. That, even allowing a slick 20 overs an hour, is good going. There were numerous fielding lapses. So many, in fact, that had it been PC (Post-Cronje) it would have raised suspicions about match-fixing.

Yardley manipulated his bowlers and claimed two new balls, but to no avail. The partnership became unstoppable. By the time the pair had put on 301 and Morris had been caught at mid-off for a memorable 182, the match was effectively over. Miller contributed a brisk 12, while Bradman continued to thread the ball through the field. At 6.15 he sportingly allowed the 19-year-old Harvey to make the winning hit. The Don had supplied a commanding 173 not out, in four and a quarter hours (apologies to all anoraks, but there is no record of the number of balls faced). In four Tests at Headingley he therefore averaged 192. It must have been tempting to take a little sod of the pitch home with him rather than the customary souvenir stump.

The Yorkshire crowd applauded, cheering the adopted hero they called 'Braddles', but there was a deep-seated disillusion. They had come to see a vintage Bradman century and more importantly an uplifting England win, but the two rarely coincided. The victory had not only clinched Australia the series 3-0, but had set a new and rather daunting record for fourth-innings run chases in Tests which acted as a major deterrent to future declarations. It stood for 28 years.

For England it was as ignominious a day as they had ever experienced, superseded perhaps only by the time in 1984 when the West Indies coasted to their victory target of 344 just one wicket down. On that occasion a half-fit Gordon Greenidge, batting on one leg, pulverised a bowling attack which included Botham and Willis for an unbeaten 214. At least England could point, in 1948, to the ravages of war which had left them as vulnerable as it had in 1920–1 – three years after the First World War – and similarly exploited. And that was why victory was so eagerly desired.

For Australia it was a triumph, achieved by prodigious talent, an unshakeable will and a powerful team unity. They were looking to re-establish themselves on the global stage after a rude interruption. Without the religious factions of the 1930s in the team, they had again set a benchmark for how the game should, or at least could, be played. And they were led by a totally uncompromising man who did not tolerate, or even comprehend, the word defeat: the Invincible Captain of an Invincible Team.

The inimitable commentator John Arlott watched the 1948 series and waxed lyrical about Bradman:

He was 40 years old, and still playing strokes impossible to any other cricketer in the world. He stood at the crease perfectly immobile until the ball was on its way to him, then his steps flowed like quicksilver out of trouble or into position to attack. He could still pull the ball outside the off stump accurately wide of mid-on's right hand to avoid a packed off-side field. He still played the ball off his back foot past mid-off before that fieldsman could bend to it. He still hit through the covers with the grace of a swooping bird. He could cut and glance, drive, hook and pull, and he could play unbelievably late in defence. Those who had never seen Bradman bat until

1948 saw a great batsman; those who knew his batting saw a new greatness.

His final performance at Headingley was in the realm of fantasy. But reality quickly bit. Australia had a match beginning the next day at Derby, of all places. It was the original plummet back to earth. There was no time for celebration. Within 45 minutes the players had showered and changed and were on a stuffy train from Leeds with no buffet car. Well, Bradman never liked drinking anyway…

A Brief Glimpse of Immortality

You know how this story ends. You won't perhaps know that the Australians had to pack five three-day matches against the counties into the 17 days between the fourth and fifth Tests. They needed them like a hole in the head. Rain ruined two of them, which was probably a blessed relief. Bradman was exhausted and missed the game against Glamorgan. He played in the following game, against Warwickshire, though, and, pointedly, was bowled for 31 by the leg spinner Eric Hollies by a top spinner he didn't appear to pick. Hollies, a Warwickshire stalwart and one of those mavericks who have taken more wickets than they have scored runs (almost invariably spinners), was not in the England squad that summer, but he took 8-107 in that innings. It won him selection for the final Test at The Oval.

Despite a showpiece century against Lancashire, Bradman was spent. He got to The Oval sensing it was the end (he had declared earlier in the year that he had played his last Test series in Australia). What he claimed not to know was that his Test average at that point stood at 100.39. He needed just four runs to reach 7000 (in 70 completed innings) and guarantee an average of over 100.

He lost the toss and Australia were consigned to field. Not for long, though. England capitulated in just over two hours. On a soft but far from difficult pitch, Lindwall (6-20) bundled them out for 52 – England's lowest total at home. After the early loss of replacement opener John Dewes (Washbrook had been hit and injured batting for Lancashire against the Australians, ironically in his benefit match), a strange hypnosis descended on England. They hardly played an aggressive shot. Hutton, who was last out for a ponderous but secure 30, struck the only boundary of the innings.

Barnes was reunited with Morris at the top of the Australian order and they were untroubled in putting together a century stand. With the score on 117, Barnes edged a wide ball from Hollies to Evans. Bradman made a measured entrance to a standing ovation. As he reached the wicket, Yardley, the England captain, led three cheers (he forgot the 'and one for luck'). Bradman, perhaps for the first time in his life, looked quite sentimental. Having flattened down a couple of divots with the back of his bat, he settled into his stance. He shuffled back and across and defended his first ball from Hollies.

The canniest spinner in England, Hollies had told a Warwickshire colleague that he would bowl Bradman a googly second ball 'because he would be expecting it first ball'. It was perfectly pitched on off stump. Misreading it, and definitely not expecting it, Bradman made a rather ungainly lunge. It spun back and bowled him through the gate for a duck. Bradman swivelled on his heel and, with a brief glance at his broken wicket, smartly departed the scene. The crowd, briefly silent in suspended animation, rose to cheer him all the way back to the pavilion. It wasn't bodyline that had finished him off, or some other brutal tactic, but old-fashioned sleight of hand at leisurely speed. He was human after all.

Arthur Morris continued on to an imposing 196 (out of Australia's 389, Hollies taking 5-131). England, while exhibiting more fight than in their first innings, were then bowled out for 188. It gave Australia another crushing victory, by an innings and 149, so Bradman didn't bat again. He ended, as most people know, with a Test average of 99.94, giving him just the vaguest hint of mortality. Well, it makes the story more real, doesn't it?

His work wasn't done, though. As the great West Indian Learie Constantine wrote, 'He pities none…if he can make any bowler look foolish, he will do it… no room for mercy, no standing back while a disarmed rival picks up his fallen weapon.' Bradman was on a mission to get through the whole tour unbeaten and there were still five county matches to go. The Australians achieved it, of course, with three innings wins and two draws. And guess what? Bradman's last three scores of the tour were 150, 143 and 153 – against decent bowling attacks as well. Decent on paper, anyway.

Over his entire first-class career he scored a hundred every 2.88 innings. For comparison, Hammond did it every 6.01 innings, Jack Hobbs 6.67, Viv Richards 6.98, Brian Lara 6.77 and Ricky Ponting 6.08. Sachin Tendulkar (5.91) is the only major batsman in the game to have scored a hundred more frequently than every six innings. In that sense Bradman was twice as good as anyone else who has played the game. And there were no helmets then, which certainly enabled players like Lara, and even perhaps Tendulkar, to be more prolific than they might have been without.

Yes, it may be wrong to compare players from different eras. But who cares? It's fun. Bradman was a total phenomenon. There is no other word for him. Writers ran out of superlatives. He had everything a batsman required – a great eye, quick feet, superb balance, brilliant judgement, a shot for every delivery and situation, a remorseless attitude and an utter hatred of bowlers. The legendary Sunil Gavaskar said once that being able to drive through the chaos of Indian streets – negotiating the wandering pedestrians, the weaving vehicles, the wild animals – was invaluable for a batsman, as it taught you to block out everything around you and focus only on the road ahead. Bradman was born with blinkers on and never ran out of gas.

He must have the last word. When, several decades later, he was watching one of many abject England attacks being mauled by Australian batsmen, he was asked how many he might have averaged against those bowlers. 'Aw, about 60,' he mused. 'Only 60?!' exclaimed the questioner. 'Well,' Bradman retorted, 'I am 85!'

6

FIFTH TEST, THE OVAL, 1953

'Four to get…Morris, left-arm chinaman from the
Pavilion End, bowls, short, a swivel pull from
Compton and…is it the Ashes? Yes! England have
won the Ashes!'   Brian Johnston, BBC TV

Was there a lower point in British sport than 29 June 1950? It is doubtful. On their debut in the football World Cup in Brazil, England lost 1-0 to the United States, a team of part-timers with a goalkeeper who drove a hearse for a living. Although it was suggested before the game that the Americans, who had only trained together once, should be given a three-goal head start, it was they who took the lead in the 37th minute. After that the hearse driver Frank Borghi foiled England with a number of brilliant saves. He should have offered them a lift afterwards. England failed to recover from the shock and were soon eliminated from the tournament.

On the same day at Lord's, the England cricketers were succumbing to a first ever defeat by the West Indies. These were players who, Fred Trueman once candidly admitted, 'we joost thought were a bunch of beach cricketers'. It wasn't a fluke or a narrow win, either. The margin was 326 runs. The young spinners Sonny Ramadhin and Alf Valentine bowled England out for a turgid 274 in the second innings. They sent down 143 overs between them in that innings, 90 of which were maidens. So if it was painful enough to lose the match, it was even more painful watching it.

Your Country Needs... You!

Britain was broke, having borrowed $3.75bn from the US (a debt which was only finally paid off in 2006), and most of the Empire had been sacrificed. A pick-me-up was desperately needed. But, after the events of the first Ashes Test in Brisbane that winter, England were concluding that the sporting gods were definitely against them. There was no Bradman, but Big G up above was making life just as difficult. After Australia's captain, Lindsay Hassett, won the toss and elected to bat on a flat pitch, the England seamers, led by Alec Bedser, performed superbly to roll them out for 228. But a huge Queensland storm was brewing and, as soon as the innings was over, it vented its wrath on Brisbane.

When England finally got to bat two and a half days later the (uncovered) pitch was a beast. Good-length balls spat at the batsmen's head or snaked into their ankles and England were soon 68-7. At this point captain Freddie Brown declared, reasoning that his bowlers could inflict equal damage before the pitch dried. He was right. In 13 overs Australia staggered to 32-7.

With still an hour left for play, Hassett returned the favour: knowing the pitch remained a minefield, he declared, setting England 193 to win. It was a masterstroke. By the end of the day England's second innings was in ruins at 30-6. Mind you, Surrey's wicketkeeper Arthur McIntyre, playing as a batsman, didn't help matters by getting run out going for a fourth. That made it 130 runs in the day for 20 wickets lost. Despite a gallant 62 not out the following morning from Hutton, batting at number 8, England were finished off by the mystery spin of Jack Iverson – making the ball break both ways by flicking it out with his middle finger, a predecessor of the Carom ball you see in the modern game.

England toiled hard in that 1950–1 series but never really recovered from their early misfortune, losing the first four Tests, though they did win the fifth. They still didn't have quite enough firepower with the ball, a fact that had been recognised by a docker as soon as their boat berthed in Sydney. 'Hey, Warr,' he shouted at England's jovial medium pacer J J Warr, 'you've got as much chance of taking a Test wicket on this tour as I have of pushing a pound of butter up a parrot's arse with a hot needle!' You've got to hand it to Aussie barrackers – they've got imagination. He was almost spot on, too. Warr bowled 73 (eight-ball) overs in two Tests and took 1-281. He didn't play for England again, though he did turn out to be a funny and perceptive writer on the game.

Finally in 1952, after 75 years of Test cricket, England's selectors (the MCC) took the plunge. They chose, shock horror, a *professional* – Len Hutton – as captain. It was regarded as a risk, not just because professionals continued to be regarded as lower -class oiks and were still obliged to change in a separate room to the amateurs, but also because Hutton was not even a county captain. Norman Yardley was in charge at Yorkshire.

Hutton was, of course, the backbone of England's batting and had been since the war. This was reflected in a favourite Yorkshire story. Two neighbours go to watch the Test at Headingley, but forget their sandwiches. One pops back to get them. When he returns he says to his mate, 'I've got bad news. 'Ouse 'as burnt down, wife's run off wi' lodger and kids are in't street in tears.' The other bloke replies, 'And I've got bad news for thee, too – ' Utton's out.'

The selectors (Yardley, Brown, R E S Wyatt and Les Ames) needn't have worried. England thumped India 3-0 that summer and discovered an exciting new strike force, Hutton's Yorkshire colleague Fred Trueman, whose bowling was as abrasive as his language. National Service meant Trueman was unavailable for the first four Tests of the 1953 Ashes, but his future BBC colleague Trevor Bailey, piqued by criticism of his ability in Australia, kept England in the series.

The first Test, just a week after Queen Elizabeth II's coronation, was spoilt by rain. Bedser's 14 wickets were to no avail. In the second, at Lord's, England, despite an indefatigable 145 from Hutton, looked doomed to defeat. Set 343 to win, they were 12-3 at the start of the last day, with a posse of Australian pacemen salivating. At 73-4 the forceful Yorkshire left-hander Willie Watson was joined by Bailey.

During the next four hours, Bailey reaffirmed his nickname of 'the Barnacle'. Nothing could prise him from the crease. He scored runs as a glacier gains inches. He defined Hutton's pre-series edict to sell your wicket dearly, in general defiance of a national campaign to make cricket 'faster, brighter, livelier'. Watson, who was also a prominent professional footballer and part of the England squad at that 1950 World Cup, was equally resolute, making a patient 109. He said afterwards, 'Trevor got his left foot out to the pitch of the ball, stuck his nose down and looked as if he would not budge for a squadron of tanks, let alone a battery of Australian fast bowlers.' Bailey was out with half an hour left for play, but the lower order held out.

At least two days' play was lost to the weather at Old Trafford, but on the last day England discovered a major flaw in Australia's make-up: their collapse to 35-8 against Laker and Johnny Wardle indicated that they couldn't play finger spin on a tricky pitch. That knowledge would be useful later.

Australia had the upper hand in the fourth Test at Headingley, and on the last day required 177 after tea to win. They surged to

111-3 and needed just 66 from 15 overs to retain the Ashes. Drastic measures were required. Hutton turned to Bailey, who said, 'Give me the ball.' He put six men on the leg side, went off his long run and bowled consistently outside leg stump.

The Aussies were initially nonplussed and ultimately furious when he took seven minutes to complete an over, but they allowed him to bowl six overs for just nine runs. The umpires, English of course, took no action, despite this tactic being, in some ways, more dubious than bodyline. The *Daily Telegraph*'s E W Swanton admitted that the method 'rankled a bit'. With Bedser typically miserly at the other end, Australia fell 30 runs short, even though they were only four wickets down. An M S Dhoni blitz would have seen off such a target in 20 balls and it seems remarkable now that the Aussies couldn't have tried something – taking guard outside leg stump, for instance, or giving the bowler the charge – but it was another 10 years before one-day cricket was invented.

The (20-Year) Party's Over

So, going into the fifth and final Test at The Oval, which began on a Saturday, it was level pegging at 0-0. (The Americans would have been asking what was the point of all this effort. But they just don't get the idea of a five-day draw, or indeed cricket in general.) England hadn't won the Ashes for 20 years – since the bodyline series – and in Britain the match was eagerly anticipated. With a spate of TV sets having been purchased to watch the coronation, it was even going to get some live coverage.

England ordered a dry pitch, which for once the groundsman heeded, and selected the recovered Trueman as part of an attack which included the Surrey spin twins Tony Lock and Jim Laker. Australia picked five seamers and left out their leggie, Richie Benaud.

Hassett knew this was a crucial omission as soon as the first ball of the match from Bedser drew a puff of dust. Trueman, rumbling in off his curving 25-yard run, began with a bouncer and, after Bedser and Bailey had made early inroads, blew a hole in the Australian middle order. Fast and furious, he was the embodiment of England's post-war rejuvenation. They had suffered for seven years at the potent hands of Lindwall and Miller with nothing to fight back with. Now they had a battering ram of their own. By early afternoon Australia were reeling at 118-5.

There was a partial recovery, but when Alec Bedser caught and bowled the all-rounder Ron Archer he had taken his 39th wicket of the series, an Ashes record. He also now had 221 Test victims, making him, at that moment, the leading Test wicket-taker of all time. Lindwall counterattacked in a stunning display of clean hitting and was last out, giving Trueman his fourth wicket. Australia had been dismissed for 275 – generally regarded as a 'nothing' score at The Oval.

For that match England boasted as good a top six as they've ever fielded. Hutton and Edrich opened; at 3 was the classical Peter May, a confirmed amateur who drove the ball regally; and at 4 the diametrically opposite Denis Compton, the great entertainer with his range of sweep shots, cuts and other ingenuity, and the first truly commercial cricketer after his £1500-a-year deal with Brylcreem. Tom Graveney, the master craftsman, was at five and Bailey the Barnacle at 6.

There were a few overs left for them to negotiate at the end of the first day, and Hutton was nearly out in the first of them. A vicious bouncer from Lindwall flew off the shoulder of his bat, ripped off his cap, which just missed the wicket, and fell short of the five slips. Bad light mercifully ended play an over later.

Sunday was a rest day. By the 11.30 start on Monday the ground was full. Thousands had been locked out. The emergence of Hutton and Edrich was greeted by a huge roar which E W Swanton in the *Daily Telegraph* strangely compared to 'the thunder that used to greet the public appearances of Der Fuhrer and Il Duce'. The England players were certainly under no illusions about how much this match meant to the British public.

Feeling the pressure, Hutton began edgily. Edrich was more certain, hooking the bouncers from Lindwall and Miller. Hutton survived to play neat shots off his legs and, after Edrich was lbw to a fast full toss, he and May put on 100. Australia fielded brilliantly, especially Harvey at cover, but the pitch was friendly once the ball was soft. Both batsmen eventually fell to the nagging left arm of Bill Johnston, who had started the day bowling at his fastest, but then settled into a long, containing spell of medium-paced cutters with the keeper standing up.

Compton and Graveney looked ill at ease, betraying a lack of understanding between the wickets. It would have been Compton's fault. He was a famously poor runner, who calculated in retirement that he had been involved in 275 run-outs. 'Compton's call of "yes" to his partner,' his Middlesex colleague J J Warr said, 'was invariably accompanied by "good luck."' A feisty afternoon spell from Lindwall with the second new ball and superb catching accounted for both batsmen and England were now 170-5, still more than 100 behind.

Godfrey Evans batted enterprisingly, hooking Lindwall for 10 off an over, and he added 40 with the predictably dogged Bailey. But, setting off for a run to backward square leg, Evans was sent back by his partner, slipped and was run out. Laker lasted only a few balls and, at the close of an attritional day, England were precariously placed at 235-7, Bailey 35 not out.

The third day was decisive. It had a substantial bearing not just on the match and the series but on the shape of things to come for the next five years. It began with Lock fending off a nasty lifter from Lindwall and being caught at backward short leg. England, now eight down, were still 38 behind. With the pitch likely to deteriorate, a first-innings lead was crucial.

Bailey was joined by Trueman, normally a compulsive hitter. Vitally he reined himself in, emulating Bailey by playing straight down the line against Lindwall and Miller, who were both busting a gut. He hung in for half an hour while 25 runs were added. After he was bowled behind his legs, Bedser, a useful number 11, was forthright, biffing Johnston's canny left-arm variations high over mid-off. The fielder, Miller, couldn't make the catch and the batsmen ran four to wild cheering. England had the lead. They eked out 30 more priceless runs, Bailey reaching his 50 in just over three hours. He was bowled on the stroke of lunch for 62. It had been another monument of application that had accumulated England a slender but significant lead of 31.

The Australians were back in straight after lunch. Five overs into the innings, Hutton played his trump card. He took off Trueman and brought on Laker, who immediately spun one back and had Hassett lbw. It persuaded Hutton to bring on Lock's left-arm spin at the other end. There was much controversy surrounding Lock's action. He released most of his deliveries with a bent arm, and his quicker ball – which fizzed through from nowhere – looked particularly suspicious. Hassett, when facing Lock in the first innings, had mischievously called down the pitch, 'Strike one...strike two?'

After Laker had trapped the stylish right-hander Graeme Hole lbw, Lock bowled Harvey driving and pinned Morris leg-before on the back foot. In between, Miller had poked Laker to short leg for a duck. The cream of Australia's batting had been skimmed off in 14 minutes at a cost of just two runs, and they were now 61-5.

The flamboyant all-rounder Ron Archer realised the danger of pushing and prodding against the turning ball, so went on the offensive. He hit Laker over mid-wicket with the spin and memorably on-drove Lock for six. The left-handed Alan Davidson supplied some meaty blows himself. This was a typically courageous rearguard action from Australia. They weren't going to surrender the Ashes yet.

Straight after tea, however, Lock dismissed both batsmen. Lindwall briefly wielded the long handle, but going for a second six was nervelessly caught on the boundary by Compton leaning against the fence. Laker and Lock had shared nine wickets and the Australians were 162 all out. England needed just 132 to regain the Ashes and, not least, beat the Australians at home for the first time for 27 years.

There were 50 minutes left in the day – one of those sessions that openers dread, when the bowlers have everything to gain and the batsmen have little. The pressure on Hutton and Edrich was enormous. The hopes of a nation, now watching intermittently on TV, rested on their bats. They could feel the crowd willing them on with every run they took, edging closer and closer to the coveted prize.

Perhaps that's why Hutton risked a second for a push past one of three short legs. There was never two in it, despite the fielder, James de Courcy, slightly fumbling the ball by the square-leg umpire. But tension scrambles the mind and Hutton was run out by a distance. It is said that the greatest silence in cricket was when the returning Bradman was bowled first ball in Melbourne during the bodyline series. The moment after Hutton was out was equal to it. E W Swanton portrayed it beautifully: 'I have not known a similar moment of complete, quiet stupefaction,' he wrote. With a regal on-drive off Miller, May calmed the situation and England got to the close without further alarms. They were 38-1.

Such was the momentousness of the fifth day that the BBC announced it was clearing its schedules and showing the match live (though that was slightly disingenuous as the first programme of the day – *Andy Pandy* – wasn't on until 3.45). The two-hour morning session encapsulated Australian cricket. Lindwall, who had had little rest from his 32 overs in England's first innings, flew at them for an hour and a quarter in an 11-over opening spell that posed great threat and yielded few runs. There was no Esky full of ice-cold isotonic fluids left at long leg for him, nor a drinks break after a handful of overs, nor a chance to nip off the field for 10 minutes feet up on the pretext of going for a pee.

Edrich and May resisted him valiantly, accumulating 25 runs in the first hour. The crowd were rapt and broke into fevered applause every time a run was scored. They even did so when May hurriedly kept out Lindwall's dangerous in-swinger.

At the other end Johnston nagged away relentlessly for 23 consecutive overs, offering nothing to hit and suffering an edge that slipped between the keeper and first slip for four and a difficult dropped chance to second slip. The ground fielding was brilliant, especially Harvey in the covers and Davidson in the gully. May had just produced the shot of the morning, a classic cover drive, when he was smartly taken at leg slip, glancing Miller. It's an underused position in cricket these days.

With half an hour to lunch, England needed 44. By the interval Compton and Edrich – like man and wife at the wicket, they knew each other so well – had managed to whittle that down by another 13.

Still Australia didn't give up and Lindwall subjected the two batsmen to another severe eight-over examination of their technique and courage, before finally, with 10 to win, Hassett sportingly put on himself and his opening partner Morris. Compton promptly struck the winning boundary. The crowd erupted in relief and jubilation; about 15,000 people poured onto the pitch, very much like the last time the England of Hobbs and

Sutcliffe had clinched the Ashes at The Oval in 1926. Three of the 1953 side – May, Graveney and Trueman – hadn't even been born then.

It is amusing watching Pathé footage of the moment, as Compton swivels to dispatch a slow long hop from Morris to the square-leg boundary. There is no ecstatic leaping in the air, ripping up stumps or kissing of the turf (or each other). He shakes a couple of Australian hands as you might at a distant cousin's drinks party and walks demurely off with Edrich, raising his bat less in celebration, more in self-protection, as he is enveloped by spectators invading the field.

The grass was soon covered by people, waiting for their heroes to emerge onto the pavilion balcony (mercifully there was no after-match presentation featuring a bunch of smug, ill-dressed administrators, one brandishing a giant Man of the Match cheque – everyone was broke). The players eventually appeared and both captains made a speech. Hassett, a bit of a wag, said, 'England deserved to win, if not from the first ball at least from the second last over [which he had bowled].' He was congratulated on his team's performance to which he responded drily, 'Yes, it was pretty good considering Lockie threw us out.' Irrespective of the controversy over Tony Lock's action, it was generally agreed that the team that had played the more attractive cricket had lost the Ashes.

There was no presentation of the urn, no triumphant bus tour round London or opportunity for an England all-rounder to pee in the Prime Minister's garden. Well, Winston Churchill, now 78, wasn't especially fond of cricket. A few drinks were sunk, of course, home truths spoken and laughs enjoyed. The final day of an Ashes series is always one of unique camaraderie after the shared stresses of two intense months. But one man did not participate. As he prepared to neck his first pint, Fred Trueman was handed two telegrams. The first informed him that his grandmother had died. The second was from his RAF station in Hemswell, Lincolnshire. It said: 'Notice Test Match finished. Expected back 23.59 hours.'

An English Bushfire

Trueman's next non-participation was much more serious. He became unpopular with the locals on a subsequent tour of the West Indies, for his unforgiving approach on the pitch – they christened him 'Mr Bumper Man' – and his brash attitude off it. Naturally gregarious, he liked a party but was often tactless. He was a bit of a womaniser, not that that is a hangable offence (although his usual parting line, 'That all right for thee, then, loov?', probably was). He was the only player docked his tour performance bonus and, despite a good season for Yorkshire in 1954, was not selected to tour Australia the following winter. The rather regimented Hutton was almost certainly instrumental in this, and the two never played together for England again.

The Northamptonshire express Frank Tyson went to Australia in 1954–5 in Trueman's place. It was a decent swap. Well, after the first Test, anyway, when Hutton won the toss, sent Australia in and they made 601-8. As decisions go it was up there with the bloke from Decca Records who rejected the Beatles audition, saying, 'Guitar music is on the way out.' Tyson took 1-160 and England were thumped by an innings.

A student of the game and a huge admirer of Harold Larwood, Tyson went to visit the great man – now resident in Sydney – before the second Test. They had a couple of beers and Larwood, who was always happy to talk bowling, advised his visitor always to bowl as fast as possible. For the Sydney Test Tyson, a tall, powerful man with a loping stride and a great gather at the crease, shortened his run and increased his pace. Stirred by a green pitch and being struck on the head by a bouncer from Lindwall, he ripped through the Aussies in their second innings, giving England a narrow victory. He matched pace with attitude. After he had bowled a bouncer to Jimmy Burke, the batsman threatened him. 'If you bowl another bouncer at me I'll hit you with this bat,' he said. Tyson sent down another bumper next ball, glared down the pitch and retorted, 'Missed yer!' He splattered Burke's stumps with a yorker soon after.

Tyson was even more devastating in Melbourne with 7-27 in Australia's second innings; it was said he 'raged through Australia like a bushfire'. On a cracked pitch where the ball leapt and snaked, the Aussies lost their last eight wickets for 34. Both Richie Benaud, who was playing, and Don Bradman, who was in the stand, declared it was the fastest spell of bowling they had ever seen, Benaud suggesting years later that Tyson was quicker 'perhaps by millimetres' than Jeff Thomson. He was christened 'the Typhoon' and 'cricket's new terror' after the match that England, aided by Brian Statham's incisive bowling into the wind, won comfortably.

In the fourth Test in Adelaide, Tyson and Statham, both bowling fast and mainly full, shared nine wickets in the match. But the Ashes-clinching contribution was supplied by a less illustrious name: Yorkshire's Bob Appleyard. A bowler of medium-paced off-cutters – like a mirror image of Derek Underwood – he was phenomenally accurate, and lethal on either wet or worn pitches. Exploiting bare patches on the fourth evening, Appleyard quickly removed Morris, Burke and Harvey at a personal cost of six runs and Australia folded the next day for 111, giving England an easy series-winning target of 94.

It was the highlight of Appleyard's quite extraordinary life. Get this. His mother left home when he was seven, one of his younger sisters died when he was 13 and two years later his father, stepmother and other two sisters were gassed to death by a faulty boiler in the bathroom. He was brought up by his stepmother's parents. He played Bradford League cricket until he was 26, then took a record-breaking 200 wickets in his first full season for Yorkshire (1951) before nearly dying of tuberculosis a year later. He not only made a full recovery, but took a stack of wickets the next year and was picked for England in 1954. Then he won the Ashes. He played only nine Tests, but took 708 wickets for Yorkshire in six seasons, average 15. Now when you hear Geoff Boycott talk in such reverent tones about the amazing Bob Appleyard (still alive in 2013, aged 88) you'll understand why.

A Perfect 10

Appleyard exposed a weakness in Australian batsmanship which England brilliantly exploited in the 1956 series: a fallibility against off spin, fast or slow. You know who we're talking about here, don't you? Jim Laker, also born and schooled in the Bradford area. He began life as a fast-bowling all-rounder, until he turned to spin while stationed in Egypt during the Second World War.

If England were undecided whether to focus their energies on seam or spin at the start of the summer, their mind was soon made up when Surrey played Australia at The Oval and Laker took all 10 wickets in the first innings. (Tony Lock took seven in the second as Surrey, the county champions for four years in a row, trounced the tourists by 10 wickets.) Dry turners it was going to be, especially as Tyson and the rehabilitated Trueman were both injured for the first Test.

It was a wet June and it took until the third Test for the plan to come to fruition. The Headingley pitch took spin from the second day and England won by an innings, Lock and Laker sharing 18 wickets. At Old Trafford, Australia were surprised to find a shaven, reddish surface instead of the grassy one they had encountered against Lancashire earlier in the tour. But even though chairman of selectors Gubby Allen had colluded with the groundsman, Bert Flack, the fickle Manchester weather was the factor that engineered the most extraordinary feat in cricket history: one man taking 19 wickets in a match.

England's captain Peter May won an important toss as the pitch was already dusting up on the first day. But Australia's spinners (Johnson and Benaud) weren't as good as England's and didn't manage to bowl them out until mid-afternoon on the second for 459. Until the effects of the heavy roller wore off, the Australian openers were untroubled. Then Colin McDonald nudged a turning ball to Lock at backward short leg. In the same over, Laker, bowling from the Stretford End, produced a peach to the left-handed Harvey that pitched leg and hit the top of off. After that the rot set in.

Lock dismissed Burke caught at slip with the first ball after tea. Laker immediately wreaked havoc with seven wickets for eight runs in four overs. The Australians, mostly back-foot players, were completely mesmerised by his immaculate control and subtle variations of length. Two were bowled and one lbw on the back foot; two were caught close in, pushing forward too hard at the ball, and one was stumped. Only Benaud tried to attack and was caught at deep mid-wicket. Australia were 84 all out and Laker had taken 9-37.

Johnson, the Australian captain, suggested that they had been 'trapped on a stinker, the fellows were angry and the batting blew up.' But May, his opposite number, saw it differently: 'The pitch was not that bad. Jim just dripped away at their nerves, realising that they had got a little obsessional about him and the wickets.' Some tried to kick the ball away but, with the newish lbw law allowing leg-befores to balls pitching outside the off stump, it was futile. Miller considered a more forthright approach and said to the short leg, Alan Oakman, 'If you don't look out, I'll hit you in the bollocks.' But he also subsided tamely, prodding a catch to that very fielder.

Laker had a deliberate method, moving smoothly to the crease in what John Arlott described as 'a constabular stroll' and then, bowling mainly round the wicket, pivoting on his front leg to get plenty of drift away and spin back. He let the ball go with an audible snap of his fingers and the close fielders could often hear it whirring through the air. With excellent command of length and flight he wasn't in the slightest bit perturbed by bowling with five, sometimes six men round the bat. In fact nothing seemed to affect him at all. After each wicket he showed little emotion, turning on his heel and, hands in pockets, chatting nonchalantly to the umpire. He was a passionless exterminator.

Australia were asked to follow on before the close of the second day and the groundsman asked Johnson which roller he would prefer. 'Please your effing self!' the captain growled. Again they made a solid start until McDonald injured his knee and retired hurt. This brought in Harvey, who hit his first ball from Laker, a full toss, to short mid-on to record a four-ball pair – in one afternoon, the ultimate ignominy. It was, said Laker, his worst ball of the season.

Australia ended the day 53-1.

Torrential rain and squally showers permitted only 90 minutes' play over the next two days, with a rest day in between. Australia crept to 84-2. On the fifth day the pitch was so saturated it was unresponsive for most of the first session and Australia got through to lunch unscathed. But the sun was drying the surface and eventually balls began to pop and turn. Straight after the interval Laker pinned Ian Craig leg before and the left-handed Ken Mackay – known as 'Slasher', an ironic nickname given his defensive mindset – was caught in the gully, also for a pair. Miller pushed and poked uncharacteristically for a while and was then bowled for a duck. Archer, half forward, prodded a catch to short leg. Four wickets had gone down for 16 runs.

McDonald, the recovered opener, was still in and reading the spin well, using the depth of the crease to get right forward and right back, which is not generally the Australian way (on flat Aussie pitches, precise footwork is not as important as it is in England). Benaud copied his method, while also making quite a play of slapping down divots in the pitch, advertising its unsuitability. He never has been one for vocal protests. He and McDonald held out for over an hour, putting on 51, and Australia were sniffing a chance of survival. Laker and Lock changed ends and were then rested for a few overs.

After tea Laker was back on from his favoured Stretford End and with his second ball snared McDonald at short leg, though the umpire took an age to give him. It is uncanny how often an interval disrupts a batsman's concentration and a wicket falls soon afterwards. (That was why Brian Lara used to go straight to the nets at tea if he was not out.) Benaud fell a few runs later, bowled playing back to a quicker ball. It was 5 o'clock and Australia were 198-8.

The end was swift. Lindwall propped forward and was caught at leg slip. Finally, wicketkeeper Len Maddocks was lbw playing back to a half-volley. It was all over, the Ashes were England's. Laker had become the first bowler in Test history to take all 10 wickets in an innings, giving him 19-90 in the match. No one had ever even taken 18 before (or since), at any level of cricket. And what did he do? He spun round, casually shook hands with the non-striker, slung his jumper over his shoulder and meandered off to the pavilion for a fag.

It was the ultimate virtuoso performance, without par in sport. Even with the collusion of teammates – which in the era of match-fixing you can't rule out – it would be virtually impossible to emulate. Given that his spin twin Tony Lock had bowled 69 overs in the match (to Laker's 68), beaten the bat constantly and taken just one solitary wicket, Laker's feat was like a footballer scoring nine out of 10 goals in an international while often laying the ball off to give others a chance. It was as close to sporting perfection in a team game as you are ever likely to get.

Besieged by press and well-wishers, he eventually got away from the ground at about 8pm for the long drive home. He stopped halfway for a snack at a pub in Lichfield where his wickets were being replayed on TV. Not a soul recognised him. And when he got home his wife Lily, who was Austrian and didn't really understand cricket, said, 'Jim, did you do something good today?' 'Not bad,' he replied with classic Yorkshire understatement and went off to feed the cat.

7

FIRST TEST, BRISBANE, 1974

'Thomson, from the Vulture Street End, glides to the wicket, hurls one down and, oooh, it leaps up at Amiss, who just jerks his head back at the last moment. Marsh has to jump to take it at full stretch above his head. Seriously fast bowling this. Keeper and slips are miles back. You can almost hear the batsman's heart beating…'

The Swinging Sixties. Yes, I know you've heard a thousand stories about them and are fairly sceptical: it's a fair bet, assuming that you were alive at the time, that you don't recall the raging hedonism everyone now talks about. But 1963 – the height of the Profumo scandal, when the showgirl Christine Keeler was found to be sleeping simultaneously with the British Secretary of State for War (John Profumo), an Antiguan drug dealer and a Russian spy – was the year of enlightenment. As Philip Larkin suggested in his poem 'Annus Mirabilis', it was the year sex, culture and sport collided to make Britain a brighter, though not necessarily better, place.

It was also the year the Beatles launched their first album, *Please Please Me*, the Rolling Stones released their first single, 'Come On', and various other bands led the encouragement to get it on, so to speak. This was facilitated by the launch of the Pill, which was by now in widespread use (no pun intended). The liberation of youth was further encouraged by Mary Quant, designer of the year in 1963, the advent of the mini skirt and the arrival of 17-year-old George Best in the Manchester United team. Best immediately made football sexy and about a thousand co-professionals jealous.

The same cannot quite be said about the cricket of the time (or ever, in truth, despite what was written about the 2005 Ashes).

Frequent Blockages

In the late 1950s England took on tour to Australia an excellent attack compromising Tyson, Trueman, Statham, Laker and Lock. They appeared to have every base covered. But because of injury those five never once played together. Tyson was anyway a spent force. It didn't help that there was friction between the bowlers (all professionals) and the management and batsmen (all amateurs). Despite the slow death of the distinction between Gentleman and Players, finally abolished in 1963, there was still a sort of latent class war going on in the team.

The series was instead dominated by defensive batting (Trevor Bailey recorded the slowest 50 in Test history in Brisbane – 357 minutes – ultimately loitering for a day and a half for 68, and sacrificing the initiative to Australia) and dodgy bowling actions. Left-arm 'chucker' Ian Meckiff took five English wickets in the first Test and nine in the second. (He was eventually called for throwing years later in South Africa and never played again.) 'It's like standing in the middle of a darts match!' Jim Laker told Neil Harvey while he was batting. But there was little public complaint. Anyway, England, who included the Surrey pair Tony Lock and Peter Loader, many of whose deliveries looked dubious, didn't have much of an argument. The former Australian captain Ian

Johnson suggested in the *Melbourne Herald* that even Trueman and Statham had 'jerky' deliveries.

Then in the decisive fourth Test, Australia produced the 6ft 5in Gordon Rorke, who not only released the ball from about 9ft in the air but also, exploiting the last days of the back-foot no-ball law, from about a yard in front of the crease. (As long as your foot *landed* behind the back line you could drag it forward to gain an advantage.) He took crucial scalps in that fourth Test, which Australia won by 10 wickets.

In fact these controversies masked the truth – that the Australians were fitter, sharper and more athletic than England, their batsmen were more adventurous and they had the incisive skills of the left-handed all-rounder Alan Davidson, a 1950s version of Wasim Akram. They also had Richie Benaud, who, quite apart from re-inventing the art of propelling leg spin from round the wicket, was a very canny captain. Years later as a TV commentator Benaud was meticulous and highly observant. He missed nothing, even when he didn't appear to be looking. Often he seemed to sense what was going to happen before it did. You can imagine all those traits being invaluable as a skipper. He was always one step ahead. He would argue that captaincy was 90 per cent luck and only 10 per cent talent. But his acute intuition was largely responsible for Australia winning the 1958–9 series 4-0.

Docile pitches and more turgid batting dominated the next few Ashes contests, many of which were stalemates, and Australia consistently retained the urn. But England still had Trueman and Statham. The fire-breathing Trueman, who modestly claimed he was 't' fastest booler who ever drew breath', constantly challenged a batsman's reflexes, his courage and his eardrums ('Ee, thou's got more edges than a broken pisspot!' he would grunt). He was the first bowler to take 300 Test wickets, a feat he achieved at The Oval in 1964. In contrast, the wiry, whippy Statham, known as

'George', a favourite Lancastrian nickname, had to be persuaded to open his mouth or bowl a bouncer. He was skiddy and very accurate and would test the batsmen's precision and patience. 'If they miss, I hit,' was his catchphrase. Almost 60 per cent of his 252 Test wickets were bowled or lbw. He was the stealthy spike to Trueman's battering ram but, with 2260 first-class wickets at 16, no less a bowler for it.

They were nullified by the indefatigable Australian opening pair of Bill Lawry and Bobby Simpson, who batted as if in a bunker, sheltering behind their bats, rarely venturing out unless the coast was clear. The left-handed Lawry, who secreted rather than scored runs, was described by the *Daily Mail* journalist Ian Wooldridge as 'a corpse with pads on'. He was certainly a masochist, sometimes returning to the dressing room black and blue after taking numerous lifters on the body. Simpson was equally obdurate, though adept at stealing quick singles and also a brilliant close catcher. This was a major boon to the slippery mainstay of Australia's attack, Graham 'Garth' McKenzie, as 60 per cent of his 246 Test victims were caught behind the wicket. Fielding and fitness were not areas in which England excelled.

England's failures betrayed the fact that the county game was in a sorry state. An overdue attempt to make it more 'swinging' was the introduction of one-day cricket. The First-Class Counties Knock-Out Competition for the Gillette Cup, to give it its full, catchy title, was launched in May 1963, with a 65-overs-a-side match (supposed to be completed in a day, but actually lasting two because of rain) between Lancashire and Leicestershire.

Sussex won the competition in its first two years, largely because of the captaincy of Ted Dexter, who had been heavily involved in setting up the concept. Not only was Dexter a dasher with the bat, but he had ingenious ideas in the field, being the first to think of getting his bowlers to aim straight and full with a funnel-shaped field setting – with the deep men set behind the bowler rather than square of the wicket.

Dexter founded Rothman's International Cavaliers – a squad of world-class players who toured England during the 1960s, playing exhibition matches on Sundays. The idea was a huge success and the forerunner of the John Player Sunday League, introduced in 1969. Dexter's imagination didn't seem to be translated into his Test captaincy, however – he often seemed bored and seven of the 10 Ashes Tests in which he was in charge ended in a draw. England had some talented batsmen in their line-up, notably Colin Cowdrey, Ken Barrington, Dexter himself and latterly Geoff Boycott, but no one seemed prepared, or able, to take the initiative. Whatever was going on in society, in the Test arena it was the era of the slow hand clap.

Dolly Mixture

The most famous Test of the 1960s was largely irrelevant in terms of the result, as Australia had already retained the Ashes for the sixth successive time. But at The Oval for the fifth Test in 1968, England, 1-0 down, drafted in the South African-born batsman Basil D'Oliveira – who had made a 50 earlier in the series – when the Northants opener Roger Prideaux was taken ill.

Cape Coloured D'Oliveira was a prodigy in non-white cricket at home, making huge scores littered with sixes (28 in one innings of 225, for instance), but because of his mixed race he was not permitted to play first-class cricket for his province. He was rescued from the abominations of South Africa's apartheid regime by John Arlott and Worcestershire, whom he played for from 1964.

Having made his Test debut against the West Indies in 1966, he was desperate to re-establish himself in the England side and stake a claim for the tour to South Africa in the winter of 1968–9.

He had rejected an obvious bribe from the South African establishment to coach there – to ensure he wasn't available for England – and was incensed by the threats of South Africa's Prime Minister B J Vorster, one of the instigators of apartheid, to have the tour cancelled if Dolly was picked.

This was the context in which D'Oliveira strode out to bat at The Oval, never mind that England were 238-4 late on the first day with the second new ball due. He survived a tricky hour that night and, having been dropped by the keeper Barry Jarman on 31 the following morning, proceeded to play an innings of smooth authority. Using a short backlift and fast hands, he punched or glided anything wide through the covers or short-arm jabbed it past mid-wicket.

John Edrich kept him company in a stand of 121, then with Alan Knott he put on 62. A paddle to leg got him to the hundred he craved and that he had promised his wife he'd make. No cricketer has ever been under such duress, which must make D'Oliveira's gallant 158 the greatest innings in the history of the game. It elicited a worried remark from the benevolent umpire Charlie Elliott. 'Oh Christ,' he said, 'you've set the cat among the pigeons now.'

He was not wrong. D'Oliveira's hundred, plus a vital wicket late on the last afternoon to help Derek Underwood exploit a drying pitch and bowl England to an unexpected victory, made him an obvious choice for the South African tour. But, buckling under more threats from Vorster, the England selectors (Doug Insole, Peter May, Don Kenyon and Alec Bedser – who assured me during an interview that he hadn't heard of the threats) did not pick him. They used his age – 33 – as an excuse. Little did they know he was actually 36. The captain, Colin Cowdrey, had promised to champion his cause but, fearing a political storm, in the end he didn't.

D'Oliveira was devastated. 'My dream has been shattered,' he wrote. 'This is what I had lived for. The chance to go there knowing I would play on grounds where before I could only sit with my sandwiches in a confined area [known at Newlands in Cape Town as 'the cage'].'

There was massive outrage at his non-selection: MPs had their say, as they invariably do, and special meetings were called, as they invariably are. No one did anything, as they invariably don't. But then, three weeks later, the medium pacer Tom Cartwright was ruled out of the tour because of injury. Despite D'Oliveira's bowling being at best a useful bonus, he was announced as the replacement. There was more fudging going on than in a Cornish dairy.

Vorster was clear what he thought of it and made an absurd declaration that this was 'not the team of the MCC but the team of the anti-apartheid movement'. If that wasn't sad enough, what was worse was that his speech, at the National Party Congress, got a standing ovation. The tour, of course, was cancelled and South Africa were cast into sporting isolation for two decades.

It's fascinating to speculate on what would have occurred if events had been different. Suppose D'Oliveira had been caught for 31 in that match, what would have happened then? Well, he wouldn't have been picked for the tour and the world could have continued to turn its blind eye, as it had since apartheid was introduced in 1948. The immense South African side, which had lost only one Test in six years and trounced the Australians 4-0 before being cast into the darkness, would have conquered the world in the 1970s.

Tony Greig (and other South African-born players) would not have ended up bolstering England. There would have been no 'I intend to make them grovel' speech, inadvertently galvanising the West Indies, and no World Series Cricket (which Greig helped set up and which included various frustrated South African stars). Cricketers' salaries would have remained languishing just above those of bus conductors and Spanish au pairs. Quite apart from all that, without D'Oliveira's century and subsequent selection, the consequences for the non-white South Africans, incarcerated in their inhumane townships, still virtually treated like slaves even 15 years later, don't bear thinking about. The power of sport, eh?

Summer Snow Storm

The rivalry between England and Australia turned nasty in 1970. Again. Ashes Antagonism replaced the apathy of the Sixties. England needed a captain with attitude to atone for the insipidness of the past, and they found him in the taciturn tyke, Raymond Illingworth. That winter he unleashed a barrage of abrasive fast bowlers on the Aussies, spearheaded by the lithe, decidedly hasty John Snow and supported by the Lancashire duo of Peter Lever and Ken Shuttleworth and a young Bob Willis. It took a while for the rewards to materialise – until the last Test, in fact – and it was at times an ugly business, but, from an English point of view, it had the desired result: Australia 0 England 2.

Illingworth was from Pudsey – the same Yorkshire town as Len Hutton – and reared in the hard school of the Bradford League. He became an expert reader of cricketers' technical and mental faculties through years of determined batting and probing off spin for his county from 1951 onwards, not to mention 12 years in and out of the England Test side. He had a vivid impression of players' methods, as is often the case with bowlers, especially spinners, though they are rarely put in charge. Misguidedly, captaincy usually seems to be a batsman's prerogative.

He got the England captaincy partly by luck – the man in possession, Colin Cowdrey, ruptured his Achilles in 1969, the same year Illingworth took over at Leicestershire. He was an instant success, tough, shrewd, meticulous. He knew the kind of players he wanted in his side, was granted them and got the best out of them. His preferred batsmen were committed, fearless, experienced, knew their own games – Boycott, Edrich, D'Oliveira, Cowdrey (recovered), Keith Fletcher and the less celebrated Brian Luckhurst of Kent, who was a great success in that 1970–1 series.

Illingworth's bowlers were aggressive, penetrative and persistent. He had the advantage, in addition to his hostile pace attack, of Derek 'Deadly' Underwood, a left-arm spinner bowling at practically medium pace, who was so accurate that his wicketkeeper, Alan Knott, was rarely required to do anything except appeal for lbw. He could plug away into the wind while the quicks rotated with it.

With due respect to Boycott, who batted superbly throughout, averaging 94, Snow was man of the series with 31 wickets (at 22). He was a sophisticated operator able to move the ball both ways and specialising in rib ticklers – balls rearing into the batsman's ribcage – which are much harder to get out of the way of than the common or garden bouncer. Several Australians made the mistake of trying to duck them, with painful results. They were constantly apprehensive of him.

Running in with an easy, languid rhythm, Snow was faster than he looked, very accurate and with deceptive changes of pace. He spared no one, was warned by the umpire in several matches, including the first ever Test in Perth, for overusing the bouncer and wasn't averse to 'sconning' tailenders (hitting them on the head). Moody and intense, he would occasionally lapse into lethargy; then Illingworth would post Boycott at mid-off to wind him up with 'My moom could 'av 'it that with 'er clothes prop' and get him going again.

After the abandonment of the third Test in Melbourne due to torrential downpours, a first ever One-Day International was staged, partly to offset financial losses. Thousands poured excitedly through the turnstiles, though when Boycott and Edrich managed just eight from the first eight (eight-ball) overs, they must have thought about heading out again. But a decent match ensued, which Australia won, and a new genre was born. In the intervening 32 years (to March 2013) there have been 1400 Test Matches and an amazing 3340 One-Day Internationals. No wonder we have so much trouble remembering any of them.

England performed superbly as a team to take a 1-0 lead in the fourth Test in Sydney. Boycott compiled an immaculate 142 not out in the second innings and Snow, with 7-40, hustled out the Aussies – who included Lawry, Ian and Greg Chappell, Doug Walters and Rod Marsh – for just 116 to give England a colossal 299-run victory.

The rescheduled fifth Test in Melbourne (after the earlier washout) was an ill-tempered affair marred by a crowd invasion. After that the Aussies, led by the safety-first Bill Lawry, were riddled with caution and lost their way. In the sixth Test they were left a day and a half to make 469 to win on a flat Adelaide pitch, but lacked urgency and finished 328-3. Lawry was summarily dropped – the first time this had happened to an Australian captain for 70 years.

Ian Chappell was appointed for the final (seventh) Test in Sydney and immediately orchestrated England's capitulation for 184. Australia engineered a lead, but towards the end of their innings their number 9 Terry Jenner ducked into a third successive short ball from Snow and was hit on the head. There were, of course, no helmets. Jenner collapsed to the ground and had to be helped off. Umpire Lou Rowan, a policeman and the man who had warned Snow for intimidation in Perth, waited until he was ready to bowl at the next batsman, Dennis Lillee, before giving him a first warning. Snow was livid, claiming that he had bowled only one bouncer that over while 'your blokes have been bowling seven'.

Illingworth joined in the argument, and the crowd grew restless and started throwing (presumably empty) beer cans on the field. Snow eventually finished the over and stormed down to fine leg in high dudgeon. He baited the crowd, more cans were thrown, a man by the fence grabbed his shirt and there was a bit of a scuffle. Illingworth went to intervene and then instinctively waved to his players to leave the field. It was a bit radical, but he was a man who was fiercely protective of his team and one who acted on hunches. In the dressing room, umpire Rowan told them that if they remained there they would forfeit the match, so after only seven minutes they returned and the game continued. Jenner came back to make a brave 30.

A concerted team effort by England in their second innings set Australia 223 to win and regain the Ashes. Snow took a wicket in his first over but then injured his hand on the boundary fence going for a catch, was taken to hospital and didn't return. But Illingworth, whose dressing-room speeches were noticeable for their succinctness – 'Come on, then, let's go,' was all he said before the final day – managed his resources brilliantly. The Aussies were winkled out for 160 – three, including the key wicket of Greg Chappell, by Illingworth himself. England had won the Ashes back after a 13-year absence, and, as it was in Australia, they had done it the hard way.

Illingworth's (and Snow's) methods weren't universally welcomed by the purists in England. E W Swanton wrote in the *Daily Telegraph* that 'the Ashes had been retaken at a heavy and wholly unnecessary cost in terms of sportsmanship'. But society was changing. This was the era of heavy metal, with machismo and chest wigs replacing peace and love and droopy clothes, and cricket was getting with the beat.

Although there were unsavoury incidents on the field, the teams got on well off it, regularly sharing beers after play; there was a healthy mutual respect. Greg Chappell summed it up, saying that Illingworth's side had 'subjected us to a mental intimidation by aggressive field placings, and physical intimidation by constant use of his pace attack, ably led by one of the best fast bowlers of my experience, John Snow.' Snow, reflecting on the tour later, wrote, 'I'm not afraid to leave a trail of fractures among the opposition – not to inflict deliberate injury, of course, but to rough up a batsman, make them apprehensive and destroy their confidence. I never let them forget the game is played with a very hard ball.'

Two very hard Australians, one a trucker's son from Perth, the other a car salesman from Sydney, observed this with great interest.

Tit for Tat

Lillee and Thomson. The names filled a batsman of the 1970s with foreboding. They had venom in their blood and they fired heat-seeking missiles which targeted the batsmen's largely unprotected bodies as a route to their stumps and their general peace of mind. 'There's no batsman on earth who goes out to meet Dennis Lillee and Jeff Thomson with a smile on his face,' Clive Lloyd said. If that's what a man with his colossal ability and stature thought, whatever must it have been like for ordinary mortals?

Batsmen knew that to show any sign of weakness or fallibility was fatal, but they also knew that leather on flesh, when delivered at over 90mph, hurts like hell. Even if you are telling yourself to get in line and repel the thunderbolts, your body is sometimes doing something different. And fast bowlers can smell fear at 1000 paces.

England had faced Dennis Lillee before, both in Australia

PUNCH'S FANCY PORTRAITS.—No. 90.

Fred 'The Demon' Spofforth as depicted in *Punch* magazine. The idea of him as a deadly insect (plus moustache) is interesting, no doubt inspired by his spindly arms and legs.

An ageing Spofforth (probably late 1890s, when he was in his mid-40s). His height doesn't look exceptional, but at 6ft 3in when the average man was only 5ft 6in, he would have been daunting to face, even with his cap on.

Like Spofforth, W G Grace was unusually tall (6ft 4in), with a colossal upper body even before he swelled to nearly 20 stone. Oddly, he had a thin, squeaky voice which must have made the calls emanating from beneath that vast beard hard to hear.

A classic shot of Victor Trumper about to unleash his flowing straight drive. The pick-up of his bat is almost like a baseballer's. Note only one (open-palmed) batting glove – he liked to really 'feel' the bat in his hands.

George Beldam/Popperfoto/Getty Images

Warwick Armstrong's surname was appropriate as he had a very powerful upper body. This is an early picture (around 1905) when the 'Big Ship' was only a medium-sized vessel. His shirt from the 1920 series (which is in the museum at the MCG) would make a decent sail.

Allsport/ Hulton Archive/Getty Images

Jack Hobbs unveiling his trademark pull shot. Even though he was meticulous with his placement, he could also hit the ball hard, as here. He has swivelled 180 degrees to play the shot, but still retains perfect balance.

The Oval, 1926: thousands invade the field after England have won the Ashes for the first time since World War I. Note the almost universal wearing of suits and bowler or trilby hats, and the lack of females or children.

Harold Larwood bounces Bill Woodfull in Brisbane during the 1932–3 bodyline tour. This is a good example of England's leg-theory field-setting that the Australians were so unhappy about. Six short legs wait for a chance, including four behind square. Following that series the law was changed to allow a maximum of two fielders behind square on the leg side.

Larwood in follow-through during bodyline, showing the power in his shoulder. He was quite wide of the crease, which made his short ball angle awkwardly in to right-handers, rather like some of the West Indian quicks of the 1980s. The Australian umpires must have got unbelievably hot in those coats.

Hammond and Bradman walking out for the toss at Trent Bridge in 1938. Walter Hammond appears slightly deferential in his body language – he was losing the 1930s battle of the thunderbats. Bradman's meticulousness is noticeable by the presence of his bat to prod the wicket with (it was allowed then). The Trent Bridge players' balcony remains the same today.

The Don batting during the 1948 tour of England (when the Australians didn't lose a game.). The photograph shows his remarkable use of the crease, getting right back and outside off stump to dispatch the ball with powerful forearms, a full follow-through and a ruthless demeanour.

Denis Compton, the first truly commercial cricketer, hits the winning runs at The Oval in 1953 to regain the Ashes for England for the first time in 20 years. Judging by the state of his hair, his famous Brylcreem wasn't working. Keith Miller, his great opponent and dining partner, is in typically casual pose at slip.

This picture captures all the explosive potential of Jeff Thomson's bowling action. A former javelin thrower, he was like a human catapult pulled back tight ready to unload. The right foot is pointing almost backwards and the ball is out of sight of the batsman behind his leg. With that pace and trajectory, the batsman didn't see much of it after release, either.

Dennis Lillee's more traditional fast bowler's action, featuring a magnificent jump into his delivery and a classic sideways-on position. It exudes menace. This is during the 1975 Ashes in England. The non-striker is David 'Stainless' Steele and the umpire the delightfully geriatric Tom Spencer.

The Ladbrokes odds during the 1981 Headingley Test (when England were 135-7 in the second innings, still 91 behind). Dennis Lillee and Rod Marsh were so intrigued they actually put a bet on and finished up winning £7,500. There were no suspicious no balls or deliberately dropped catches though …

Ian Botham traps Ray Bright lbw first ball during his 5-1 spell at Edgbaston in 1981. Geoff Boycott nicknamed him Guy the Gorilla after this celebratory pose. He has the perfect power-packed physique for a cricketer. The umpire is Don Oslear.

A young Shane Warne bowls during the Lord's Test in 1993. Although bowling round the wicket to a right-hander is a mainly defensive option for a leggie, it was an attacking one for him because he was so accurate and spun the ball so much. You can almost hear that ball fizzing through the air. He doesn't look a lot like this now.

The ball of the century – Warne's first in an Ashes Test, Old Trafford, 1993. It completely bamboozled Mike Gatting, a fine player of spin, although the non-striker, Graham Gooch, observed, 'If it was a cheese roll it wouldn't have got past him.'

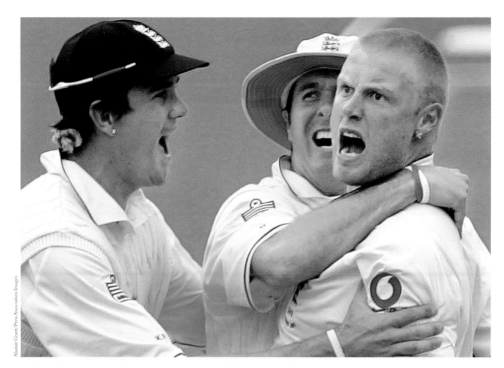

Andrew Flintoff's desire and intensity during the 2005 Ashes are beautifully captured. There was something almost primeval about the way he celebrated every time he took an Australian wicket. Here he's being congratulated by Michel Vaughan and Kevin Pietersen, showing just a glimpse of the 'dead mongoose' haircut under his cap.

Ricky Ponting works another one to leg at the Melbourne Cricket Ground in 2006. He was a fantastically nimble player, very quick into position, though later in his career he sometimes got his head too far over to the off side. But his hand-eye co-ordination was so good he still rifled the ball through or over the leg side virtually at will.

Glenn McGrath tormented England for 13 years, taking 157 wickets at a phenomenal average of 20.92. This picture illustrates how close to the stumps he bowled, the long levers that gave him his deceptive pace and the merciless expression as he relentlessly pursued another victim.

during the 1970–1 series when he made his debut as something of a tearaway, then at home in 1972 when he was already a fearsome assailant. He excelled in that series – partly because of a season in the Lancashire League the year before – moving the ball around at great pace, though his consistency was slightly overshadowed by the dramatic exploits of Bob Massie. At Lord's on his Test debut Massie swung the ball prodigiously both ways to take 16 wickets in the match, a new Australian Test record. Soon after, his swing mysteriously vanished and so did he.

Lillee himself was then on the sidelines for a while with a serious back injury, but now in 1974 he was back in a third incarnation as, he hoped, a refined assassin. Echoing John Snow, he said, 'I try to hit a batsman in the ribcage when I bowl a purposeful bouncer, and I want it to hurt so much that the batsman doesn't want to face me any more.' But, after his injury, no one was convinced his bowling had the teeth to back up his tongue.

Jeff Thomson was new. He had only played one previous Test – against Pakistan two years previously – and bowled a heap of rubbish. England had seen him and his funny slingy action in the match against Queensland, prior to the first Test. They found him a little unconventional, but otherwise were singularly unimpressed, even though he had said on TV, 'I enjoy hitting a batsman more than getting him out. I like to see blood on the pitch.' When asked about playing against the English he said, 'Stuff that stiff-upper-lip crap. Let's see how stiff it is when it's split.' Sounded like a nice bloke.

By the sound of it the pair were perfect ammunition for Australia's captain Ian Chappell, an uncompromising, dyed-in-the-wool Aussie whose team talks were littered with the c-word if he was referring to the Poms. He had inherited the suffering of his grandfather, Vic Richardson, in the bodyline series and owed it to him and his country to avenge it. Or, as he put it, 'stick it up 'em, like my granddad would have done.' But even he didn't know at the outset whether they would.

Mike Denness, a magnanimous Scot, was England captain. It was a strange choice based largely on his success, mainly in one-day cricket, as Kent's skipper. Though an elegant stroke-player, he lacked real fight – he was what Boycott would call an 'airy-fairy' player – and his election to the job so piqued Boycott, who was hoping for it himself, that he made himself unavailable for the tour of Australia. As things turned out, Boycott would have been a better choice. Or even his mum, for that matter.

England therefore had a new opening pair – Warwickshire's Dennis Amiss, a correct, fluent player who always looked bedraggled because he sweated profusely, and the workmanlike Brian Luckhurst. John Edrich was shifted down to number 3 as a sort of third opener. After Denness and Keith Fletcher came the engine room of the side – the towering, swaggering Tony Greig at 6 and the brilliant, mercurial, eccentric, starched-collared Alan Knott at 7. The main bowlers were Bob Willis and Derek Underwood, with men like Chris Old as support – if they could get him on the field. But before the first Test in Brisbane he had an injured hand. (The mind boggles as to what he had done, given that once he excused himself from playing with 'I sneezed and I've gone in the neck.)'

Australia won first use of a Woollongabba pitch prepared by Clem Jones, the Brisbane mayor, who had sacked the groundsman 10 days before. It helped the bowlers a touch and England did well to restrict Australia to 219-6 on day one. Several batsmen were out hooking. On the second morning they let the position slip and Australia's last three wickets added 81. Greig resorted to bouncing Lillee, who gloved a catch to the keeper. It wasn't the smartest move. 'Just remember who started this,' grunted Lillee, skulking off.

England began batting on the second afternoon. They were confident, believing that there were not too many terrors either in the pitch or, with Lillee still feeling his way back from injury and Thomson a rookie, in the Australian bowling. They were in for a rude shock. Looking more like a Hell's Angel with his piratical hirsuteness, Lillee was menacing enough off his long, marauding run, then hurling the ball down, but Thomson was genuinely frightening. Gliding a short distance to the wicket, he did an odd chassé with his feet before his body jack-knifed backwards at the crease. Momentarily his right hand practically touched the ground behind him and his front foot pointed at the batsman's head. Then in a whiplash of arm the ball was catapulted up the other end. It was like the sudden release of a sapling bent double.

It generated ferocious speed and lift off the surface: several times in Thomson's first two overs keeper Rod Marsh had to leap high to take a ball that almost ripped his hand off. 'It hurts, but I love it!' he said. Luckhurst fell tamely, glancing a catch down the leg side, but Amiss got a brute which climbed almost vertically from a decent length, jammed his thumb into the handle of the bat and was caught at third slip. The ball, that is, not his thumb. Suddenly England were 10-2.

Denness' first delivery from Thomson struck him directly on the shoulder blade almost before he had moved – 'It was very painful,' he said – and he flirted unconvincingly outside off stump, playing and missing. It had become clear by then that Thomson had been under orders to bowl within himself in the Queensland match prior to the Test. His speed now was extreme and made worse by the ball being invisible to the batsman behind his body as his arm reached back before release. And he was erratic, with the odd wide thrown in among his throat balls. That made him even more awkward: the batsmen didn't know what to expect.

When Thomson was rested, Denness, perhaps mentally relaxing to the slower pace of Max Walker, shouldered arms and was lbw. Fletcher, after a couple of boundaries, played on to Lillee. Edrich hung around tenaciously, but England were 57-4.

Lillee greeted Greig with the inevitable bouncer. It flew past his nose and was taken by Marsh at full stretch above his head. Greig wandered down the pitch and provocatively patted a spot not far from Lillee's end. The bowler was steaming. Bombarded with more short stuff, Greig sliced his first runs over the slips for four, drove another boundary, looking to get leg-side of the ball and flay it through or over the covers. He played and missed a bit but seemed unconcerned. In fact he was relishing the battle. Edrich defended bravely and fiddled runs; at stumps on a compelling, sometimes alarming day, England were 114-4, still nearly 200 behind.

The following morning Edrich was out early, steering Thomson to slip, though it emerged later that his hand was so badly bruised he could hardly grip the bat. Undaunted, Greig counterattacked, cuffing short balls over the slips or through cover. He slashed a short ball from Thomson to third man to bring up his 50. If it was pitched up he drove it imperiously with a big booming follow-through, then mischievously tapped the middle of his 3lb bat or ostentatiously rehearsed the upper cut to the bouncer he knew was coming next.

Underwood, once a walking wicket who had now made himself into a handy tailender, kept him determined company, though he didn't enjoy Greig's habit of signalling four himself after bunting one past extra cover. 'For Christ's sake, don't do that, matey,' he said (Kent players always used the word 'matey'). 'Think of the poor bugger who's batting the other end.'

Greig took no notice, thumping another boundary past cover and indicating four with a big sweep of his arm. Then, after

Underwood was out, he pretended to head a Lillee bouncer after it had passed. He knew that riling the bowlers was the best way to disrupt them. The next ball flew over the keeper's head for four byes. Two expansive drives off successive balls from Lillee brought up a thrilling hundred. Finally a huge drive at Lillee ended in a thin edge to Marsh. Greig had carved 17 boundaries in his rollicking 110, almost exclusively through, or over, the off side; he had won over the entire ground and probably, at that very moment, Kerry Packer, the man who was going to turn cricket upside down and bankroll his life. But England were soon 265 all out.

Australia had been metaphorically winded and their second innings was slow to get going. In the remaining two and half hours' play they pottered to 51-2, a lead of 95. On the rest day that followed, everyone was able to catch their breath, or soak their battered bodies. It had been a humdinging three days, like cricket on speed.

The fourth day was hot and humid. Willis quickly disposed of the obdurate Ian Redpath, but none of the England faster bowlers could make the ball fly like Lillee and Thomson, and that was their only success before lunch. Underwood was restrictive, but Ross Edwards – fluently – and Greg Chappell – circumspectly – both made 50s. The arrival of the happy hooker Doug Walters and the forthright Rod Marsh gave the innings impetus. They 'flagellated' the England attack, according to Frank Tyson, who was commentating on TV, and after tea Ian Chappell declared, leaving England 333 to win and, of more immediate concern, an awkward 35 minutes to bat that night. This became two overs when Thomson unleashed three short balls and the umpires decided the light was too dim to handle this sort of bowling.

The light was irrelevant: a bank of 5000 megawatt bulbs wouldn't have helped England, unless they had been placed between the bowler and the batsman. Even watching some of those deliveries on YouTube 39 years later, you'd prefer to do so behind the sofa. It was a horror movie. Luckhurst was first to go on the final morning, offering no footwork and a limp bat to guide Lillee to first slip. Edrich, after a pain-killing injection, stuck it out bravely for 40 minutes, taking his hand off the bat in agony every ball, until he was late getting into line against Thomson and was bowled off-stump. Amiss, also battling with a hand injury, survived for an hour until he received a second vicious snorter from Thomson. Rapid and angled in on a goodish length, it took off and flew to third slip via the shoulder of the bat. Amiss called it his 'trapdoor ball', because it literally appeared from nowhere. Denness, struck on the arm first ball, exhibited some defiance, though he was rarely in line and on 27 he edged an attempted cut.

Greig came in at 92-4. 'Right,' said Ian Chappell to his bowlers, 'is there any danger we can actually try and knock his stumps over instead of trying to knock his fucking block off?' His brother Greg, noticing the batsman's soft footwear, added, 'Hit him in the sandshoes, that'll slow his footwork down a bit.' Thomson produced a wicked, fast yorker which bent in late through the air and was too good for a man of 6ft 7in with a high backlift expecting something at his head. It cannoned off his pads and spread-eagled his stumps.

Knott, Lever and Underwood pluckily kept the Australians in the field until after tea; then Thomson finished them off, giving him figures of 6-46 and Australia victory by 166 runs. 'Thomson and Lillee Too Good for Brittle England' was the *Daily Telegraph* headline the next day. Without reflecting the fear the pair had spread, it pretty much summed up the rest of the tour.

Battered and bruised, England summoned a batting replacement for the next Test in Perth. The man to answer the call was Cowdrey, a veteran of six Ashes tours and now 41. Amid some ridicule he gamely arrived after a hazardous 47-hour journey and, when Amiss and Edrich were ruled out, batted at number 3, introducing himself to Jeff Thomson in the middle with, 'Hello, I don't think we have met – my name's Cowdrey.' The bowler wasn't impressed, but Cowdrey did win over the Aussies with two determined innings.

Not that it did England much good. They lost the second Test by nine wickets, Thomson taking seven more scalps in the match, spreading more unease and famously striking the replacement opener David Lloyd so hard in the groin that it knocked his abdominal protector inside out and thrust the fragile items it was supposed to be protecting through its ventilation holes. It was quite a business prising everything apart, after which he was helped off in agony – though he has dined out since on his claim that 'it proved I could play Thommo with my cock.'

After an exciting drawn third Test, Australia emphatically wrapped up the Ashes in the fourth at the Sydney Cricket Ground, Lillee and Thomson again doing much of the damage in the 171-run win. Several batsmen were hit and Edrich, who took over the English captaincy when Denness stood down, suffered two broken ribs, though he returned from hospital to make a valiant 33 not out.

Australia also had a comfortable win in the fifth Test at Adelaide, giving them a 4-0 advantage. England had failed to reach 300 in any innings in the series, Lillee and Thomson had shared 58 wickets and inflicted all manner of mental and physical scars. Lillee was fast, mean and precise. He knew how to nail an opponent. He was a ruthless executioner. Thomson was faster, looser, ultra-vicious. Like a human torpedo. He was more of a random destroyer.

The ferocity with which Thommo hurled the ball into the pitch from where it reared up at the batsman's throat was terrifying.

On a practice pitch at the University of Western Australia his speed was timed at 99mph, which is rapid enough, but fast bowlers (of which I was an occasional version) know that the adrenaline of a match (or the persecution of a batsman) always makes them bowl 5mph quicker. He almost certainly propelled the world's first 100mph delivery, 30 years before Shoaib Akhtar and Brett Lee. It gave the batsman about 0.4 seconds to get into position and play his shot (or take evasive action). And this wearing a cloth cap, a towel on the thigh and a flimsy box that would have been more use as a soap dish. It is a miracle that no one was maimed for life. It was hardly surprising that when they arrived home from the 1974–5 tour, some England batsmen had the tortured expressions and nervous dispositions of men who had been to war.

> *Ashes to Ashes*
> *Dust to Dust*
> *If Thomson doesn't get you*
> *Lillee must.*

And they did.

The Soporific Sixties had given way to the Savage Seventies. It was Bodyline – the Sequel. Casualty departments were on red alert. And there was no danger money for batsmen. Just a regulation £30 a day. Pitiful.

8

'...Bowled 'im. It's all over and it's one of the most fantastic victories ever known in Test cricket. Bob Willis — eight wickets. England have won this match after one of the most astonishing fight backs you will ever see.' Richie Benaud BBC TV

David 'Stainless' Steele symbolised England's mid Seventies response. (No, that wasn't his age, despite his elderly appearance — it's the decade we're talking about.) Steele, bespectacled, silver-haired and slightly eccentric, was actually only 33 when Jeff Thomson greeted his appearance at Lord's in 1975 with 'Who's this, then, Father fuckin' Christmas?' and he had the best defence available (Boycott was still in self-imposed exile).

He was a relic of the Jack Hobbs era — lunge forward, plant your front foot up the wicket, head over the line and try to smell the leather. He did, too, when the Aussie pacemen whistled a few past his nose. He withstood their attack nobly and survived for 19 hours in the series (not including getting lost in the Lord's pavilion on the way out to bat), averaging 60. Australia still won the 1975 series 1-0, but a determined England, now captained by Tony Greig, had at least staunched the bleeding.

Pheasant Shooting

At the time of the Centenary Test in Melbourne in March 1977, England and Australia had played each other 225 times. England had won 71 Tests and Australia 88. Australian players were still being paid about as much as dressing-room cleaners, and England's weren't doing much better, on £200 a match. Rumours were rife that a big cheese was poised to buy up all the best players and set up a rival to Test cricket.

Nothing, however, was going to spoil the party celebrating a hundred years of Anglo–Australian rivalry. An impressive 218 ex-players assembled to watch the match at the MCG – venue of the inaugural Test – including Bradman, of course, and two octogenarians, Jack Ryder of Australia and England's Percy Fender, opponents in the 1920–1 Aussie whitewash. It was a superb occasion, attended by the Queen and the Duke of Edinburgh, and the cricket lived up to it.

Australia, put in by Greig, were rumbled for 138 and the opener Rick McCosker had his jaw broken by Bob Willis. Lillee and Walker countered by routing England for 95. By the end of the third day Australia had piled up nearly 400 in their second innings. It looked like another inevitable Aussie win.

England had a team meeting on the fourth morning, and players were canvassed as to the approach they should take. When it came to Derek Randall, the madcap Notts batsman piped up, 'I think we should rise like a pheasant!' There were quizzical looks around the room and then someone said, 'Don't you mean phoenix?' 'Oh yes,' Randall replied, 'I knew it were a bird beginning with F.' He did his best, however, compiling a memorable 174 in England's pursuit of the 463 needed for victory. It was a riveting innings, a mixture of cricket and circus. He swatted a Lillee bouncer to the fence, then did a little jig. A further bouncer clonked him on the forehead, after which he doffed his cap to the bowler and bowed theatrically. He did a backward somersault after swaying out of the way of another short ball. In between he peppered the boundaries with pulls, drives and exquisitely timed clips off his toes. He gave England a genuine chance of winning until he was fifth out with 117 needed. But Lillee had the last word, knocking over Underwood and lastly Knott to bowl England out for a valiant 417. Australia had won by 45 runs, uncannily exactly the same margin by which they had won the first ever Test a century ago. Statisticians loved it. So did everyone else.

Except, perhaps Kerry Packer, the TV mogul, who, a month later, announced the creation of World Series Cricket (WSC), starting with a sequence of matches between 'Australia' and the Rest of the World. Former Australian captains such as Richie Benaud and Ian Chappell had been heavily involved in setting up WSC, most of the Australian team had been signed up and Tony Greig had helped recruit five England players, among others. He was going to lead the World XI. He was summarily sacked as captain of England.

Australia tried to deny that the Packer controversy was the reason they lost 3-0 to a Mike Brearley-led England side that summer (1977), but it can't have helped. There wasn't much team unity, with some players contracted to WSC and others not. The pivotal moment, however, came in the third Test and concerned an Englishman: one I T Botham.

The Australians, it must be said, already knew something of Botham. He had been in Melbourne during the Centenary Test on a young player's scholarship. He was drinking in a bar one night with former players from both sides when he heard Ian

Chappell being derogatory about England. This went on for a while and eventually Botham confronted him. Botham claims Chappell wouldn't back down, and neither would he, so Botham clocked him one. Chappell went flying.

More insults were traded before Chappell departed, initially pursued by Botham with his I'll-see-you-outside head on. Mercifully a passing police car intervened before the situation escalated, but the two have barely exchanged a word since. The trouble is they're too similar – both loyal, patriotic, uncompromising, intransigent, even got the same Christian name. Silly, really.

This was the backdrop to Botham's Test debut on 28 July 1977, coincidentally on the great Garfield Sobers' birthday and at the ground which was the West Indian's second home, Trent Bridge. It was a sort of passing of the all-rounder's baton and Botham began as he meant to go on.

First he strangled the Australian captain, Greg Chappell, with a long hop (how he must have wished it had been Ian), then, bounding in with great enthusiasm, took four more legitimate wickets in his next six overs. Add in a spirited 25 in England's first innings, batting at number 8, and it was clear that England had found something.

It was even clearer when Botham took 5-21 in the next Test at Headingley – though, rightly, that match is mainly remembered for someone else. Geoff Boycott, in his second comeback Test, made his hundredth first-class hundred on his home patch. The pitch was so flat even his moom could've made roons on it. But it was a fantastic achievement and an emotional day. He went on to be last man out for 191 (he was on the field the entire match), setting up England's innings win and the regaining of the Ashes. Boycott had administered a slow torture in retribution for the brutal killing by Lillee and Thomson; often those lingering deaths are actually more painful.

Reversing the Charges

By the beginning of the 1980s England and Australia had played each other nine more times. First England, still under Brearley, beat an Australia shorn of its stars by Kerry Packer 5-1. Then a full-strength Australia beat England 3-0, though, because it was a shortened series, the Ashes were not at stake, much to the Aussies' chagrin. Two and a half years after his debut Botham had accumulated 1336 Test runs, including six hundreds (average 40), and 139 Test wickets (average 18), plus any number of stunning slip catches.

With a great eye and a simple method he stood tall and hit colossally – and straight, too. He rarely played across the line, except when flicking off his toes. He was fearless and his driving on the up was imperious. From a bouncy run-up and strong body action he was an innings-wrecker with the ball, swinging it both ways, late and at pace. He could rough a batsman up if he wanted to. Think Jimmy Anderson with attitude. He had become a tour de force and he was only 24. Then, when Brearley declared his unavailability for future tours, he was made captain, partly on Brearley's recommendation. That's when the trouble started.

Botham had the misfortune to take charge not against an Australian Third XI, decimated by WSC, but against the 1980 West Indies. This was their side: Greenidge, Haynes, Richards, Bacchus, Kallicharran, Lloyd, Murray, Marshall, Holding, Roberts, Garner. The original 90mph hit-man Colin Croft was first reserve. You'd be hard pressed to beat that lot if you picked the best 11 from all of cricketing history (partly because at least five of them would be in it). So, in five Tests at home and then four away against those West Indians, Botham's England didn't conjure a win, though they did manage a few draws.

Being 24 – and Botham – meant he wasn't an ideal leader. He was an instinctive cricketer who, though he pulled his weight in matches, wasn't a great believer in training or practising particularly hard compared to others, and he struggled to see other people's perspectives. In the West Indies, for instance, Graham Gooch often liked to go for an early-morning jog along the beach before play. After England had lost a couple of Tests – despite courageous innings from Gooch – there was a team meeting which Botham took charge of. Gooch claims one of the recommendations he made was that early-morning runs should be banned, so that the players had more energy in the matches. 'But Skip, the morning jog is how I get myself going before a day's play,' Gooch explained. 'Yes,' Botham retorted, 'but you keep falling asleep in the bar!'

When the team arrived back from the Caribbean beaten and battered, there were calls for Botham to be replaced as captain. England were losing and his form had noticeably declined. Added to that, he was due in court to answer a case of alleged assault (no, not on Ian Chappell), though he was later acquitted. In early summer 1981 he was reappointed for the one-day series against Australia, which England lost 2-1, and also for the first Ashes Test.

Australia, now captained by Kim Hughes, were back to full strength, though the only Chappell present was Trevor, the youngest sibling, who was mainly famous for the underarm delivery he had 'bowled' earlier in the year – on brother Greg's instruction – to stop New Zealand winning a One-Day International. In the Test at Trent Bridge Dennis Lillee, slower but cleverer, helped Terry Alderman, an artful swing bowler, to exploit a green pitch better than England's array of seamers, and England missed six catches. Botham, who dropped two of them, scored one and 33 and took 3-68 in the match. On the first Sunday ever used for Test cricket in England, they succumbed to a four-wicket defeat.

The anti-feeling was growing, fermented by unsupportive press headlines like 'Botham Must Go! in the *Evening Standard* on the morning of the Lord's Test. The British press are nourishing when things are going well but predatory when they are not. They smell a victim and the vultures dive in. It is incredibly demoralising and is the reason the papers are now banned from dressing rooms. Botham says he had already made up his mind to resign before he was trapped lbw for 0 during a fiery spell from Geoff Lawson that finished off England's first innings.

Having promoted himself up the order in the second to go for quick runs and an intended declaration, he was clean-bowled first ball, sweeping the left-arm spinner Ray Bright. A dreaded pair in the Lord's Test. He walked back to dead silence in the pavilion and Long Room. At such times even in county matches, as normally encouraging spectators deliberately avoid eye contact or bury their faces in a newspaper or pretend to be asleep or actually are asleep, and you are aware of the stern expressions of Bradman's and Jardine's and W G Grace's portraits on the Long Room wall, you feel useless, a liability, desperate to crawl into a hole and disappear. It was the lowest Botham ever felt in an England shirt and he said after the match, which was drawn, that he couldn't carry on if he was going to be appointed one match at a time. He jumped before he was pushed.

At 8.30 that night, Mike Brearley's phone rang in his Highgate flat. The caller was immediately cut off. This happened several times. Eventually the operator asked if he was happy to accept a reverse-charge call. He said he was. It was the chairman of selectors, Alec Bedser, ringing from a faulty payphone in a pub. (Or that's what he said. Maybe he had mistaken those golf driving-range tokens for coins.) 'We'd like you to captain the side for the rest of the series,' he said. Brearley accepted immediately.

It wasn't a universally popular selection. Some of Brearley's mail was supportive, but some was critical. His batting was regarded as a potential weakness (I have never subscribed to this

– I always thought he was a very well-organised player, and once saw him make a superb hundred against Willis on a difficult Lord's pitch) and Ian Todd in the *Sun* suggested that his elevation was an insult to Botham. One letter he received said simply, 'If you want to know a fish is bad, look at its head.'

The next Test wasn't for another nine days and Brearley's county side, Middlesex, had no match in the meantime, so he was obliged to play for the Second XI against the RAF to get some practice. He made a few runs against an assortment of Lt Cols and Wing Cos. After that there was a selection meeting. Bob Willis had been struggling slightly both with his dicky knees and with illness – call it crease-itis, he bowled 32 no-balls at Lord's – and was not initially picked for the third Test. He was later added to the 12, but still almost did not get selected for the match. Brearley wanted him, but some of the other selectors didn't. Many believed his time was done.

Once at Headingley, Brearley, training to be a psychoanalyst, approached Botham, with whom he had always had a strong father/son-type relationship. He asked him if he wanted to play. Unbeknown to Botham, it was a rhetorical question. He said, 'Of course I bloody want to play, Brears.' 'Great,' Brearley replied. 'I think you'll score a century and take about 12 wickets.' He was a clairvoyant as well as a shrink.

The Miracle of Headingley

The first sessions of the match were Australia's. They won the toss and on an indifferent day of strong breezes, and a pitch that looked a little suspect, made 203-3. The resourceful opener John Dyson got to his hundred just before the close before being yorked by Graham Dilley. Botham took one wicket and seemed to be running in more slowly than in the past. Brearley was half wishing he himself hadn't agreed to this sudden return.

The great thing about Brearley was that he treated everyone differently. I played under him for three years with Middlesex and saw that he understood how to galvanise people, locking onto their individual psyche. He studied character and it felt as if he could see inside your brain. He had different techniques for different personalities – not just the stick for one and a carrot for another, he was more subtle than that. He used gentle persuasion for some, controlled anger for others; there would be the incentive of, say, a Sunday off or maybe an introduction to the attractive brunette in the Tavern Bar for a fast bowler from whom he needed one more big effort. He might ask a young player his opinion, making him feel more important.

He used humour, too, to lighten someone's load. He had an infectious laugh and giggled a lot, even after dishing out a rollicking. When he remonstrated about the dressing-room card school and demanded more attention on the match from those who batted lower down the order 'instead of playing silly games of pontoon!', there was an embarrassed silence. Then John Emburey said, 'OK, whose deal is it?'

Luckily Brearley could see the funny side, but he was very sincere and thought deeply about the game. Sometimes, when something had gone wrong and he lost his temper, he could be quite scary. Once when the Middlesex batsman Roland Butcher negligently ran two others out, including Brearley himself, in the space of two overs, he stormed onto the dressing-room balcony at Lord's, still in his pads, and shouted, right across the field, 'You cunt, Butch!'

Brearley had massive respect for Botham, but liked to goad him, challenging him to respond, understanding that his vast ability needed a bit of cajoling from time to time. During the first day at Headingley he had seen Botham's little jump into the crease before delivery, which seemed to be inhibiting his pace, and started calling him the 'Sidestep Queen'. Botham would only have accepted this from someone either intellectually or physically superior. There weren't too many of the latter (even then he was an ox of a man with calves like chimney pots), so Brearley, who had two degrees, one a first in Classics from Cambridge, had more chance than most. On the second day Botham was bounding to the crease and running in straighter, as he used to. He took five more wickets, giving him 6-95, and Australia declared at 401-9, leaving them time to dismiss Gooch before the close.

The pitch was mottled and ridged and, overall, England were dispirited, knowing that Australia had made about double what they should have. That was confirmed when the home side collapsed to 87-5, mostly to unplayable deliveries from Alderman and Lawson. Then Botham strode in and immediately played with abandon, encouraged by Brearley from the balcony. There were a few false shots, but some memorable ones too until, having just reached his 50, he nicked a lifter from Lillee to give wicketkeeper Rod Marsh his 264th Test victim. This was a world record (overtaking Alan Knott) achieved by a true, fair dinkum Aussie, trenchant and aggressive but totally honest on the field (he never appealed unless he was absolutely convinced it was out), disarming and humorous after play. A thoroughly decent bloke. 'Caught Marsh bowled Lillee' ultimately appeared in the scorebook 95 times, the most by a bowler/fielder combination in Test history.

England were all out at tea on the third day for 174. It wasn't a terrible score for that tricky surface. With two hours left for play and a rest day to come, Kim Hughes took the obvious step and asked England to follow on. Gooch was immediately out for 0. Fortunately for England bad light curtailed play early. It did not curtail play particularly early at the Botham residence, however. Both teams decamped there for his traditional Saturday night Leeds-Test barbecue (which still happens even now – he stands, defying the evening chill in a pair of shorts and an apron, quaffing wine, turning fat, juicy sausages and holding court). That evening chez Botham ended at midnight with many of the players merrily embroiled in a rugby scrum on his lawn.

On Monday morning, after the rest day, many of the England players, including Botham, checked out of their hotel. They were expecting the match to be over sometime after tea. This still looked likely at 3pm, when England were 135-7, another 91 short of avoiding an innings defeat. In the morning Brearley, batting at 3 had got a good ball from Lillee, and Gower and Gatting seemed almost mesmerised by Alderman. But for a courageous partnership between Boycott and Peter Willey, the situation would have been even worse.

When England's number 9 Graham Dilley joined Botham in the middle, Brearley had showered, changed and packed up his kit, though he put on a cricket shirt to keep up appearances. The match odds were flashed up on the electronic scoreboard – England 500-1. In their plight that seemed almost generous. The story about Lillee and Marsh giving the Australian team coach driver a tenner and a fiver respectively to have a piece of that is familiar. What is not so well known is that the Aussies had already asked the dressing-room attendant to get the champagne in. He was a fledgling pro golfer called Ricci Roberts – the same Ricci Roberts, in fact, who now caddies for Ernie Els. There was an ironic consequence of that as the match unfolded.

Initially it was the helmeted Dilley, rather than the bareheaded Botham, who went on the attack. In such a hopeless situation there was nothing to lose. With a big backlift he laid back and thumped a couple of balls only fractionally wide through the off side. His whirling bat scored 22 of the first 27 the pair put on. Botham was more circumspect (suggesting later, only half joking, that he was playing for a not out). But after Dilley had again flogged Lillee through cover, Botham followed suit. Using Gooch's bat – 'He hadn't used it much in the match and I thought there must be a few runs left in it' – he drove Alderman down the ground and glided him through the slips, eased Lillee silkily backward of point and cuffed Lawson over gully. He was buoyed by a couple of streaky boundaries, an overthrow for four from an aborted quick single and a big drive that skewed off the inside edge to the mid-wicket fence and brought him his 50. The crowd were loving it and he was beginning to.

Sensing Alderman was tiring, Botham heaved him over long on – an ugly but effective stroke – and another mid-wicket hack flew over the slips. Almost unnoticed, England were now only four runs behind. Botham then stepped back and flayed a lifting delivery from Lillee like a tracer through backward point. It went so fast to the boundary no one moved. England were in the lead. In the dressing room, the players were starting to look at the weather forecast, wondering if, just possibly, rain was predicted for the final day and they would only have to hang on for the rest of this fourth day to have a chance of drawing the match. It was a faint hope.

A mishit hoick off Alderman brought up the hundred partnership – in just 70 minutes. A saunter up the pitch to Alderman and a booming straight six brought up Richie Benaud's great commentary line: 'Don't bother looking for that, never mind chasing it. It's gone straight into the confectionery stall and out again.' (It shows how long ago it was: confectionery stalls are making a comeback.)

Dilley, swinging heartily, was bowled by Alderman off the inside edge for a rousing 56. The eighth wicket had put on 117 in just 80 minutes. But still England were only 25 ahead. This brought in Chris Old. The left-handed 'Chilly' was an unpredictable batsman. He was a fragile character, apprehensive of any bowler above medium pace, and was often dismissed flailing tamely at the ball, his body retreating to the leg side, well out of harm's way. But he actually had a phenomenal eye and, four years previously for Yorkshire, had scored one of the fastest hundreds in first-class history – in 37 minutes, though some of it was off 'gimme' bowling to set up a declaration. He could strike a mean ball. There was no problem with his ability. It was all a matter of what was going on in his head.

In this instance, he applied himself, willed on by the team, notably Peter Willey, who had practically threatened him with potential violence before he went in (Willey's Popeye forearms meant he wasn't a man to mess with). He wedged a bat handle against the image of his backside on the dressing-room TV to keep it in line. Old managed a lively 29 as he and Botham added a further 67. Kim Hughes lost the plot – scattering his fielders everywhere and failing to bowl his spinner, Bright (who had dismissed Botham for 0 in the previous Test) – and the bowlers lost their rag, Lawson sending down two beamers.

Botham, seeing it big, attempted a massive hit off Lawson on 99; the ball sliced off a thick edge and scooted to the third-man boundary. His hundred, made in one session, had taken 87 balls and his second 50 just 30. He raised his arms in triumph. The players stood to applaud him on the dressing-room balcony, Brearley clapping and then forcibly gesturing him to stay put. He did. After Old was bowled, he protected the number 11 Willis from the strike for the last 20 minutes and they had added a further 31 by the close.

The score was 351-9, Botham was 145 not out, his highest Test score. It was the sort of swashbuckling innings, played without a helmet or any inhibitions, that belonged to another era. It turned the clock back to the beginning of the century, being reminiscent of Jessop's famous assault on the Australians at The Oval in 1902.

It was beautiful for its simplicity and fearlessness. It was almost anarchic. It had enabled the last three wickets to put on 216 so far and England were 124 ahead. They celebrated their dramatic recovery in the best Yorkshire way, with pints of Tetley's and huge portions of 'baby' haddock – which overlap the plate both sides, making you wonder at the size of the 'mother' – at the famous Bryan's fish restaurant, up the Otley Road.

It's probably difficult to recall where you were when all this was going on – Monday 20 July 1981. Yes, yes, I know, you were playing with Lego…ancient history and all that. But I remember it all too well. I was playing at Lord's for Middlesex v Worcestershire; we were batting and I was so captivated by the TV coverage that, at 6pm, I forgot to pad up as nightwatchman (actually it was deliberate, as Worcester had a ferocious Barbadian pace bowler called Hartley Alleyne) and I got a right rollicking from our stand-in captain, Phil Edmonds. It could have been the first ever instance of a nightwatchman being timed out (or beaten up by the captain, who had a fiery temper). Luckily we didn't lose a wicket before the close.

'Botham's Miracle!' declared several papers the following morning with typical hyperbole. 'The greatest comeback since Lazarus,' wrote Pat Gibson in the *Daily Express*, though Botham dismissed it later as 'one of those crazy, glorious, one-off flukes'. It was a sunny morning, too, ideal for posting a few more runs. But in a classic anticlimax, Botham added one sumptuous boundary when play began, before Willis was caught at slip and England were all out. Australia required 130 to win. They were still overwhelming favourites.

In the dressing room Brearley said, 'More aggression, more adrenaline, more encouragement for the bowlers. The Australians will be nervous now.' He decided to open with Botham and Dilley. Willis, wicketless in the first innings and still hampered by overstepping – particularly common at Headingley, where the ground undulates disconcertingly – would be first change.

Botham conceded eight from his first two balls, but then got a wicket (Graeme Wood) with a half-volley. Dyson and Chappell progressed with relative comfort for a while and Willis, bowling uphill and into the wind after Dilley's fruitless spell, could find no way through. He asked to bowl from the other end and, after some consultation, Brearley gave him his head. Simultaneously, the clouds rolled in. It was 56-1.

Willis, running in increasingly like a man possessed, arms pumping, afro bouncing, eyes like a zombie, produced a snorting bumper to Chappell, straight at his head, which he could only palm to the keeper, Bob Taylor. In the last over before lunch he made one bounce to Hughes, who edged low and left of third slip, where Botham took a fine rolling catch. In the same over Graham Yallop couldn't keep down a nasty kicking delivery and Gatting at short leg dived forward to grab it. There was no quivering of the ground. He was looking svelte that year. At lunch Australia were 58-4.

Old, whose naggingly accurate support up the hill into the breeze is easily ignored, bowled Border soon after lunch off the inside edge. In eight overs on the trot he conceded only 11 runs. He was a superb bowler when mind and body were in sync.

After being hooked for four, Willis claimed Dyson, attempting to repeat the shot at one that didn't get up much; it caught his glove on the way through to Taylor. Two overs later Marsh top-edged a hook and Dilley, backpedalling rapidly down the hill at fine leg, judged an awkward catch superbly, just inside the rope. The score was 74-7. Lawson soon edged to Taylor, whose excited leap in the air belied his 40 years, and it was 75-8. Willis, still no-balling occasionally but completely in the zone, had taken six wickets in six overs. Christopher Martin-Jenkins, unusually commentating on TV, declared in that measured, patrician voice, 'England are on the brink of an absolutely sensational victory.'

Not so fast. Lillee was a canny and unorthodox batsman and he fashioned a different way of playing. He made room to persuade the short, wider balls over slip or slash to third man. The fuller, leg-side ones he flicked over square leg. Emboldened, Bright smacked Old twice through mid-wicket. In four overs they scored 35 of the 55 Australia needed to win. For England it was crisis time. If Australia won here, they would go two up, with three to play. Golfers know it's pretty hard to come back from there. In the Ashes it's even harder.

Gatting spoke to Brearley, suggesting that Willis – known to everyone as 'Goose' for the way his head jerked repetitively forward as he ran in – must bowl straight at Lillee. It didn't matter what length. Willis did so and Lillee, trying a more orthodox shot, scooped it in the air to mid-on, where Gatting moved smartly in and took another excellent rolling catch. He was engulfed.

The drama wasn't over. Botham, replacing Old, twice had the number 11 Alderman missed by Old at third slip. Brearley, well versed in cricket history, suddenly wondered if this Test would be remembered for the same reason as the famous one in 1902 when Fred Tate dropped the vital catch. But Willis was irresistible and soon afterwards detonated Bright's middle stump with a rapid yorker. The fast bowler who had been written off by the press days earlier hared manically off towards the dressing room, pursued by his delighted teammates. He had taken a phenomenal 8-43 to seize England victory by 18 runs and level the series 1-1. It was only the second time in history that a Test Match had been won by a team following on (after that crazy match at Sydney in 1894 – see page 47). It was the definition of daylight robbery.

Hordes of photographers and well-wishers descended on England's poky dressing room, where Willis was so drained from the exertion that, according to Botham, 'he looked about as ecstatic as a man who just realised he had forgotten to post his winning entry on the pools.' The broadcaster Peter West attempted to interview Willis afterwards, but failed to get much out of him as he stared zombie-like over his shoulder. But the guy with the toughest job was the dressing-room attendant Ricci Roberts. He had to approach the Australians and negotiate a price for their pre-ordered champagne so that England could buy it off them. You can imagine their reaction. The fact that he managed it suggested he had a bright future in international politics. But he took the undoubtedly more lucrative option and became Ernie Els's caddy.

The triumph reinvigorated both the series (the Stock Exchange ground to a halt during the game) and Willis' career. In his own mind his future had been in serious doubt before the match. Brearley said, 'I didn't think Willis could still bowl like that. He surpassed himself.' He went on to play another 30 Tests, captain England and exceed Fred Trueman's record of 307 Test wickets.

Botham was reborn as a barnstorming all-rounder and the scourge of Australia, giving everyone something to talk about other than Lady Diana Spencer's wedding dress for her marriage to Prince Charles a week later. He had Brearley to thank for his calming, guiding, encouraging influence. For Australia's captain Kim Hughes there was nothing but utter bewilderment. 'We didn't do much wrong…except lose,' he said dejectedly. The only consolation was that things couldn't get any worse.

Except that they did.

An Irresistible Force

The Edgbaston Test began the day after Charles and Diana's wedding (during which, incidentally, Clive Lloyd, playing for Lancashire against Middlesex, butchered 91, much of it off my bowling). It was a decent morning for batting, with a very patriotic feel, many spectators wearing Union Jack hats or waving St George's flags. England squandered it, being bowled out for 189, and were roasted in the press. Australia battled hard to accumulate a lead of 69, Brearley constantly hampering them with smart bowling changes and field settings.

England fared little better in the second innings, despite Boycott's three-hour vigil for 29. A bit of adventure down the order from Emburey and Old got them past the 200, but Australia needed only 151 to win – 20 more than at Headingley, but the pitch was smooth and the outfield like glass.

Willis and Old reduced Australia to 29-3, but Border and Yallop stabilised the situation and Border in particular looked entrenched; at 105-4, Australia seemed certain of victory. Brearley, casting round for bowlers with Botham appearing strangely diffident, was about to call on Willey to partner the excellent Emburey. He was egged on by umpire Dickie Bird, who said, 'It's all over, skipper. Best thing you can do is put the twirlers on so we can get away early.'

Out of the blue, Emburey made one bounce at Border, who gloved to short leg to end his three hours of resistance. It was now 105-5. Still just 46 to win. Brearley summoned Botham, telling him to keep it tight for Emburey at the other end. He did as he was told. And he finished Australia off in the process.

Bowling round the wicket to the left-handed Marsh he burst through his attempted drive, spectacularly ripping out his middle stump. Next ball he hustled one on to Bright, trapping him lbw. '114-7!' exclaimed Richie Benaud. 'And the crowd have gone quietly berserk.' Lillee almost edged the hat-trick ball and was out a couple of overs later, caught at the second attempt by Taylor. Each wicket Botham celebrated with a puff out of his chest and a biceps flex. Very King Kong (he was soon christened 'Guy the Gorilla').

It was suddenly 120-8.

Roared on by the 10,000 in the ground, he bowled the debutant Martin Kent off his pads. Three balls were enough for Alderman and, a nanosecond after shattering his wicket, Botham raced up the pitch, grabbed a stump and charged to the pavilion. He had taken 5-1 in 28 balls. Australia had lost their last six wickets for 16 and the match by 29 runs. All of England were celebrating, scientists were accepting that lightning does strike twice and anoraks were telling anyone who was interested that it was the first Test anywhere in the world since 1934 when no batsman had made a 50. The Aussies, now 2-1 down, had, according to Botham, 'lost their bottle'. It certainly looked like it. 'I suppose my mum'll speak to me,' said Kim Hughes, desolately. 'Reckon my dad will, too. And my wife. But who else?'

Hughes regained his credibility temporarily at Old Trafford when England, despite bolstering their batting with the addition of Chris Tavaré, were knocked over on a flat pitch for 231. Botham was out first ball, smartly caught in the gully off Lillee. The Australians started brightly, with Wood taking 16 off Willis's first two overs, causing Fred Trueman, who was scathing about any England fast bowler, to say on radio, 'I should be ashamed to draw my pay if I bowled like this in a Test!' Willis took the wickets of Dyson, Hughes and Yallop in his next six deliveries. 'Well...I don't know what's going off out there!' stammered Trueman (invariably his default when he was proved wrong).

Botham's observation about bottle had proved to be accurate. The tourists flopped to 130 all out. Willis, Botham and the newcomer Paul Allott, who had already made a career-best 52 not out in England's first innings, shared nine wickets. Tavaré, as dashing a batsman in county cricket as he was dour in Tests, anchored England's second innings. He crawled to 50 in over five hours as wickets fell around him.

England were 104-5, 205 ahead, when Botham walked in. Carefully he played himself in, scoring just three singles from his first 30 balls. He took a couple of fours off Bright, after which Australia claimed the second new ball. Botham, wanting to avenge his first-innings dismissal to Lillee, went on the rampage. He hooked him for three sixes in two overs, twice while ducking his head at the last moment and not looking at the ball. 'He plays that shot very well!' exclaimed Benaud on TV. 'He doesn't bother looking at it, just swats it away as if he was smashing a fly.' He drilled one back past Lillee so hard it was the bowler's turn to duck. It was intimidatory batting. Going up on his toes he flayed him through backward point. Alderman was launched back over his head and then, when he dropped a tad short, was slapped far over deep mid-wicket into the crowd as if he were an off spinner.

Botham plundered 66 runs off eight overs. These were not lucky runs. This was clean-hitting, calculated audacity. His fifth six – a sweep off Bright – brought up his hundred in 86 balls. To celebrate he smote the left-arm spinner over the sightscreen and shortly afterwards was gone in a blur of power and bravado. It was a command performance that elicited, in Brearley's words, 'a rare Antipodean awe at the prowess of an Englishman.' In *The Times*, John Woodcock, who had been watching Test cricket for 40 years, asked, 'Was this the greatest innings ever?' Botham had scored 118 out of a partnership of 149 with Tavaré, whose share was just 28. England were now 354 to the good.

Knott and Emburey weighed in with perky 50s, setting Australia a remote 506 to win. They threatened at one point when they were 210-3, but Emburey took two quick wickets and the seamers chipped in. Though Border illustrated why he was to become one of the great Australian batsmen with an undefeated 123, Willis took the final wicket half an hour after tea on the last day to regain the Ashes. In a crazy three weeks one man had turned the series upside down, sending Australia into complete turmoil. Botham, said John Woodcock, 'had been able to scale heights beyond the reach of ordinary men.'

He wasn't finished, either, getting through 89 overs in the final Test at The Oval despite back spasms, and taking 10 wickets in the drawn match to give him 34 in the series to go with his 399 runs. He appeared fearless, though, in common with many great sportsmen, this was a bit of a façade and he often needed praise and reassurance (don't we all?). He couldn't have achieved his miracles without Brearley, who departed Test cricket with a farewell 51 at The Oval and who, Botham said, 'encouraged me when I needed it and restrained me if he thought I was in danger of overstepping the mark. Most important, though, he listened to me.'

The 1981 Ashes set Botham up for life. He had become not only a national hero but the permanent bogeyman of Australia, a distinction which lasted right up to his retirement. In his final first-class match for Durham against Australia, in 1993, he was sending down some mediocre fare, but the Aussies were still in awe. 'What's he tried now?' asked Merv Hughes, who was unsighted in the pavilion. 'One that Boony couldn't reach!' Shane Warne said. 'He'll snare one in a minute, you bet,' said Hughes reverentially. (He didn't, in the end, for about the first time ever.)

Brearley retired with a proud captaincy record (played 31, won 18, lost four) to a new life in psychoanalysis, though he also wrote a defining book, *The Art of Captaincy*, and continues to contribute insightful pieces to the *Observer*. Many of the other heroes that summer – Gower, Willis, Boycott, Gooch, Gatting, Allott – are still actively and lucratively involved in the game, though Graham Dilley died of lung cancer aged 52 and Chris Old was recently seen working behind a checkout at Sainsbury's in Truro.

Most of all, though, the series revived English cricket, which had been in the doldrums, dropping to 10th on the list of participation sports (below tennis and bowls). Just as W G Grace had hauled cricket to the heights of public consciousness in the 1880s, so Botham's Ashes did a century later. The parks were awash with bats and balls and inspired a generation of kids to play cricket instead of Space Invaders.

Cricket's private, often mysterious world needs a classic drama every so often to remind those of us ritually immersed in it, and to demonstrate to the uninitiated, what a fantastic game we've got. The 1981 Ashes led eventually to Botham being touted round Hollywood by his agent. It wasn't him they needed. It was his scriptwriter.

INTERLUDE

*'That ball had as much impact on cricket in the
Nineties as the Wonderbra had on women's fashion.
It breathed new life into an old tactic. Everybody
wanted one to enhance their basic assets. Its jaw-
dropping qualities made normally strong, impressive
men hyperventilate.'*

As with the fashion and music of the decade, it's best to draw a
veil over most of the rest of the 1980s Ashes Tests. The only
alternative to the wrist-slitting material from the likes of the
Smiths and the Stone Roses seemed to be the synth-abuse of the
Pet Shop Boys and Dexy's Midnight Runners with their appalling
crimped hairstyles and naff shiny suits. Ian Botham defined the
era with his rather embarrassing highlighted blonde mullet. When
he ribbed Kevin Pietersen about his dead-skunk hairdo in 2005,
he had obviously forgotten about that.

Botham remained the key performer in the Ashes contests of
the 1980s. If he flourished, then, generally, so did England. On the
1982–3 tour he struggled to make an impact with either bat or
ball. But for a dramatic last-gasp win in Melbourne, when
England's current chairman of selectors, Geoff Miller, grabbed a
slip catch off a rebound from Chris Tavaré to give England victory
by three runs, they would have lost the series 3-0.

Gatting on Top

In 1985 in England, Botham roared in to bowl with renewed zest and took 31 wickets in the series. He also contributed explosive cameos with the bat, the most outlandish of which was at Edgbaston when he marched in – admittedly at 572-4 – and then hit his first and third balls back over the bowler Craig McDermott's head for colossal straight sixes. Australia's selectors obviously believed they had the powers of recovering lost youth, picking 35-year-old Jeff Thomson and 38-year-old leggie Bob Holland. Both flopped and so did the team, losing the series 3-1.

Then in 1986–7 England, after stuttering performances against the Sheep Shearers of Queensland, the Grape Pickers of Adelaide and the Gold Diggers of Perth (three Country XIs), were famously written off by, among others, the English cricket writer Martin Johnson, who said in the *Independent*, 'It seems to me England have only three major problems – they can't bat, they can't bowl and they can't field.'

Botham quickly disproved that by spanking a morale-lifting 138 in the first Test in Brisbane, which England won at a canter. After that he was injured, but came back for the decisive fourth Test and, despite bowling a lot of medium-paced dross, demolished the Australia lower order after Gladstone Small had dealt with the top five. This gave England an unassailable 2-0 lead in the series, and the captain, Mike Gatting, was depicted on the front page of the *Daily Telegraph* being doused with champagne. He deserved his moment of glory, having placed a considerable amount of attention on fielding (England took some vital, breathtaking catches that series) and given an assortment of gifted but often awkward characters straightforward direction, such as 'If you get in, stay in,' and 'If you're going to get pissed or get a girl, do it before midnight.'

It remains an anomaly that those were the only two Tests Gatting won as England captain (out of 23, though that was a better record than Botham's 0 out of 12). It wasn't entirely Gatting's fault. He bravely stood up to a dodgy Pakistani umpire (Shakoor Rana), but was then surprisingly sacked the following summer for taking a woman to his room, an act which was deemed inappropriate for an England cricket captain. Whereas it is the kind of act deemed practically compulsory for a West Indies cricket captain or an Italian Prime Minister.

Most surprising of all was that Gatting retained his status as the last England captain to win the Ashes for the next 18 years. Australia's 1986–7 defeat obliged them to examine their sporting infrastructure thoroughly. After the initial press furore, with headlines like 'Can Pat Cash Bat or Bowl?', there was some sensible analysis, sowing the seeds for the birth of the Australian Cricket Academy. All the great players that Australia unearthed in the next decade came through this finishing school. Gatting inadvertently kick-started a sporting revolution Down Under. He was made an OBE in England for his achievements (which some suggested stood for Order of the Branston Empire, owing to his love of cheese and pickle). The Aussies should have given him a knighthood.

How you regard the next eight Ashes series totally depends where you are from. If you are Australian you will think they represent the apex of sporting achievement. If you are English you will see them as a catalogue of unmitigated disasters. Between 1987 and early 2005, England beat Australia just once when the Ashes were still at stake (Edgbaston 1997). Jokes such as 'What do you call a Pommie who can't bat or bowl? An all-rounder…' rained down like confetti and the newspaper headline 'Is there anyone in England who can actually play cricket?' was pre-set and ready to roll.

During the 1989 series England, still obliging their players to lurch about the country between Tests playing three-day county matches on dodgy pitches, selected 29 players. Yes, *twenty-nine*. (See if you can name them, without looking it up. I'll help you: one was Alan Igglesden, and another is now MCC's head of cricket, John Stephenson.) Australia, whose first-class programme was based around four-day matches on flat tracks, picked just 12. They won the series 4-0.

That tells you two things. First, that England were seriously short of talent. Second, that, as Tony Greig often said to the amply conked Bill Lawry in the famous Channel 9 commentary box, 'The England selectors couldn't pick your nose, Bill.' (It is permissible to substitute Nasser Hussain for Bill Lawry as this story unfolds.)

The series was defined by England failing to take a wicket for the entire first day at Trent Bridge (Australia were 301-0) and by Allan Border, who had metamorphosed from Mr Genial playing for Essex to Captain Grumpy, reacting to a request for a drink from England's Robin Smith. 'What d'you think this is, a fuckin' tea party?' Border retorted. 'No, you can't have a fuckin' glass of water!'

England struggled without Botham, who had a fractured cheekbone. He was missed not just for his skill and total self-belief, but also for his iron constitution, enabling late-night socialising with members of the opposition which he instantly recovered from and they usually didn't. (His comment when four Australians were dropped in India recently for not handing in a self-improvement questionnaire was a classic of Botham derision: 'A form asking how much sleep you got during a match?' he hooted. 'Sleep?!')

His absence helped Australia's left-handed opener Mark Taylor, rather unfairly nicknamed 'Tubby' (he was slimmer than Gatting), pile up 839 runs in the series, while the swing bowler Terry Alderman took 41 wickets. No wonder he always ran in looking as if he was smiling. There was a lot of dissatisfaction in England at the time, not only with the running of the cricket team, but also with the governance of the country in general, following the introduction of the poll tax. A piece of graffiti daubed on a political slogan summed up the summer. Underneath 'Thatcher Out!' someone had written 'lbw Alderman'.

They Were All Warned

By the beginning of the 1990s, Australia, now as intent on challenging the dominance of the all-conquering West Indies as on beating the Old Enemy, were systematically improving. England, hampered by the fading powers of their 1980s stars, were drastically in decline. There was a conflict of attitudes in the England camp. On the 1990–1 tour of Australia, the disciplined Graham Gooch and Mickey Stewart ran the team along slightly inflexible lines. Debonair players such as David Gower and Allan Lamb preferred a more laissez-faire outlook. It was where the professional approach of the modern era clashed with the remnants of amateurism. The Tiger Moth incident, when Gower and the Derbyshire batsman Johnny Morris boarded two old biplanes from a nearby airfield to fly over the ground while England were batting in an up-country match, brought this discord to a head. It was a rather puerile thing to do, but the England management were too heavy-handed – publicly disciplining and fining the two men – and both the tour and Gower's career unravelled after that.

Gooch, whose wholehearted dedication was admirable, remained captain for the 1993 Ashes in England. Behind him he had assembled men he thought were tough and committed. These included Michael Atherton, Gatting, Smith and Alec Stewart (and not Botham, who was about to retire, nor Gower, Lamb or

Morris). These batsmen were all hardy individuals with sharp reflexes who, apart from Atherton, had endured a battering at the hands of the West Indies pacemen and were hungry to take revenge on lesser fast bowlers. The Australians had Merv Hughes – known as 'Fruit Fly' (Australia's favourite pest) – but his huge girth, walrus moustache and expletive-laden language rendered him more a comic figure.

Thus when Australia had managed just 289 in the first Test at Old Trafford and England's openers Gooch and Atherton had put on a reassuring 71, they were anticipating building a decent position. After Atherton was dismissed by the persevering Hughes (actually a far better bowler than he appeared), Border summoned the leg spinner Shane Warne for his first Ashes bowl. It was the 28th over of the innings and Gatting was on strike.

Gatt devoured spinners almost as eagerly as he did spotted dick and custard. Belying his stockiness, he was quick on his feet and masterly at feigning a charge down the pitch, then laying back to cut the resulting short ball to the boundary. He hoodwinked slow bowlers and celebrated such successful initiatives with a triumphant little cough. He was positively salivating at the sight of the blonde, plumpish figure who was about to bowl, and imagining a few easy runs before tucking into the sandwiches at tea.

Warne's exploratory first ball was floated down on the line of leg stump. With the spin imparted it drifted slightly outside leg stump, dipping in length as well. Gatting would have attempted to sweep it if it hadn't been the bowler's first delivery. Instead he thought it better to have a little look first, so he thrust bat and pad out towards the ball for a regulation block. To his surprise it bounced sharply, ripped away at 45 degrees from a perfect length, slipped past the outside edge and cannoned into the stumps off keeper Ian Healy's gloves. Or so he thought. But Warne's and

Healy's reactions and, crucially, umpire Bird's grim expression, suggested something different. The ball had actually bowled him off stump. Having stood for some seconds in total disbelief, Gatting eventually made his way off, with Richie Benaud on commentary saying, 'Gatting still has absolutely no idea what's happened to it.' Gooch, the non-striker's, wry observation that 'if it was a cheese roll it wouldn't have got past him' does the ball (and Gatting) a disservice. It was such a phenomenal delivery he would have had trouble playing it even if he had seen it on Youtube several times first. After his tea.

That ball had as much impact on cricket in the Nineties as the Wonderbra had on women's fashion. It breathed new life into an old tactic. Everybody wanted one to enhance their basic assets. Its jaw-dropping qualities made normally strong, impressive men hyperventilate. There is no real parallel on a sporting level. The closest would be the basketball player Michael Jordan's 'hangtime,' which, like Warne's big leg break, seemed to defy the laws of science. Interestingly Warne chose Jordan's number – 23 – to wear on the back of his Australian (one-day) shirt. David Beckham later did the same when he went to Real Madrid. It is a number that has a special resonance in sport since Jordan's use of it, and is always the most sought after: it symbolises a player with unique powers.

Warne bamboozled 34 England batsmen that series (which of course Australia won 4-1) and the headline 'Hung, Warne and Slaughtered' was a repetitive theme that summer, that decade. He went on to torment virtually every player on the planet, so that by the end of the 1990s he had 356 Test wickets, already the most ever taken by an Australian. More significantly he had been exceptionally frugal, conceding just 2.5 runs an over. As Richie Benaud, a great friend and adviser to Warne, said, in his inimitable way, 'For a leg spinner, that's quite remahkeble.'

Warne's emergence symbolised the metamorphosis going on in Australia. Pre-1990s, outsiders still visualised it as a tough land full of hard men labouring in the outback or hunting crocodiles, quaffing beers round the barbie at night. Their spiritual hero, aside from Paul Hogan, was the bristling moustachioed, throbbing-templed medallion man Dennis Lillee – who was, of course, a fearsome fast bowler.

Warne did the most to cast off that clichéd impression. Now Australia was seen as urban and sophisticated, full of glistening shopping malls and smart professionals sipping lattes or eating sushi. Warne didn't burst blood vessels to achieve his goals. Instead he tormented opponents with a flick of the wrist and a flashing smile. He moved mountains with twirling fingers rather than toiling elbows.

He could make five apparently identical deliveries all do different things: the hard-spun leg break which fizzed past your edge; the top spinner which could jump up and bite; the wrong'un – making you look a fool as it spun in the opposite direction; the slider – one that didn't spin; and, deadliest of all, the back-spinning flipper which floated down innocently, looking like a long hop, then skidded wickedly on, pitching and whistling 'Waltzing Matilda' before crashing into your stumps. Quite a repertoire.

Warne's relationship with the old Australian leg spinner Terry Jenner was symbiotic. Jenner, who had fallen on hard times and been briefly imprisoned for embezzlement, had been rejuvenated by his work with Warne and had become known as the 'Spin Doctor'. Warne benefited hugely from the older man's close monitoring and wicket-taking nous. They constantly worked on little ploys together. Jenner was like a retired conjurer teaching his son the tricks of the trade.

Warne brought theatre to the game, teasing batsmen with his sleight of hand and then tricking them out of their wicket.

He was a brilliant con-man, a light-fingered wicket thief. He was
astute, too, spotting minor alterations in a batsman's approach. At
Lord's in one series he realised that Michael Atherton took guard
a fair way across on middle, so concentrated on a leg-stump line
and bowled him behind his legs with his notorious 'pickpocket'
delivery. To counter that, Atherton took a leg-stump guard at
Trent Bridge. Warne noticed, changed to a wider line outside off
stump, making the batsman reach for the ball, and had him caught
behind instead. His control, his artistry, his constant threat in any
conditions explained why Australia lost just two Test series out of
23 between 1993 and 2001. It also enabled Australia emphatically
to end the West Indies' 15-year domination of the game, the task
Warne was originally fast-tracked to perform.

He was the chief reason Australia won six Ashes series in a row
by handsome margins. If he had changed sides, the story would
have been reversed. To him, as to all Australians, the Ashes are
special, as he explained: 'No matter how good or how bad England
are playing or how well Australia are doing, it's always the same.
It's been drummed into you since the age of about five that if
you're Australian you have just got to beat the Poms.' (Whereas in
England it's drummed into you from the age of about five that
you have got to beat the taxman.)

But Warne was only the principal cog in Australia's gleaming
machine. The rest was made up of pairs of wheels spinning off
each other. At the top of the order, the manic Michael Slater
would be attacking from one end, the mellow Mark Taylor
accumulating from the other. Mark Waugh caressed the ball about
with effortless ease, his twin brother Steve, known appropriately
as 'Tugga', cuffed and clipped it with severe efficiency. Ian Healy
rabbited and hassled behind the stumps, calling out, 'Back to the
nets, idiot!' when some callow opponent lost his wicket. Taylor
stood beside him at slip, quietly chewing gum and gobbling

catches. The ruthless exterminator Glenn McGrath probed away relentlessly, conducting a forensic examination of a batsman's technique, in partnership with Warne's teasing and winkling.

When wickets weren't falling they'd dry up the runs – McGrath metronomically accurate, often using the bouncer as a dot ball; Warne going round the wicket and aiming into the rough – until the batsmen lost patience. Or spinner and keeper would indulge in a bit of irrelevant banter in mid-pitch: 'Oi, Heals, what hole are we playing today?' 'Ninth at The Capital, Warney.' 'What club are you gonna use?' 'Nine iron, mate.' It was meant to amuse and confuse. Anything to upset the batsman's concentration. The opposition were ritually hunted down. There was no remorse.

All Change, Please, and Mind the Gap

A sequence of England captains looked on with a mixture of envy and exasperation, knowing that the English system, which compelled players to have more allegiance to their county than to their country, had no chance of competing. First it was Graham Gooch, who resigned the captaincy to Michael Atherton. Aged just 25, Atherton was not only still learning the game himself, he also had to manage, select and practically coach the team (with some help from David Lloyd) through six Tests and three One-Day Internationals a summer, while still playing 10 County Championship games and 15 one-dayers for Lancashire.

When the onerous demands of that and trying to see off McGrath had turned him into the oldest looking 20-something in Britain, he handed the reins to Alec Stewart, a lively sergeant-major type who quaintly called his dad (Mickey) 'manager' even at home. Stewart, fit and focused, was, however, a hopeless tosser, to coin a phrase, and lost all five during the Ashes of 1998–9 in Australia. He handled capably the tasks of captaining, keeping and batting at number 4 against such uncompromising opponents; it was the others who let him down. Despite Warne's absence through injury, England had surrendered the Ashes by Christmas. A crystal replica of the famous urn was presented to the Australians to keep until, it was said, England could win it back. At the time an announcement that Ian Botham and Ian Chappell were adopting a child together would have sounded more likely.

Stewart gave way to Nasser Hussain, a reformed member of the brat pack. Hussain was a fine, backs-to-the-wall batsman, but he was so highly strung he couldn't sleep, arguing that, if he nodded off the night before an innings, the trauma of walking out to bat would soon be upon him. He was therefore easy to wind up, and the Aussies often had a field day. Ian Healy greatly enjoyed baiting him with lines like 'Let's have silly point right under Hussain's nose' and then positioning the fielder quite some distance away.

A strong leader, however, Hussain assembled an impressive team for the 2001 Ashes in England, augmented by the eagle-eyed coach Duncan Fletcher. England were on a roll and, with the injury-prone pace pair of Darren Gough and Andrew Caddick finally on the field together, had a chance, despite Australia's 15-match unbeaten run. This was the biggest Ashes series since, er, the previous one.

It went the same way, of course. Slater lashed Gough's first over of the series for 18, heralding a new, indecent haste in Aussie batsmanship. The imposing left-hander Matthew Hayden wasn't averse to sauntering up the pitch to the pace bowlers and savaged anything short; at number 3 Ricky Ponting was the best hooker and puller in the game. Then came the Waugh twins, followed by the languid caresser of boundaries Damien Martyn, and then Adam Gilchrist, surely the best number 7 in Test history.

Wielding his bat like a samurai sword, Gilchrist sliced a tiring attack to ribbons, specialising in sizzling square drives and clean strikes over long on. He hit more sixes in Test cricket (100) than anyone and was largely responsible for Australia's run rate usually surpassing four an over. It was like cricket on speed and it bought Australia's bowlers extra time. Not that they needed it. With an attack led by McGrath, backed up by the rapid Brett Lee, the slippery Jason Gillespie and Warne, matches frequently finished early. Having won the third Test on the Saturday to go 3-0 up, Australia sealed the fate of the 2001 Ashes in just 11 days, as Warne reminded everyone, cavorting around on the Trent Bridge balcony showering people with champagne.

This was Australia's seventh Ashes series win in a row and the red-tops led the clamour for the urn to be transported to Australia and left there forthwith. There was again much gnashing of teeth about the English 'system' (i.e. the counties), which Australia's coach John Buchanan, who had spent a year with Middlesex, called 'the true servant of mediocrity.' Funny, it did England all right until the mid-1980s, and then what happened? Well, everyone else improved and we stood still.

Changes were afoot. Central Contracts, introduced in the year 2000, largely at the behest of Duncan Fletcher, began to have an effect. The players who were likely to play for England were withdrawn from county games. This incited inevitable ire in the shires, who conveniently ignored the fact that without the television income from England's games there wouldn't be any county teams. As a result the international players were fresher, better prepared and less inclined to lounge around checking the county scores on Ceefax. England had also decided that 'if you can't beat 'em, hire 'em.' So Rod Marsh, the man who had once called English bowlers pie chuckers, became head of the English Cricket Academy (his remit was to turn sausage rolls into Beef Wellington) and Tasmanian Troy Cooley joined up as bowling coach. England were captained by a guy born in India, and coached by a Zimbabwean and two Australians. Smart use of the remnants of Empire, if you ask me.

The hopes of a decent Ashes contest for the 2002–3 series in Australia were high. Australia were as hard as nails under Steve Waugh's gimlet-eyed captaincy. They allied physical supremacy to sly comment on the field – Waugh called it 'mental disintegration' – throwing in observations like 'He likes a little airy drive, this bloke!' or 'Check that extravagant backlift!' to disturb a batsman's concentration and avoid the match referee's censure. But England had some quality and verve too: a decent hand of fast bowlers – Gough, Caddick, Hoggard, Harmison, allied to the emerging all-rounder Andrew Flintoff – and solid, aggressive batting in the shape of Trescothick, Vaughan, Butcher, Hussain and the ageless Stewart.

Alas, the hopes were dashed as soon as England arrived. Flintoff had failed to recover from a double hernia operation and was sent to the Australian Cricket Academy to get fit. Gough was unable to play following a knee operation and was sent home. Various other players were carrying injuries. Then Hussain made his calamitous decision to field first in Brisbane, and Australia's new intimidating opening partnership of Hayden and Langer feasted on nervous bowling. The zesty Simon Jones eventually dismissed Langer, but then, to cap it all, he ruptured knee ligaments horribly, diving in the outfield, and had to be sent home as well. Australia won the first Test by 384 runs and, despite batting of the highest calibre from Vaughan, who made three big hundreds in the series, it was all one-way traffic from there.

The Ashes were sacrificed (again) on 1 December, the earliest point ever, and Hussain admitted England had been poor. You could look at it another way and say Australia had been superb. This 2002 side surely challenged the 1948 Invincibles as the best Australian team in history. Langer and Hayden strutted around bullying the opening bowlers; Ponting was the consummate number 3, able to bunker down and steer the team through a storm, but also to set the spinnaker and capitalise on a fair wind; Mark Waugh, and then when he retired Damien Martyn, made runs with the nonchalance of someone out for a beach stroll, while Steve Waugh dug in and drilled the ball square of the wicket with relentless satisfaction.

Various players came and went at number 6, but the Aussies didn't really need one with the unstoppable Gilchrist at 7, followed by a quartet of bowlers – Warne, Lee, Gillespie and McGrath – who were all ace snipers, gunning batsmen down wherever they reared their unfortunate head. The mercurial Warne could be relied on to keep it tight from one end, while the pacemen battered away like an incessant sea at the other, exposing any weakness. It was the perfect formula. As an 11 they were bonded by an insatiable desire to win, and they had an astute coach, John Buchanan, who helped streamline that desire.

Between 2000 and 2005, that team played 20 Test series, won 17 and lost just one – the gripping encounter in the subcontinent when India won a dramatic second Test in Calcutta after following on. They were a supreme side with more illustrious players – Hayden, Langer, Ponting, the Waughs, Gilchrist, Warne and McGrath – than any team could ever have fielded. Only Clive Lloyd's 1984 West Indies could even run them close.

The only things that could stop them were the onset of age and a highly skilled, disciplined and aggressive opponent hell bent on ending 16 years of total humiliation. Cue the 2005 Ashes…

9

SECOND TEST, EDGBASTON, 2005

'"Bowden!!...Kasprowicz the man to go...Harmison has done it. Despair on the faces of the batsmen...and joy for every England player on the field!" [Richie Benaud, Channel 4] And, one might add, for every England fan watching, listening or praying...'

What were you doing in the summer of 2005? Enjoying a cheap Greek holiday before the country went belly-up? In Paris witnessing Lance Armstrong win his seventh Tour de France title? (Don't tell me you knew all along...) 'Finding yourself' in Thailand? Well, if you were in the UK you would have to have been imprisoned in a Scottish croft by a weird religious sect or employed on a submarine (as one England fan was) not to have been at least partially touched by the Ashes.

It was a series that had almost everything. Drama, intrigue, controversy, stunning debuts, sad farewells, unexpected beginnings and gripping endings. A duel between a shaven-headed English man-mountain, Andrew 'Freddie' Flintoff, and a bottle-blonde Australian conjurer, Shane Warne – brawn v brain...well sort of...that turned into an epic. It was absolutely compelling from start to finish. England hadn't won an Ashes series for 18 years (a span of eight series and 44 Tests) – when a couple of the current side were still in nappies – and had gone to extensive lengths to prepare for the challenge.

Cracking Up

They had done a lot of work with an Australian fast-bowling coach, Troy Cooley, who knew the opposition inside out. They introduced a special spin-bowling contraption known as Merlyn, which was able to replicate any spinner's deliveries they chose, to their practices. And they drew on the inspiration of a number of people, including Alan Chambers, a renowned polar explorer, who talked to them about motivation and handling adversity. Australia, who had been impregnable for most of the previous decade, were hell bent on keeping England in their place and hauled their wearying bodies through a Queensland boot camp, much to Warne's undisguised chagrin.

It was shaping up to be a battle to the death as an ageing warrior (Australia) sought to defend the prize from a younger, more thrusting challenger (England). This was going to be sporting rivalry at its most vivid and intense – a five-match series compacted into six breathless weeks. Also it was to be the last live cricket on British terrestrial TV (raising many objections in Parliament, where there are a surprising number of cricket anoraks) after the subscription channel Sky had won exclusive live rights for the foreseeable future.

England's build-up to the 2005 Ashes series actually began in 2004. It was late September in Birmingham, the time of year when most people are bringing their geraniums in for the winter and West Bromwich Albion fans are going to early-season relegation battles. It is certainly not the time of year for major cricket matches between England and Australia.

But that was the month that the ICC had scheduled the Champions Trophy – that vital competition no one wants to play in, watch or cover – and this was the semi-final at Edgbaston between cricket's two oldest adversaries. A lot of people hadn't noticed, including BBC Radio, where the preview of the encounter was the sixth item on the sports news behind reflections on the death of legendary football manager Brian Clough two days earlier and updates on various footballers' eyelash injuries.

It was a cool dank morning and a good toss for Michael Vaughan to win. England, who had won all seven home Test Matches against West Indies and New Zealand that summer, were noticeably pumped up. Steve Harmison gave early notice of his threat with a vicious bouncer at Adam Gilchrist. Andrew Flintoff and Darren Gough were also hostile and England's fielding was tigerish. Vaughan even effected a run out.

But it was England's batting that really took Australia by surprise. Marcus Trescothick cracked four fours off one Glenn McGrath over, prompting speculation that the bowler's powers were fading, and Vaughan, often ineffective in one-day cricket, savaged Brett Lee with a series of daring pulls and creamy drives. Chasing 258, England coasted home by six wickets. 'Come on, is there anyone in Australia who can play cricket?' asked 'Machine Gun' Mike (Walters) in the *Daily Mirror*.

Australia played down the defeat – as they would – arguing that they were rebuilding without Shane Warne, who had retired from the one-day game, and that they were playing out of season. But the cracks were appearing. More importantly, as it was the first time England had beaten Australia in a one-dayer in six years and 15 attempts, it allowed Vaughan's team to believe that the Aussies were not invincible.

That thought sustained England through a demanding winter in South Africa and helped to crystallise their plans for the following summer – namely, to play an aggressive brand of cricket and get in the Australians' faces. It had served them well so far, with eight Test wins in a row (seven at home and one in South Africa), a settled team including a fast and feisty bowling attack and, in Freddie Flintoff, a bullish all-rounder.

Flintoff's inspiration, Ian Botham, was refreshingly positive: 'When I first started commentating on England we couldn't beat the Eskimos. Now they're playing good cricket they have the best chance to beat the convicts for 20 years.' He was further encouraged by the emergence of the South African-born Kevin Pietersen, who had pulverised his former compatriots for three one-day hundreds in the winter and was now managed by a company Botham had set up. 'Great player, but someone get that dead mongoose off his head,' Botham said, referring to the wild blonde streak in Pietersen's hair.

As for the Australians, they arrived in England in June 2005 exuding their usual air of superiority. Their ex-players cast serious aspersions on England (Flintoff couldn't bat, the middle order was weak and untried and Warne would sort them out, the fast bowling was overrated and the spin non-existent). Warne inevitably boasted that he had a 'new' delivery. And, having promised to hunt down the England captain everywhere he went, Glenn McGrath reverted to his default 5-0 prediction, though it had got to the stage where he couldn't say anything else without it being seen as a sign of weakness and self-doubt. Kerry Packer's Channel 9, the brash, perennial home of Australian cricket, was so confident of an English trouncing it hadn't even bothered to buy rights to the Tests. They were to be shown instead on SBS, a minority, government channel with an inclination for alternative programming. It was a bit like putting the Ashes on BBC4.

In June 2005 England hit the Australians hard, first at the Rose Bowl for the inaugural Twenty20 match between the teams. Darren Gough tore at the Australians like a man possessed, memorably bowling a bouncer at Andrew Symonds first ball, hitting him on the shoulder to leave a calling card and completely ignoring the chance of going for a hat trick by aiming at the stumps. After six overs Australia were 31-7 and they went on to lose by a distance. 'THRASHES' yelled the *Sun*. England had put down their marker.

This continued in the one-day series that followed. In one game, Simon Jones fielded a drive off his own bowling from Matthew Hayden, tried for a run out and accidentally hurled the ball into Hayden's shoulder. Hayden had a hissy fit and squared up to Jones, flexing his ample biceps. Jones wouldn't back down and was bravely supported by Paul Collingwood, who was about half Hayden's size. This England team were not going to be bullied.

In the next game at Bristol, Pietersen pulled off one of the great batting heists. He rescued England from almost certain defeat with a brilliant 91 not out, destroying the Australian attack with clean, audacious hitting. Once, depositing a decent delivery from Jason Gillespie miles over long on, he made the Australian seamers look like club trundlers – or, in the case of the long-haired Gillespie, a guy who'd got lost on his way to the Glastonbury Festival. Pietersen left an indelible mark on both the Australians and in the Test selectors' minds.

After that Australia stumbled from one mishap to another, and by the time the Test series arrived the teams were neck and neck with the pundits, though the *Sun* inadvertently gave the Aussies a bit of extra motivation by depicting their quick bowlers holding handbags under the cheeky headline 'Is that all you've got, Sheilas?'

The cracks in the Australian foundations were getting serious as they were buffeted from all sides. An interesting parallel was with a significant geological event in Australia. One of the Twelve Apostles: giant, 20-million-year-old limestone stacks and celebrated landmarks off the Victoria coast – had recently collapsed from the incessant pounding of wind and waves. Was it an omen?

Do Not Adjust Your Set

In the few days preceding the first Test at Lord's, the build-up turned into a media frenzy with numerous player prognostications and opponents' piqued responses. Much of it focused on Flintoff, whose insistent fast bowling, in particular, had become an intimidating weapon. He had never before trained it on the Aussies in a Test Match. But buoyed by Flintoff's presence, Michael Vaughan deliberately riled the Australians in the pre-match captains' briefing by rejecting Ricky Ponting's suggestion that, in the case of disputed catches, the batsman should accept the fielder's word. Previously, he had agreed to the idea.

A combustible atmosphere was developing. The day before the game, with ticket prices reaching £1000 a pair, Australia's Justin Langer, a black belt in Taekwondo, could be seen sparring with himself on the Nursery Ground and forecasting a heady conflict. The next morning, when Australia won the toss and elected to bat, this latent animosity exploded onto the field. The hostile Steve Harmison, provocatively given the first over ahead of the more sedate Matthew Hoggard to test the Aussies' mettle early on, fizzed a bouncer into Langer's shoulder with the second ball of the match. In his opening spell he also clanged both Hayden and Ponting on the head, cutting the Australian captain's cheek. There was a conspicuous lack of concern from the England fielders.

The Australians tried to counter this attack with some aggression of their own. The first session was like two prize fighters who had been chained up in their corners for too long being suddenly let loose to grapple feverishly with each other. With Australia 97-5 and recovering in their corner at lunch, it was certainly first blood to England. By tea they had been routed for 190 by England's zesty, four-pronged seam attack. The great edifice was crumbling before our eyes.

And then normal Australian service was resumed. McGrath, a peerless exponent of the Lord's slope, reduced England to 21-5. The openers Trescothick and Strauss were quickly seen off, caught in the slips, with Trescothick becoming McGrath's 500th Test victim. Vaughan, after a brief verbal spat with Ponting, was castled, as was Ian Bell. And Flintoff's first Ashes innings lasted just four balls. 'I've waited eight years for that,' he said, sitting disconsolately in the dressing room unbuckling his pads. On his Test debut, Pietersen at least offered some forthright resistance, before England closed the first day on 92-7 and everyone could catch their breath. The hordes of colour writers crammed into the Lord's media centre – the ones whose task is to convey the mood of the day, not just report the events – had reams of material.

The next morning, despite Pietersen memorably launching McGrath straight back over his head into the Lord's pavilion, and also creaming Warne into the grandstand, England were obliterated for 155 and conceded a lead of 35. This was systematically increased thanks to lamentable English fielding, which gave Australia seven lives to howls of dismay from English fans experiencing Ashes déjà vu. 'Vaughan Again Losers!' blasted the disloyal *Sun*. Chasing an impossible 420 to win, England were mercilessly tripped up by that old double act McGrath and Warne and fell flat on their faces to lose by an emphatic 239 runs.

McGrath, the Aussie terminator improbably nicknamed 'Pigeon' for the birdlike pitter-patter of his run-up, was sensing another tame English submission and he was not alone. The *Sydney Telegraph* proclaimed, 'Our message to pathetic Poms: is that all you've got?' There was a distinct and surprising sense of disappointment from Australian quarters. They had begun to find their team's dominance a little tedious and they were relishing the prospect of a decent contest for once. To them, Lord's was the ultimate anticlimax.

The Greatest Test?

A 10-day gap before the second Test at Edgbaston gave England time to mull over what had gone wrong. It turned out to be crucial. They realised that Pietersen, untrammelled by the litany of failed Ashes campaigns, had shown them the way. There was a visible aggression in their net practices as a sequence of batsmen charged at the balls issuing from the ingenious Merlyn machine and launched them into the distance.

It was still just a machine, of course, and the story at Edgbaston may well have been the same as at Lord's but for two unexpected events before the start of the Match. The first was Glenn McGrath treading on a stray ball in fielding practice. He went over on his ankle and crumpled to the ground in agony, white as a sheet. He was carted off and would clearly be out of the match. It was later dubbed the ball of the series.

The second was Ponting putting England in when he won the toss. Despite McGrath's absence giving his seam attack a rather pop-gun appearance and despite having the best spinner in the world to exploit a fourth-day pitch, he based his decision on historical data about the Edgbaston pitch when the teams first arrived. In other words he had made up his mind two days earlier. It was as absurd as Nasser Hussain deciding to field first in Brisbane in 2002–3 (Australia finished the first day on 364-2) and Hussain smiled ruefully when reminded of it.

It was the opportunity England craved. The pitch was flat and benign when the teams emerged to the strains of 'Jerusalem', and Trescothick sounded the timpani when he took three boundaries, all struck imperiously through the covers, from Brett Lee's second over. Gillespie and Michael Kasprowicz, who had expected to be carrying the drinks all tour but had been drafted in for McGrath, were treated with something approaching relish by two left-hand batsmen who gorged themselves on anything short and wide.

When Warne got an early bowl, Trescothick deposited him into the sightscreen and Strauss was down the wicket giving him the charge. This was a better headrush than anything available on Birmingham's Broad Street on a Friday night and the Edgbaston faithful, always very vocal in their support of England, urged their approval. The England openers put on 112 before Strauss was bowled by Warne; undeterred, Trescothick struck 18 off Lee's final over of the morning and England took lunch at 132-1.

Trescothick was eventually caught behind for an initiative-stealing 90. But, spared the law and order of McGrath, the England batsmen gambolled about in the afternoon, like children skirmishing on their father's preciously manicured lawn when he isn't home. Vaughan kept up the momentum and Pietersen exhibited more of his unique repertoire, including a one-legged flick past mid-on from a yard down the pitch, whipped up like a topspin forehand. It was immediately christened 'the flamingo shot'. When Vaughan was out, Flintoff marched in with renewed vigour but began uncertainly. A botched drive off Warne skewed agonisingly in the air just out of reach of mid-off and bobbled to the boundary to relieved cheering.

It was the slice of luck Flintoff needed. Emboldened, he smote Warne back over his head for a huge six and swung a full toss over mid-wicket for another. When Lee bounced, Flintoff hooked – without looking at the ball: it pinged off a top edge and into the seats beyond square leg. Pietersen himself unleashed shots of extreme ingenuity, especially an off drive against Warne played almost squatting, like the lunges you are supposed to do in the gym to strengthen your quads. Flintoff employed his muscularity to plant Lee for another big six over square leg. Soon after he recorded his maiden Ashes 50. The partnership evoked memories of the cavalier Viv Richards and the cruder Ian Botham putting bowlers to the sword together in the halcyon days of Somerset CCC.

It was too good to last, but Flintoff and Pietersen's liaison of 103 and some meaty blows from the tail enabled England to finish the day 407 all out. This ebullience was not just a heady response to being put in, but also a stark contrast to Test Matches of the previous generation when 300 runs in a day was regarded as indecent. 'You don't understand this, do you?' said Tony Greig on commentary at one point to Geoff Boycott. 'You're right! It's fun, though,' Boycott replied. In fact it was the first time for 40 years that England had gone past 400 on the opening day of a Test Match. The innings contained 10 sixes. Edgbaston is an intimate ground which has become the spiritual home of the England team and the crowd trooped home sated. England had exorcised their Ashes demons, at least temporarily.

The match continued at the same breakneck speed on the second day. Vaughan set interesting fields, challenging Matthew Hayden's ego with a man at silly mid-off to Matthew Hoggard. Insulted at such impudence, Hayden made to shift him first ball with a booming drive, but instead ladled a tame catch to extra cover. It was a huge moment for the England bowlers, who had been bullied by this 'Incredible Hulk' in previous series. After that Ponting was busy at the crease and Langer bristled with intent, but Vaughan kept the scoring in check with men set deep at cover and square leg to cut off the boundaries.

The discredited left-arm spinner Ashley Giles, a local hero but seen by Australians as a spare part and by a *Guardian* journalist as a wheelie-bin, had the satisfaction of dismissing Ponting, Michael Clarke – a reputedly fine player of spin – and Warne himself, bowled charging miles down the pitch. Vaughan ran out Damien Martyn, a freak moment many believed meant the gods were on England's side. Adam Gilchrist hit crisply and was looking dangerous, but Flintoff generated some hostile reverse swing and made sure he ran out of partners. Australia conceded a lead of 99.

Trescothick and Strauss emerged again on the second evening to ecstatic applause, although seasoned England watchers were bracing themselves for the inevitable collapse. It was not long in coming. Warne was calling Strauss the 'new Daryll' after the South African Daryll Cullinan, who had always been his bunny. (Warne was fond of saying, 'What colour's the couch?' when Cullinan came into bat, intimating that the dressing room was where the batsman preferred to be and would be heading to shortly. To his credit, Cullinan wasn't averse to the odd witty retort. After Warne had been out injured and then banned for a while and, slightly out of condition, eventually encountered Cullinan at the crease again, the spinner, salivating over the prospect of an easy wicket, said, 'I've been waiting two years for this!' To which Cullinan replied, 'Look's like you've spent most of it eating.')

So, after England had progressed easily to 25-0 in the evening sunshine, Warne was summoned to bowl the seventh over of the innings and the last of the second day. With four men round the bat he sent an exploratory first ball down the leg side to Strauss. The second, bowled from round the wicket, went to the other extreme: it barely pitched on the cut strip, it was so wide outside the left-hander's off stump. Strauss walked across his stumps, bat held high above his head, intending to watch it pass harmlessly in front of him through to Adam Gilchrist.

The ball had other ideas. It landed in the bowler's footmarks, gripped and spun literally at 45 degrees. Strauss watched helplessly as it passed in front of him, sneaked behind his back leg whistling g'day, and crashed into leg stump. Warne punched the air in triumph. Michael Slater laughed manically on commentary. Strauss wasn't laughing. He knew that he would now be 'Daryll' for the rest of the series. Probably for ever. Even his wife would start calling him that. He had most people's sympathy as Hawkeye couldn't replicate the ball, suggesting this amount of deviation was impossible. It was a 'computer says no' delivery. Unplayable. At least England's nightwatchman Hoggard survived the rest of the over.

Warne, surrounded by star-struck hangers-on in the hotel bar later, beamed at the mention of his wonder ball. 'I felt after the way we had played I had to make a statement and turn one as much as I could,' he said. There was some debate about whether it was the biggest turner he had ever produced, although Richie Benaud, commentating on his last Test series in England after 40 years behind the mic, thought a delivery to Shivnarine Chanderpaul in Sydney might have spun as much. The papers dubbed it a 'Double Gatt' – suggesting it spun twice as much as Warne's famous Ashes curtain raiser (to Mike Gatting) in 1993, and no reference at all to the fact that its victim was now twice the size he was then.

On the third morning, however, it was Brett Lee who perpetrated the expected collapse. In nine balls he ripped out Trescothick, Hoggard and Vaughan. Suddenly England were 31-4. It could have been 31-5 as Pietersen earned a reprieve after appearing to get a faint glove on his first delivery. His luck ran out when, as he attempted to sweep Warne, the ball cannoned off his pad and arm and he was given out caught behind by umpire Rudi Koertzen. Ian Bell suffered a similar fate soon after and England were 75-6.

Flintoff marched out purposefully as usual, passing the dismissed batsman well before he had left the field. But he was soon in considerable pain after appearing to wrench his shoulder driving Warne. There was a lengthy delay while he had treatment. Crucially he survived the 20 minutes to lunch and was then stuffed full of painkillers.

What happened in the next three hours was reminiscent of Headingley '81. Watching Warne winkle out the England tail,

Flintoff knew he had to take action. With last man Simon Jones for company, and appearing to feel no ill effects, he picked up Kasprowicz (by the way that's a stroke, not a dead lift), depositing him into the stand beyond mid-wicket. He did the same again two balls later, sauntering across his stumps and, with a clean swing of the bat, sending the ball into the cheap seats and the crowd to communal yelps of delight. The left-handed Jones, a clean hitter with a good eye, added some lusty blows of his own. There was more than a hint of Botham's mesmerising partnership with Graham Dilley at Headingley all those years ago. If they'd still had a man with a steering wheel operating the Edgbaston score box, he would have been giddy

It was a thrilling assault climaxing with a shot that seemed as bionic as Warne's ball to Strauss. Lee flung down a 94mph missile, but Flintoff, clearing his front leg and swinging mightily, smote it soaring back over the bowler's head with interest. It flew like a stone out of a giant catapult, soaring over the sightscreen, bouncing on the roof of the pavilion and landing behind it on the forecourt. It was the biggest hit anyone had ever seen at Edgbaston. It was so huge that, on TV, Geoff Boycott laughed uncontrollably, and he doesn't often do that, even at his own jokes. In another parallel with Botham, rekindling his memorable assault on Craig McDermott at the same ground 20 years earlier, Flintoff thumped a boundary next ball, followed by another monstrous six. It was stirring stuff.

Flintoff and Jones frolicked for an hour, putting on 51 for the last wicket. Flintoff's four sixes brought his match tally to nine (better than Botham ever managed in the Ashes) before he finally missed at Warne and was bowled for a barnstorming 73. Warne, the consummate sportsman, yelled, 'Well batted, Freddie, well played, mate!' above the din of the crowd's ovation. Australia now needed 282 to win.

There were 44 overs remaining in the third day's play. This time Hayden and Langer made untroubled progress towards a half-century opening stand. Things looked ominous for England. Again it was Flintoff who transformed the situation. Thirteen overs had been bowled when Vaughan asked him to mark out his run.

Still on a high after his batting, he pawed at the ground at the top of his mark, like an impatient bull getting ready to charge. In his sights was the diminutive left-hander Justin Langer, the original Aussie tough nut. Flintoff had begun to perfect the art of bowling round the wicket to left-handers, landing unusually tight to the bowler's stumps and maintaining a straight line, compelling the batsman to play, before slanting the ball away towards the slips. Batsmen found his awkward angle, his relentless accuracy and his bat-jarring hostility very hard to handle.

Instinctively he sensed his moment. The first ball was sharp and straight, but Langer, quick footed, drove it to cover. The second was a touch shorter and had all Flintoff's brute force behind it. It bounced higher than Langer expected and cannoned off the top of his bat into the stumps. It was the breakthrough England needed.

But next came the redoubtable Ponting. He had looked dangerously good in the first innings before unexpectedly succumbing to Giles. Now he took guard and looked around. His eyes narrowed with focus and determination as he settled into his stance.

Flintoff knew Ponting was a shaky starter. His first ball was fast and angled in; it rapped the Australian captain on the pad as he lunged over-elaborately forward. Flintoff, the England players and half of Birmingham yelled for lbw. Umpire Billy Bowden ruled correctly that it was too high. The next ball, on a perfect length and line, curved away. Ponting, hurried by the pace, thick-edged it along the ground to slip. The fifth nipped in and took him on the pad again. There was only a half-hearted shout from the bowler this time and the crowd drowned it out. The sixth was just wide enough to be left alone. Ponting, initially relieved to have survived the over, suddenly realised a no ball had been signalled as the bowler overstretched, striving for extra pace.

Flintoff stood at the end of his run, feet together, both hands on the ball, and prepared to bowl again. He positioned the shiny side on the left, hoping to make the ball reverse swing away. He thundered in, accelerating to the crease before hurling it down in a bone-juddering explosion of effort. The delivery, fractionally outside off stump and a touch fuller, invited the drive. Ponting thrust the bat at it, looking for his first run, but it left him late in the air, took the edge and was pouched by wicketkeeper Geraint Jones. Flintoff, the veins round his temple engorged with adrenaline, let out a primeval roar, audible above the racket of the crowd and was engulfed by his teammates. He had claimed Langer and Ponting in one of the most intensely compelling overs ever bowled in Test cricket. Australia were 48-2.

It required strong men to withstand this attack, but Hayden and Martyn remained composed and eased Australia's frazzled nerves, taking the score to 82. Then Hayden drove loosely at a swinger from Simon Jones and edged to a diving Trescothick, and Martyn clipped lazily in the air to mid-wicket. Now Michael Clarke and Simon Katich restored order, stabilising the innings. Slightly against the run of play, Giles deceived Katich with lack of spin and with 15 minutes left till stumps Gilchrist ladled a catch to mid-on. Very uncharacteristic. The nightwatchman Gillespie lasted just two balls – out lbw to Flintoff – and Australia had declined to 137-7. The game was up.

What separates the great from the very good is their self-belief, their bravado, their sheer iron will, in a crisis. So, cool as you like, Warne saunters in, walks across his crease first ball to the marauding Flintoff and nonchalantly flicks a single on the leg side. Clarke, Warne's great buddy and admirer, does exactly the same. An over from Giles follows – the last scheduled one of the day. There are no developments, but England, with Australia on the ropes at 140-7, claim the extra half-hour, hoping to finish the match in three days. The crowd, who've already experienced more twists and turns than a driver in the Paris to Dakar rally, now have to gird themselves for even more excitement.

The England players, trying to conceal their apprehension, urge the bowlers on. 'Come on, lads,' Strauss calls out from silly point, 'they're really struggling here.' Warne, affronted by the indignity of a possible three-day defeat, glares at him. 'There's only one person who's struggling here, and that's you,' he retorts. 'You're fucking shit!' The bowler sledging the batsman – well, that's commonplace. But the batsman sledging the fielders? That's unique.

Warne adds to the effect by sauntering up the wicket next ball and planting Giles over mid-wicket for a huge six. He adds another a ball later, for good measure. Clarke sizzles with activity at the crease. Another 34 runs are quickly added. England's expectations have been dashed and with Harmison about to bowl the day's last over the momentum has shifted back fractionally Australia's way. They still need over 100, but the bowlers seem suddenly spent and the pitch is playing no tricks.

Harmison bowls a series of awkward lifters to Clarke, who negotiates them jerkily. We have come to the last ball of the day. If Clarke survives, Australia still spell danger for England. Harmison comes lolloping in to bowl. Clarke is expecting another short one. He edges back in the crease as the ball is released, but, unexpectedly, given that Harmison is to craftiness what Kevin Pietersen is to modesty, he sends down a superbly disguised slower ball.

Even more unexpectedly, it is on target. Clarke pokes at it forlornly, but is completely beaten. The ball slides past his groping bat and clean bowls him. Harmison punches the air in celebration while giving off the distinct impression that he is more surprised than anyone. Flintoff, looking more intimidating than ever and delighted that his mate has made such a vital contribution, is beaming from ear to ear.

'INFREDIBLE' is the *Sun's* summing up of an amazing day.

The fourth day dawns bright and sunny as the teams take the field – at 10.30am, at the behest of Channel 4, so that their daily 6pm scheduling of *The Simpsons* isn't disrupted. Australia, with Warne now joined by Brett Lee, require 107 to win. England need two wickets. Even though the day's play could be over in two balls, Edgbaston is packed. There is not a seat to be had. And that crowd goes on to witness one of the great sessions of Test cricket, the sort of compelling struggle of mind, matter and naked patriotism that elevates a Test Match above any other form of sporting contest.

England, of course, were confident of wrapping the match up quickly with their battery of quick bowlers operating on a tricky fourth-day pitch. But Warne was like Bradman. In his subconscious dictionary the word 'defeat' did not exist. Having made two hundreds for Hampshire that summer, he had his own ideas about how Australia were going to achieve victory, clearly visible when he carved a couple through the covers early on. He led the rapid accumulation of 24 runs from the first four overs.

Lee, more than a tailender himself, drove and pulled heartily and the target was soon down to 62. Then Warne, going back and across to try to work Flintoff to leg, lost his footing and disturbed the stumps with his right leg. He was out hit wicket for an artful 42. Strauss had had the last laugh. With only the walking wicket Kasprowicz to come, England were home. Or so it seemed.

Kasprowicz somehow survived a couple of excellent yorkers and Lee managed to farm the strike for a while. He took affirmative action, scything Flintoff through the covers and thumping Giles over mid-wicket for four. Emboldened, Kasprowicz wafted the spinner over mid-off and sliced him past slip. Suddenly the target had been brought to within sniffing distance: just 27 runs required. How were England feeling now? Vaughan still looked calm and the coach, Duncan Fletcher, remained inscrutable behind his wraparound sunshades.

Harmison was brought back on. He was fast but a touch wayward and an attempted yorker veered down the leg side, evaded Geraint Jones's grasp and went to the boundary. It was poor keeping and the fact that Jones had spent his childhood in Australia was not lost on the more vociferous spectators. A tricky chance to the normally safe Simon Jones at third man – from a Kasprowicz upper cut – was also grassed. At the critical moment England's nerve was beginning to fail them. Although Flintoff rapped Lee painfully on the fingers, requiring treatment, he then also fired one way down the leg side, beyond Geraint Jones's reach. As it was also a no-ball, it cost England five precious runs. Now it was just six for victory. England, to all intents and purposes, had lost.

This was the opposite of a relaxed Sunday morning. The tension was unbearable. Fifteen thousand people in the ground and millions on TV and radio were glued to the action, barely able to believe what was happening. With Australia now favourites to go 2-0 up in the series, England's obituary writers were poised. The football premiership season was due to start the following weekend and English cricket's shop window would close – with its imminent transfer to satellite TV – possibly for ever. British sport was about to become a monoculture dominated by Wayne Rooney, Wenger-bashing and the WAGs.

There is a strange dynamic about valiant last-wicket partnerships, however. When, at the beginning, the last pair face an impossible task, their situation is liberating. With no expectation, there is a licence to play shots. Nothing will be lost by having a swish. It is a strategy known in the vernacular as 'shit or bust', though no one has ever accurately explained why this should be.

But a new mentality percolates the batsmen's subconscious if such an approach comes off. Sixty to win becomes 20, the unobtainable is suddenly, tantalisingly, within reach. With possibility comes pressure. It transforms the batsmen's attitudes. Caution and responsibility suppress a free spirit. They start leaving wider balls they would previously have had a dart at, push and poke rather than plunder and pummel. Anxiety transfers from bowlers to batsmen.

The next two overs yield just two quick singles. Four to win. English ignominy is just one hit away.

The batsmen have a mid-wicket conference. Vaughan talks to the bowler, Harmison, and tinkers with the field. He has kept the slips in place and men saving the one, but has also left a deep square leg and a cover point out on the fence. It turns out to be a masterstroke.

The first ball of the 65th over is an attempted yorker. But it is wide and overpitched. Lee's eyes light up and he flays it through the off side for the winning runs. Except that he hits it precisely to the deep-cover fielder, Simon Jones. Five yards either side and the match, probably the series, would have been over. But Jones fields the ball cleanly and throws it back. The batsmen have crossed for a single. Three to win.

Kasprowicz is now on strike. The field close in. Harmison bowls a straight, shortish ball. Kasprowicz goes up on his toes and defends competently. The next delivery is banged in short and lifts awkwardly at the batsman's ribs. Kasprowicz tries to get inside the line to fend it off, but it catches his glove as he takes evasive action and carries through down the leg side to the sprawling Geraint Jones. Even before umpire Bowden raises his absurdly crooked finger, England know they have won.

The moment was beautifully captured by Richie Benaud on commentary. 'Jones!… Bowden!!… Kasprowicz the man to go… Harmison has done it. Despair on the faces of the batsmen…and joy for every England player on the field!' And, one might add, for every England fan watching, listening or praying. And particularly for Channel 4's advertising department who, now the series had been so spectacularly revived, could triple their rates.

The fielders embraced wildly, Flintoff lifting Vaughan some distance off the ground, jeopardising his ribs, before turning his attention to the figure of Lee, sunk to his haunches in despair. In a classic vision of sporting solidarity – captured and reprinted all over the world – the victor consoled the vanquished, stooping to place a hand on his opponent's shoulder to offer heartfelt words of commiseration. Although Flintoff is fond of jovially telling everyone that what he actually said was, 'Ha ha! It's 1-1 now. You better get ready!'

Ironically, replays of the final dismissal, pored over (by me!) in the Channel 4 VT truck once the clamour of the moment had abated, revealed that Kasprowicz's hand was off the bat when it was struck. Technically he should not have been given out. But there was no Decision Review System then and, to be honest, no one really gave a monkey's, not even the Australians. They accepted defeat manfully – even, mark you, their media – recognising they had been beaten by a better team and acknowledging that anything was better than the tame English submission they had become accustomed to. 'Now we have a series,' celebrated *The Age*. Beneath all the ruthlessness and bravado, you see, Australians do have a heart. Well, an aorta, anyway…

Before the last exultant Brummie had staggered home, arrangements were already underway to make a DVD of what was now being billed as The Greatest Test. Not only was it the closest ever finish in an Ashes encounter, but it had more surprises than a Stieg Larsson novel. There had been parallels with the England rugby team's victory in the World Cup final – against Australia – two years earlier. The same white-knuckle ride, culminating in a pulsating finish. Harmison's winning wicket was the Jonny Wilkinson drop-goal moment, and both matches had made tub-thumping warriors (Martin Johnson and Andrew Flintoff) into people's champions.

Flintoff had become an overnight hero, and the papers devoted reams of copy to the lad from Preston who had given up alcohol and chips to become, they suggested, the new Ian Botham. The *Guardian* printed a huge picture of Flintoff, over which was written: 'In Affectionate Celebration of English Cricket which was reborn at Edgbaston on 7 August 2005.' Little did they realise how true that would turn out to be.

The Great Escape

There was no time for bathing in the afterglow. The third Test at Old Trafford began in four days. Miraculously Glenn McGrath was declared fit to play, having needed a Zimmer frame five days earlier. The decision reeked of desperation, and it looked like it, as he finished the first day wicketless, though he clean bowled Michael Vaughan with a no-ball and was unlucky that the Australian slips suffered a bad attack of dropsy. Vaughan, whose batting technique had been questioned after his failures in the first two Tests, was inspired here by the bravery of the England team mascot, a terminally ill boy who had defied expectations of his imminent death. He made a regal hundred. 'Technique's a load of bollocks!' he exclaimed later in the hotel bar.

The abrasive Old Trafford pitch was perfect for reverse swing and England's quartet of marauding fast bowlers exploited it brilliantly. More than one Australian batsman was bowled or lbw shouldering arms as the ball bent in the air unexpectedly late. England had become exceptional at getting the ball in the right, ragged state for this sort of bowling, allowing one side to become badly scuffed and kept scrupulously dry. The Australians had no answer and conceded a significant lead which the England batsmen capitalised on. Australia were left three and a half sessions to make 423 to win. Or rather, England had 108 overs to bowl them out.

Mercifully Manchester produced its best weather (partly cloudy) for the fifth day and the ground was full by 9.30am. An estimated 17,000 people were turned away. One old steward said he couldn't remember anything like it since the halcyon days of Lancashire – Clive Lloyd et al. – in the 1970s. 'These days we have to lock 'em in,' he said. The England players were given rapturous receptions when they came out to warm up; most of the Australians too, though Warne – their pantomime villain – was hissed and the long-haired Gillespie got cackles of 'Where's your caravan?'

When play began, Langer fell early and Hayden was given a thorough working over by Flintoff before being bowled behind his legs. Martyn and Katich made little headway. When Gilchrist was again undone cheaply by Flintoff's round-the-wicket attack, it looked as if the game was up for Australia.

In one of his finest hours, however, Ponting defied everything the bowlers threw at him. Busy at the crease, he scored fluently through the leg side and read the reverse swing superbly. As the bowlers tired he cut and drove with alacrity. Clarke kept him company in a stand of 81 and then Warne was at his impudent best, messing up the bowlers' lines and lengths with nifty footwork and familiar bravado. At the beginning of the last hour Australia needed just 109 to win with three wickets left. They couldn't, could they?

No, not quite. It was Flintoff – who else? – who finally saw off Warne, finding his edge; the ball ricocheted off Strauss' knee and was acrobatically caught by Geraint Jones, making amends for some earlier lapses. Flintoff went from flat on his back to fully upright in one acrobatic move, suggesting a potential future as a Cossack dancer. England now had 10 overs to get the last two wickets. With granitic impenetrability, Ponting stood firm. The scar from the Harmison bouncer at Lord's was still visible on his right cheekbone, but his spirit seemed unbreakable. He looked as if he could bat for ever.

Then, with the last ball of the 104th over, Harmison got a short ball to brush Ponting's glove as he shaped to play to leg. England appealed manically, supported by most of the 21,000 people in the ground. Ponting lingered, adopting that 'What me, guv?' look, abiding by the famous cricketing rule – allegedly invented by Australians – that you only walk when your car breaks down. Despite Billy Bowden being a New Zealander, he felt more sympathy than satisfaction in giving him out. Ponting, head bowed, looked totally forlorn. He had resisted England for almost seven hours. It was a monolith of an innings. But now he had given England four overs at Australia's last pair of Lee and McGrath.

Lee survived the first of these competently, McGrath the second edgily. A huge lbw shout against Lee in the penultimate over from Flintoff went, correctly, in the batsman's favour. It was down to the final six balls: Harmison to McGrath, the 6ft 5in bloodhound pursuing the original rabbit. Again the tension was unbearable. Almost spent, Harmison was off target with the first and crucially McGrath got a single off the third. Lee calmly negotiated the next two. 'One ball, one wicket' declared the big screen, as if anyone needed reminding. It was an anticlimax. Lee clipped the final delivery, a low full toss, to the boundary. The match was drawn. Rarely can one dull word have been more inappropriate for such a titanic struggle.

In the context of the series, what happened next was even more significant. The Australian team erupted as one on the balcony to congratulate themselves on their escape. It had huge symbolism for Vaughan. Recognising the importance of 'taking the positives from the game', as captains like to say, he drew his team together on the pitch. 'Look at that dressing room,' he said. 'Australia are celebrating a draw. They are there for the taking.'

By now the whole country was caught up in this summer-long dispute between intransigent fathers and impudent sons. Half Britain's households followed it on TV, BBC Radio put its wall-to-wall football coverage on hold. Virtually every paper asked whether cricket was the new football. ('Ye gods, let's hope not, we don't want our sport invaded by mercenaries, crooks and morons!' was the universal reply.) People were following it all over the world. There were stories of fans using coat-hangers on foreign beaches to pick up weak radio signals. Of expensively received commentary on a mobile phone in Nevada and on a laptop in Sierra Leone. Of a home-made satellite in the Malaysian jungle, of text updates read out on a Royal Navy submarine deep down in the Pacific. Of Eskimos rigging up aerials above their igloos. Well, maybe not. All over India, they were gripped. In China, they began discussions about whether to add cricket to the national curriculum (true). And in Australia there was a national investigation into the art of reverse swing (what is it and why can't we do it?) and the economy was seriously affected as thousands stayed up all night to watch the drama unfold and then fell asleep at work. Whatever happened to the Great Australian Sickie?

SECOND TEST, EDGBASTON, 2005

Hallelujah!

There were 10 days between the third and fourth Tests. But at Trent Bridge there was no let-up in this absorbing melodrama. McGrath was absent, this time with an elbow injury, and Gillespie had been dropped. Australia's fearsome opening pair for the last seven years were now carrying the drinks. Flintoff, drawing on this and his own inspiration of Elton John's 'Rocket Man' played in the dressing room (his dire musical taste was perennially stuck in the 1970s), compiled his first Ashes century. It was an innings of considerable sense and restraint, neither of which qualities you would normally associate with Flintoff. England totalled 477.

Incisive bowling, dodgy umpiring and brilliant catching – notably a one-handed horizontal screamer by Strauss at second slip to dismiss Gilchrist – enabled England to bowl Australia out for a paltry 218. It was mid-afternoon on the third day and Vaughan asked his bowlers how they felt. The reaction was energetic, so Australia were made to follow on for the first time in any Test Match for 17 years.

Their batsmen initially responded well, but then, on the fourth day, Ponting was run out by a direct hit from England's 12th man, Gary Pratt, a specialist cover fielder. He was deputising for the injured Simon Jones, but England had made frequent use of substitutes as fielders constantly nipped off for toilet breaks. It was a practice Ponting didn't approve of. Now, as he made his way up the pavilion steps, his frustration exploded in a burst of invective at Duncan Fletcher on the England balcony. It was the most vivid piece of Aussie sledging all tour, and it was aimed at the England coach! It showed how much the Australians had regressed. Fletcher smiled – about the first time he had done so in public in six years in the job.

Another jaunty innings from Warne, who twice launched Giles for six before being stumped off the same bowler, gave

Australia a slender but intriguing lead of 128. It was 3.45pm on the Sunday afternoon when England set off in pursuit. It was still the fourth day, so time was not an issue.

Nerves were, though. After a purposeful start, England suffered a terrible attack of stage fright. Trescothick was out to Warne's first ball and Vaughan to his seventh. When Strauss was snaffled at silly point and Bell caught unwisely hooking, England were 57-4. Pietersen and Flintoff played sedately for a while and brought up the hundred. But an inspired spell from Lee saw them both off and Geraint Jones skied a catch to deep mid-off. England were precariously placed at 116-7.

Thirteen were wanted. It may not sound many, but when at one end there is a guy whistling them down at 93mph and at the other the greatest wicket thief who ever lived and neither batsman has a clue which way he's turning it, 13 feels more like 113. Those batsmen were Ashley Giles, whom Warne had dismissed four times in the series already, at a personal cost of eight, and Matthew Hoggard, a cardboard cut-out of a batsman whose only shot was a static forward defensive, and even that didn't come with a guarantee.

The huge stakes were enough to turn any Englishmen's legs to jelly (and there were plenty of those in the England dressing room, as a squad of super-trained men could hardly bear to watch). The reality was that if Warne somehow winkled out the last three wickets (and the only men to come were Harmison, who was a jibbering wreck, and Simon Jones, who could barely walk) it would be 2-1 to Australia. Then England could only draw the series and the Ashes would remain in Australia's grip for yet another two years.

And that was the thing about the Australians. They were like giant cockroaches. Uncrushable and crawling back to bug you when you thought they were dead. Clinging on to the edge of the cliff, forcing you to prise every last claw from the rock face before it would fall.

'Character' was what England needed to show now and that is what they did. Hoggard shuffled into line and nobly repelled Lee; he ultimately dredged a cover drive from the schoolboy memory bank to get to within four of victory. Giles, from Planet Ordinaire, inhabiting a different galaxy to Warne, still had the nous and self-belief to survive the great leg spinner's traps and nudge him through mid-wicket for the winning runs.

The outpouring of emotion had rarely been seen on a cricket field before. So many men were hugging and kissing it could have been the Mardi Gras. Some could barely speak. Flintoff was so overjoyed he was almost hyperventilating. Hoggard and Fletcher, who were barely on speaking terms, embraced. Some of the players' parents were in tears. The crowd's cheers lingered long after the presentation ceremony. At London's Royal Albert Hall, the start of Verdi's *Requiem* was delayed as news of England's victory filtered through and 6000 concertgoers stood and cheered. In Suffolk a church organist, improvising on a dirgy theme and listening to the radio commentary on an earpiece while the parishioners filed in for evensong, broke into the 'Hallelujah Chorus' when England won. For all the England supporters who had lived through the years of thin and thinner, this victory, which put England 2–1 up in the series, was truly a gift from God.

And then the reality dawned. England would still have to win or draw the final Test at The Oval to make the Ashes secure. There was plenty of claw-prising yet to be done.

They Don't Think It's All Over

All of which meant that the Oval Test was billed, with lashings of hyperbole, as 'the biggest cricket match in history'. The nation was gripped by cricket fever. There were reams of coverage in the papers, with reflections and predictions and profiles and the state of Simon Jones's injured ankle getting more column inches than David Beckham's broken metatarsal a couple of years before. Camera crews followed Flintoff to the supermarket (reaffirming a cricketer's accessible appeal. You wouldn't catch Rio Ferdinand nipping down to Tesco – sorry, Morrisons – would you?). There was even a girl's guide to cricket in the *Sun*. And still a week to go till the actual match. The wait was agonising.

In the end Jones failed to recover and, beset by injuries from there on, sadly never played for England again. After much debate, Paul Collingwood was summoned as his replacement to strengthen the batting. McGrath was declared fit again for Australia. The *Sun* added to the nation's general anxiety by headlining their preview piece with 'It's Not All Over Till the Fat Laddie Spins'.

Settling everyone's nerves, Vaughan won the toss and batted first. Despite Warne's brilliant mixture of leg spinners and sliders, England posted a decent 373, anchored by Andrew Strauss's second hundred of the series, finally silencing Warne's 'Daryll' reminders. Australia's harassed openers, Hayden and Langer, compiled their first century stand of the series in reply – but then strangely went off for bad light on the second evening, apprehensive of Flintoff's pace. It was a very un-Australian decision, illustrating how rattled they had become. Much of the third day's play was lost to the weather, costing the Aussies crucial time.

On the fourth day, a magnificent spell of exceptional intensity by Flintoff, bowling unchanged through a damp morning, cut through the Aussie middle order like a giant chainsaw, each wicket celebrated with a ferocious pumping of arms and beating of chest. Ably supported by the loyal Hoggard, Flintoff turned a potential deficit into a slender lead. By the end of another rain-interrupted day England had extended that to 40 for the loss of Strauss – to Warne, naturally.

The fifth and final day of the series was dubbed the most important day in English sport since the 1966 World Cup final. Quite a moment for Richie Benaud, doyen of cricket commentary since about that time, to be uttering his last words on British TV. The former Australian captain had become a national treasure in Britain, and there were tributes everywhere. That's the uniquely special thing about the relationship between the English and the Australians. We hate each other with a passion. But we love each other more. Surprisingly for the leader of the cream jacket brigade, Benaud was wearing blue.

McGrath gave England immediate jitters with a vintage early-morning spell, removing Vaughan and Bell in successive balls. Pietersen survived the hat-trick ball – a bouncer – but only by dint of umpire Bowden detecting that it flicked his shoulder rather than his bat. Pietersen could also have been caught behind before he had scored and definitely should have been on 15, when a flying edge went straight towards Warne's bucket-like hands at first slip. Unaccountably, he fumbled it. Given the events of the next three hours, he had effectively dropped the Ashes. It was a wicked irony.

Pietersen survived uncomfortably until lunch, looking very tentative against a fired-up Lee. Trescothick and Flintoff both fell to the irrepressible Warne and at the interval England were 127-5. That gave them a lead of only 133. If they subsided now there was plenty of time for Australia to get the runs. The match, the series, English cricket's sanctity, were *still* in the balance.

At lunch Vaughan took Pietersen aside. He recommended a positive approach, encouraged him to go out and play his natural game. Pietersen was transformed. He rifled Lee's fourth ball after lunch over deep square leg for six, then hooked and pulled 16 off Lee's next over, one delivery of which registered at 97mph. When Pietersen brutally flat-batted a rapid, only slightly short ball back past the bowler baseball-style for another boundary, the non-striker Collingwood could only look on in a mixture of admiration and fear for his own safety. Sensibly, he said nothing, realising that Pietersen was in what sportsmen like to call 'the zone', which actually means they have gone temporarily deaf.

There followed a further sequence of outrageous shots – the most memorable a shimmy up the pitch and monumental drive high into the new stand off Warne – which finally quelled Australia's spirit. Pietersen went to his maiden Test hundred with an extravagant off drive and, with the help of Ashley Giles, continued to plunder the bowling for another hour, taking England past 300 and to safety. It was an innings of near genius – only Brian Lara, of modern players, could have emulated it – and it was recognised as such by Warne running halfway to the boundary to congratulate him when he was out.

It was appropriate too that Benaud should have been on commentary for the last time when Pietersen was bowled. It was the ultimate moment of the series, the outcome was now decided. He described the dismissal succinctly, gave his brief verdict on the innings, finished, 'And now the two men in the com box are Mark Nicholas and Tony Greig,' and was gone.

When England were eventually bowled out for 335, there was about an hour left for play. There was no point in Australia batting again, and common sense should have prevailed, but the umpires stuck rigidly by the laws and took the teams out. Then they took them off for bad light. Still they would not declare the match was over. The end was a charade as the umpires finally strolled out alone and theatrically removed the bails. It was a tame end to a tumultuous six weeks. But nothing was going to inhibit the ecstatic celebrations of players and spectators as cheering, fireworks and 'Land of Hope and Glory' rent the air and the Ashes urn was finally held aloft by an English captain after 16 years of hurt.

It was a mesmerising series that elevated cricket into the nation's consciousness for all the right reasons and, in retrospect, the Australians would concede they were the most mesmerised: by England's sustained skill and sophistication, by their superb use of reverse swing, by the attention to detail from their carefully appointed support staff (the Aussies didn't have a specialist batting or bowling coach), by Vaughan's smart, ruthless leadership, by Flintoff's relentless battering with the ball – especially against the left-handers – and Pietersen's remarkable bravado with the bat. And by the English public's impassioned support of their team. The Australians had received a very disturbing wake-up call. The dismissive jokes such as 'Why don't Aussies need vaccinations when they go abroad? Because they never catch anything' were still ringing in their ears as they made their dejected way home, while the English team careered around London on an open-top bus.

But if you have ever been to Australia you'll probably know that there are few things in life more dangerous than a wounded kangaroo...

10

SECOND TEST, ADELAIDE, 2006

'*Pietersen settles over his bat, tapping aggressively in the crease. Warne, round the wicket, bowls, outside leg stump, Pietersen sweeps and…is out! Bowled! Incredible piece of bowling by Warne. Another batsman's pocket is picked! K P's on his way and England are in some trouble now…*'

The epic 2005 Ashes would have been a good place to end this Odyssey. It was the ultimate Test series, keeping everyone gripped right up until the last session of the last day. But Shane Warne is a man who likes to have the last word. 'Mate,' he said in Mumbai, commentating on the India–England Tests, 'you can't do a book on the greatest Ashes Tests without including our win in Adelaide in '06. Winning having conceded 550 in the first innings…that's one of the greatest victories of all time!' OK, Shane, if you say so.

It is all totally subjective, of course. But it's a good story, and that Test had a major influence not just on the 2006–7 series, but also on the two that followed it. It was a wonderful example of the ebb and flow, the unpredictable drama, the physical and mental energy expended, the harsh exploration of an individual's character, that make a five-day Test Match so special. Especially one between the old enemies. So here goes.

The Ball of the (Next) Century

Australia returned home at the end of that 2005 series with their tails dragging on the ground. They knew they had been ambushed by a younger, fitter, hungrier, better prepared adversary. Almost immediately they were on a mission to set the record straight. Ricky Ponting's face was fixed in a steely glint wherever he went, and over the next 14 months – through the boot camps and psychology sessions and strategic recruitments (the bowling coach Troy Cooley lured back from England, for instance) – an intense desire to reclaim the Ashes flourished in every member of what was still a richly talented squad. England's 2005 blueprint was adopted and enhanced. Success in various tin-pot tournaments reinstalled a winning habit. And the squad were under instruction not to befriend or even engage with the England players until the mission was complete.

While Australia reconstructed, England unravelled. Andrew Flintoff was bowled into the ground and broke down. So did a number of other bowlers. The four-pronged Ashes-winning seam attack of 2005 – Harmison, Hoggard, Flintoff and Jones – never played together again. Michael Vaughan's suspect knee gave way and needed an operation, leading to uncertainty about who would be captain. Flintoff, who hadn't played for six months, finally got the nod over Andrew Strauss for his up-and-at-'em mentality. And then, in England's riskily short build-up to the Tests, Marcus Trescothick, their assured opener, returned home suffering from stress. It left just three players in the side – Giles, Harmison and Hoggard – who had played a Test in Australia before.

But despite being littered with great players, Australia – average age 33 – were christened 'Dad's Army' and questions were asked about their fitness. So the hype before the first Test in Brisbane was massive. Everywhere there were excited predictions that this would be another humdinger of a five-match contest as the

Aussies sought to avenge their 2005 defeat. The forecasts were wide-ranging. Although Australia were apprehensive of what Flintoff and possibly Pietersen might be capable of, they were slight favourites. Yet Mr Partisan himself, good old Bill Lawry, thought England would win.

It took just one ball – yes, *that ball* – for the bubble of expectation to burst. Or at least let out a slow, unstoppable hiss. Harmison, unfit through lack of activity and unnerved by the nationalistic fervour before play, which included the unprecedented singing of the national anthems, ambled in gingerly to bowl the first ball of the series to Justin Langer. Flintoff caught it smartly at second slip. Unfortunately for England, not via the batsman: it had barely landed on the cut strip. It was possibly the worst delivery ever bowled in a Test Match, certainly at the start of one. Geoff Boycott thought his mum would have struggled to reach it with her clothes prop. It couldn't have been more of a contrast to Harmison's first ball in the 2005 series, which had singed Langer's nostrils, and it symbolised the mess England were in.

It may be hard to understand how a bowler that good (number 1 in the world three years before) could send down a delivery that bad. But tension causes the body to do strange things – scale the heights as well as plumb the depths – and Harmison had always had an unconventional action and a rather floppy wrist. He had in fact bowled some equally woeful deliveries in a Test against Pakistan at Old Trafford the previous summer, almost as if he were suffering the 'yips'. He received special attention from England's new bowling coach Allan Donald to try to cure the problem. A delivery style like his requires a lot of pre-match grooving and, it emerged later, he hadn't put the work in.

That ball was manna from heaven for the Australian headline writers and pun artists. 'The nation that brought us bodyline began the most eagerly anticipated Ashes series ever with a shock new tactic – Shoddyline,' wrote Robert Craddock in the Sydney *Daily Telegraph*. The man who delivered it was 'Grievous Bodily Harmison' no more, as his first-innings figures of 1-123 proved. Australia gorged themselves on the English bowling, making 346-3 on the first day. The remorseless Ponting helped himself to 196, pushing them around, spearing and devouring them as if they were peas on a plate.

England were bled dry and dismembered by the Aussies, losing by 277 runs, at a venue which had become known as 'the Gabbatoir', so often had visiting teams been ritually slaughtered there (Australia hadn't lost a Test in Brisbane for 18 years). For TV channels that had paid vast sums for the rights to the series and had trailed them with expensive ad campaigns, it wasn't a promising start.

The Wizard of Oz

There was little time for England to regroup – the Adelaide Test began four days later. The teams were unchanged. England, clinging to their 2005 formula, had resisted a clamour to replace the ineffective Ashley Giles – who hadn't played for six months before the tour – with the burgeoning talents of the 'Sikh of Tweak', Monty Panesar. It was a crucial mistake.

Flintoff at least won the toss. England slipped to 45-2 in the face of the naggingly accurate Stuart Clark, who seemed to make the new ball wobble disconcertingly in the air. But the third-wicket pair of Ian Bell and Paul Collingwood dug in, despite Warne's derisive comments. He called Bell 'the Sherminator' – after a ginger-haired geek in the film *American Pie* – and was generally scathing about Collingwood, nicknaming him 'Caddyshack' to suggest that he was more of a bag-carrier than a bat-wielder.

Bell eventually succumbed for 60, but Collingwood confounded the sceptics, as well as Warne. Many thought that with his low pick-up and limited back-foot shots he would struggle on bouncier pitches Down Under. The consensus was that the OBE he received for his belated appearance in the 2005 Ashes would stand for One Brief Errand and that he would revert to being a semi-permanent 12th man. These fears looked like being confirmed in the first innings in Brisbane, when he was swiftly removed for five. But having survived for half an hour in the second innings, poking and prodding at balls like a man trying to fend off a bull with a toothpick, he suddenly located a couple in the middle and was away. He was then only denied a first Ashes hundred by a rush of blood to Warne on 96.

And now in Adelaide he was undislodgeable. He batted the rest of the first day. It was not the sort of white-knuckle ride that empties bars; instead it provoked more than one request from the members to 'have a go, yer mug!' It was more a study in abstinence and resourcefulness. To draw analogies with golf – his favourite pastime – Collingwood didn't have much of a drive, but he knocked it where he wanted to, bumping and running it onto the green, getting down in two from anywhere. His short game was masterly. His most distinctive shot in that innings was adapted from the golf course. It was a straight-arm punch into the leg side off the back foot, mainly against spin, that you could call the Uphill Putt. It got him tantalisingly two runs short of a hundred by the close of play, in partnership with the friskier Kevin Pietersen.

From the eighth ball of the second morning, a half-volley on his legs, Collingwood chiselled three runs and brought up his century, his third in Test cricket. The England dressing room and travelling supporters were joyous, cheering a popular, hard-working player who had become the team Labrador, willing to do anything for the general cause.

Sixteen overs later he was joined on three figures by Pietersen. It was not K P's most fluent innings. His ambition was contained by a very slow pitch and Warne's concentration round the wicket into the rough. There were few extravagances. But he kept picking off runs, favouring the sweep against Warne, and he and Collingwood ploughed on, pushing England past 400, then past 450. It was mainly sedentary progress. When, on the stroke of tea, Collingwood danced down the wicket to Clark and planted him back over his head, he had a double hundred, the first by an Englishman in Australia since... Wally Hammond, 70 years before! All those prolific batsmen and great names in the interim – Hutton, Compton, Cowdrey, May, Dexter, Boycott, Gooch, Gower, Atherton, Thorpe, Stewart, Vaughan – and yet it was the jaunty, unprepossessing all-rounder from Shotley Bridge, County Durham, who had done it. He had certainly earned his OBE now.

Soon afterwards he played a tired stroke and was out for 206, then Pietersen, having accumulated an increasingly authoritative 158, ran himself out. It cost England a bit of momentum and with around an hour left for play on the second day Flintoff declared at 551-6. Not only was this an outstanding response to having been butchered in Brisbane, it was also felt that England had built themselves into an impregnable, potentially winning position to level the series. It had the first day of Edgbaston 2005 written all over it.

Ricky Ponting had other ideas. If Pietersen's height and exceptional reach were placing new demands on bowlers' direction, then Ponting's relentless pursuit of runs placed new demands on their devotion. In this mood Ponting was a batsman to make you want to give up bowling. On the third day, on a pitch as dead as a flattened possum, there seemed no way through. It was like bowling at Ayers Rock.

In mid-morning, he did offer one chance. England, led by the admirable Hoggard, had managed to winkle out Hayden, Langer and Martyn with only 78 on the board. Ponting had eased his way serenely to 35 when he hooked Hoggard in the direction of deep square leg. It was a slight top edge, but it went fast and direct to Giles, just above his head. He barely had to move. For a Test cricketer it was a fairly straightforward catch. Giles was a little slow reacting and fluffed it. He hung his head in despair. He must have sensed that would be England's one opportunity to put the Australians under real pressure, and he was right.

In Australia, Ponting's combination of perfect vision, nimble footwork, fast hands and an insatiable appetite for runs had only ever been exceeded by the Don. He might have been the untidiest player in the Australian shed, but there was a controlled precision about his batting. He religiously re-marked his guard every ball, smoothed away any perceived impurities in the surface, stood balanced and poised at the crease.

He eschewed risk, but his innings were never boring. There was beauty in their construction. His strokes had power but they had deftness too, as he neatly deflected straightish balls through gaps and toyed with carefully orchestrated field settings. On this occasion he was never going to let England escape from the basic error of dropping a straightforward catch. He went on to make a commanding 142. The series which had been billed as Australia against Flintoff was turning into England v Ponting.

With Michael Clarke also supplying a purposeful century and 'Mr Cricket', Michael Hussey, illustrating why he was averaging about 80 in Test cricket, Australia pulled close to England's impressive total. When they were bowled out late on the fourth day, they were only 38 behind.

With ball paying total homage to bat on this deceased pitch, the teams at virtual parity and the third innings only just beginning an hour before the end of the fourth day, the match was heading for an inevitable stalemate. Australia, once famous for possessing the fastest pitches in the world, had started to produce the slowest. This one at the Adelaide Oval was a tortoise – fast bowlers were operating with the keeper standing up – and the WACA in Perth, venue for the third Test and once the Rottweiler of pitches that went for the batsman's throat, had become a poodle that licked his feet. The chances were, that both this Test and the next would be drawn, leaving everything to play for in Melbourne and Sydney. The TV rights holders and ad executives were feeling better.

England's batting was lively in that last hour of the fourth day, motoring along to 59 for the loss of Cook. Strauss was especially positive, clipping and cutting Brett Lee for boundaries and being noticeably aggressive against Warne. Surviving a close lbw shout second ball, he swept the spinner confidently off the stumps, eased him through cover and used his feet to hit him wide of mid-on. Bell, unaffected by the 'Sherminator' barbs, was also fluent. England finished the day almost a hundred ahead with batsmen queuing up to fill their boots on such an obedient lapdog of a pitch.

The crowd for the fifth day wasn't large: the Australian public seemed to have consigned the match to a draw, too. The grassy banks alongside the Bradman Stand and in front of the main scoreboard were populated largely by travelling England fans basking in the sunshine of a gorgeous Adelaide day.

And then the sky fell in. England's progress mysteriously stalled. Strauss' fluency, in particular, was replaced by caution: he scored only three runs in the first 40 minutes. Hypnosis had overcome England, though that is perhaps to deny credit to Warne. In the Australian dressing room before play, Ponting had canvassed opinion about how to approach the day. Warne was one of the last to speak. 'I said it was really important not to give runs away in the first hour. If we managed that and took a couple of wickets I really believed we could win the game. A few of the others weren't so sure. I thought the big wicket was Pietersen. He could hurt us. But the Adelaide pitch goes through an amazing transformation between the fourth and the fifth days. It suddenly gets quite rough. I felt it was now doing enough for me and we could control the other batsmen. I was confident of taking care of the rest.'

Warne opened the bowling at one end, Stuart Clark at the other. Warne, bowling over the wicket to Strauss, aimed mainly into the rough outside his off stump, ruling out the sweep as a run-making option and, with the ball now turning various amounts, making shots against the spin tricky. Surrounded by close fielders but with two men out on the leg side should he think of having a dip, Strauss mainly hid the bat behind the pad, managing just one single off Warne in his first five overs.

In Warne's sixth over Strauss shimmied up the pitch, attempting to work to leg. The ball spun and ricocheted off his pad and was taken at short leg. He stood there looking unconcerned, but was given out caught by Steve Bucknor. Replays showed Strauss' bat hadn't been anywhere near the ball. It was a dreadful decision. It would undoubtedly have been reversed, but the Decision Review System hadn't yet been introduced (though I never understood why the third umpire, once he'd seen a glaring error like that, couldn't quickly message the men in the middle before the batsman had got halfway to the pavilion). Little moments were going Australia's way.

As Collingwood and Bell defended, and Warne ooohed and aaahed, the number of overs bowled in the morning (13) overtook runs scored (11). 'They were batting as if they were making sure they didn't lose,' Warne suggested, 'rather than thinking, "If we get a quick 150 or so here we could actually put them under pressure."'

Bell angled Warne backward of square on the off side. Collingwood called correctly for the run, Bell started, hesitated, retreated, then set off. Michael Clarke's throw was wide of the bowler's stumps. Warne caught it and then underarmed the stumps from two yards out, hitting middle with Bell well short. It was 70–3 and the run-out was evidence of England's scrambled minds.

Then came the killer blow – the wicket of Pietersen conjured up by Warne. 'K P had been saying, "You'll never bowl me round my legs, I'm too good a sweeper." But that was on a flat pitch. I felt I had a chance now it was the fifth day and the ball was turning. The night before I had told Pup [Michael Clarke] I was going to try it first up. You have to bowl that delivery a bit more round arm, to get it fuller into the rough with lots of side-spin. Occasionally it works, most often it doesn't.'

The ball, Warne's first to Pietersen, summed up their contrasting personalities. Both were super-confident. But Warne was smart. On this occasion, Pietersen definitely was not. 'The Ego', as the Aussies liked to call him, had strutted to the wicket clearly intent on repairing the damage. He had not factored in the vagaries of a fifth-day pitch. Warne was aware of that. He put two men out on the leg-side boundary but left the area immediately behind the batsman open, giving him the chance to play the paddle sweep shot he favours.

The delivery landed exactly where Warne intended, invitingly full and outside the leg stump. Pietersen accepted the bait and went for the sweep. The ball bit in the rough, made a right-angled turn, sneaked under Pietersen's swishing blade, stole round his body and crashed into off stump. It was the famous pickpocket delivery and it had just fleeced another victim.

Warne punched the air and indulged in a jubilant bout of finger-wagging with Clarke as Pietersen trudged disconsolately off. 'It was crucial because we had got rid of the danger man the way I had said we could. It was the confidence-booster we needed to convince the doubters that we could win. There was a mindset shift. Now all of our team believed we could do it, and England knew they were in the shit.' To put it bluntly. They were 73–4.

The next four overs produced just four singles, with Flintoff also strangely tentative. Then he too perished, flashing half-heartedly at Lee. England, with Collingwood marooned on one from his first 45 balls, staggered to 89-4 at lunch. They had scored just 30 runs in two hours, with one solitary boundary, and lost three big wickets. A Toohey's cold beer ad flashed up on the big screen: 'Sends shivers down a Pom's spine.' Exactly.

Geraint Jones at least tried a little aggression, striking two fours off Lee after lunch before being snapped up in the gully driving at a wide one. Neither Giles, caught at slip off a big, ripping leg break that pitched outside leg, nor Hoggard, bowled by a delicious googly, detained Warne for long. The innings pottered along for another 15 overs, producing just 20 runs. It was like slow torture.

'What's a Pom's best stroke?' asked one local. 'Sunstroke!'

Two lbws from the habitually miserly McGrath finally put England out of their misery by tea. 'Like medieval royals with syphilis, they went suddenly mad,' wrote Greg Baum in *The Age*. They had been dismissed for 129 from 73 overs. Collingwood, whose inexperience led him to be over-defensive, remained 22 not out after over three hours of dogged resistance. Warne's figures for the day were 27-11-29-4. A truly mesmerising spell. He had done what he said he would. Now it was the batsmen's turn. Australia had the final session (36 overs) to make 168 to win.

A target like that is actually easier to make than 168 in a day. It obliges the batsmen to be purposeful, rather than taking their time attempting to eke out runs, as England had done, and grinding to a complete halt. (Remember Parkinson's Law – 'Work expands to fit the time allowed for its completion'?) England also didn't have a dangerous spinner to utilise a fifth-day pitch. Just the honest Giles, principally a containing bowler. Panesar, who could certainly have made life difficult for the Aussies, was stuck twiddling his very large thumbs in the dressing room.

Australia, marshalled by Ponting and an eager Hussey, got home in a smooth flow of shots and sharp running, with three overs to spare. They won through the power of positive thought. Believing is nine-tenths of enacting. Just because they had conceded 550 in the first innings didn't mean they couldn't get something out of the match. At least that was Warne's view and his enthusiasm is infectious. It wasn't the most exciting of victories, or the result of perfect planning, but it was a brilliant piece of opportunism. It wasn't that England were spineless. If anything they showed too much spine and not enough spring.

'Dad's Army 2 – Dud's Army 0' declared Melbourne's *Herald Sun*. Gideon Haigh put it more prosaically in the *Guardian*. 'Adelaide '06 deserves to haunt this generation of England cricketers, just as Headingley '81 once haunted Australians. Having waited 15 years to recapture the Ashes, they donated them back in an hour.'

Partners in Wicket-Crime

Effectively it was true. There was no stopping Australia after that. Panesar, eventually picked for the third Test in Perth, took a wicket with his seventh ball and five in the innings. But he was collared on the fourth day by a rampant Adam Gilchrist, who capitalised on the foundations laid by Hussey and Clarke to spank a 57-ball century, narrowly missing Viv Richards' record for the fastest Test hundred of all time.

A euphoric Australia won that third Test by 206 runs, thereby regaining the Ashes. This led to the rather unedifying sight of their players embracing and then parading in front of sections of the crowd before they shook hands with England. It was disrespectful, but the will to win tends to supersede any social considerations in modern sport. Only Warne had the decency to commiserate with England before joining in the celebrations. He had always been a one-off.

He announced his impending retirement from Test cricket before the fourth Test, which turned his home ground, the MCG, into the Shane Warne Show. He bowled Strauss through the gate to take his 700th Test wicket (almost double the most by an Englishman – Botham's 383). Strauss would really struggle to shake off the 'Daryll' tag now. Warne took seven wickets in the game, made 40 not out and won the Man of the Match award as Australia triumphed by an innings. Then in Sydney it was his perennial partner in wicket-crime, McGrath, also retiring, who first cornered then mugged six England batsmen to set up Australia's 10-wicket victory there.

What a way for Australia's greatest pair of bowlers to finish their careers, with a 5-0 whitewash of England – the first and only time since 1921. It was what you might call a proper shellacking. Critics lambasted England's selection policy, their fitness, their 'excessive' number of support staff, the presence of the WAGS plus kids which sometimes made the outfit look like a Thomas Cook tour group –and it does make you wonder about priorities when you see an England fast bowler trying to feed a wriggling toddler his Cheerios before heading off to the ground. But, in truth, Australia were too good, the intensity of their cricket too great, centred round their two champion bowlers.

Over their entire Test careers Warne and McGrath had now taken 1001 wickets in partnership (9.63 per Test), enabling Australia to win the Ashes six times and score a hat trick of World Cups en route to global domination. It wasn't just the wickets they took, of course, but the hypnosis they inflicted – encapsulated by that Adelaide victory. The robotic McGrath was the Terminator, lasering in on batsmen's weak spots until their resistance buckled; Warne more the Trickster, toying with a batsman, turning him, twisting him, tripping him, never letting him escape, a cat playing with a mouse until it was time to gobble him up. He'd swallowed

195 English mice (the most in Ashes history) by the time he'd finished. No wonder he was looking ever so slightly porky...

The Ashes...No Sweat

The departure of this deadly double-act made the Ashes a level playing field again. In 2009, England had a scare in Cardiff when the last pair – Anderson and Panesar – had to hold out for 11 overs to deny Australia victory. But after that they asserted their home advantage. Under the new 'Andocracy' – an intelligent, industrious pairing of Andrew Strauss (captain) and Andy Flower (coach) – there was a new unity, a highly scientific approach and a last tumultuous contribution from Flintoff. Australia, weakened by the retirement not just of Warne and McGrath, but also of Hayden, Langer and Gilchrist, hung on grimly, but ultimately handed the urn back at The Oval due to an inferior bowling attack, especially the lack of a decent spinner.

That weakness was brutally exposed back in Australia in 2010–11. England arrived better prepared than any previous touring team, having conducted an extensive and meticulous 12-month build-up, including an arduous training camp in dense German forest. Keeping ahead of the game, they had a machine that could replicate any bowler on the planet (yes, even Mitchell Johnson's enigmatic variations!) and a coach for each discipline, including a fielding expert who monitored every player's biomechanics in microscopic detail. The result was a squad of real athletes, excellent movers, catchers and throwers. Barely a dud among them.

The team was replete with confident, battle-hardened and skilled performers. James Anderson, for instance, was now an exceptional exponent with new ball or old on any surface and could land it on a beer mat. There was no danger of him missing the cut strip with his first delivery. He was supported by three giant fast bowlers (Stuart Broad, Steven Finn and Chris Tremlett) of 6ft 6in and more, all highly disciplined, and by the big spin, charisma and reliability of Graeme Swann. England did have a sort of Harmison moment when Strauss, having won the toss in the first Test at Brisbane, was out to the third ball of the match for a duck.

But he recovered his composure to make an important century in the second innings, laying the foundation for England's extraordinary 517-1. Alastair Cook's 235 not out broke Bradman's record for the ground in an undefeated second-wicket stand of 329 with Jonathan Trott.

They were not especially pretty to watch, but their run-making was as remorseless as Trott's perpetual re-marking of his guard and they would not be deflected from their purpose. Australia's inaccuracy and dearth of spin bowlers were illuminated every time the ball went to the boundary (60 times in that innings) when the face of Warne, now a commentator, was flashed up on the big screen after the replay, advertising McDonald's chicken burgers. The departure of a great player invariably leaves a daunting shadow.

Some of the Australian bowling was so bad that Bill Lawry laughed on commentary. By the last day of the Test the Queensland public were so disillusioned they had exited in their droves. The only people left in the ground were English fans and one disgruntled local who, when Ponting posted a short mid-on fielder, shouted, 'Oh very good, Punter! The last time someone took a catch there was 1921!' Ponting's picture was on the back page of one paper the next morning with 'CLUELESS' daubed across it, though little of the fiasco was actually his fault.

England's laying of their Gabba ghost gave them vivid self-belief, which they translated into a superb performance in Adelaide. It began with an Australian run-out in the first over of the match — a neat reversal of the mishap between Bell and Collingwood four years before — as Shane Watson sold Simon

Katich down the Torrens. Trott threw down the stumps and Australia were 0-1. Such moments reveal a lot about a batting team's confidence and unity. Or lack of it. Equally it tells you something about the focus and desire of their opponents.

A ball later Anderson produced the perfect out-swinger to Ponting and the Aussies were 0-2. The stunned silence must have been similar to that which had accompanied the famous Bradman dismissal to Bedser on the same ground 64 years earlier. When Clarke edged the first ball of Anderson's next over to second slip it was 2-3. Ponting would have been tearing his hair out if it hadn't been securely glued on by experts.

It was a sensational start and England's cricket was almost flawless for the next four days. The bowling and catching were clinical and the batting unrelenting. Cook, with his unique ability to remain focused and accumulate piles of runs without ever breaking into a sweat, batted for seven hours in temperatures of 38°C and never once had to change his gloves. Pietersen converted his 150 into a commanding double hundred, as he should have done four years earlier. England declared on 620-5, which meant that in a week Australia's attack had conceded 1137 runs and taken just six wickets. 'What do you call an Aussie with a hundred next to his name?... A bowler' went the joke.

Graeme Swann's prodigious spin and strong character came to the fore in Australia's second innings; by the end of the fourth day they were a beaten team. England completed their innings victory by midday on the fifth, a sweet experience for the six players (Strauss, Cook, Pietersen, Collingwood, Bell and Anderson) who had been suffering Adelaide-itis ever since that fateful turnaround there in 2006. When a massive thunderstorm broke over the ground that afternoon, a semi-inebriated Collingwood celebrated by diving across the saturated tarpaulin covers in his undies. It was a cathartic moment.

England in that match were peerless. The Australian press, to their credit, conjured a humorous take on the emerging gulf between the teams, with a neat twist on Bill Woodfull's famous line during the bodyline test in Adelaide almost 80 years earlier. Over a large picture of Australia's departing number 11, Peter Siddle, the caption declared, 'There are two teams out there on the field. Only one is playing cricket. That team is England.'

Producing such immaculate performances take their mental toll, and England were rather offline in Perth; they were caught out by a wonder spell from Mitchell Johnson, who had temporarily realigned his radar. Vitally they saw it as a mere blip and arrived at the climax of the Australian sporting year – the Boxing Day Test at the MCG – with their confidence still intact.

They even had the gall to put Australia into bat. What a nerve, in the cauldron of Australian sport, where 80,000 salivating Melbournians come to watch the latest batch of fleshy visitors boiled alive! Unfortunately for them, it was their own team who were roasted on the Christmas spit that year. In a blaze of ugly shots the Aussies were dismissed for just 98 before many of the portable barbies had even been fired up. By the end of the first day England were 59 in front without losing a wicket. 'If Carlsberg sponsored cricket, they would do days like this,' said a delighted Strauss after play.

England won handsomely by an innings on the fourth morning to retain the Ashes. To have done so in Australia for the first time since 1986 – after five failed attempts – was arguably a greater achievement than Vaughan's team regaining the urn at home in 2005. There was an overwhelming feeling of redemption among the players as they performed the Sprinkler – an oscillating dance based on the rotation of a lawn-watering device – in front of the massed ranks of the Barmy Army. (This happened, incidentally, some time after the players from both sides had shaken hands.) Strauss, a thoroughly decent man who prides himself on honesty, good manners and respect, but who also hates losing at anything, be it cricket, golf or arguments about four-man attacks, became only the third post-war English captain – after Hutton and Brearley – to win the Ashes both home and away. Warne would have to give up calling him Daryll now.

What of Australia? It was the beginning of the end for Ponting, who was pictured walking back to the pavilion on the front page of the *Herald Sun* beneath the words 'We were ~~Awful, Hopeless,~~ A DISGRACE.' He was injured anyway and temporarily handed over the captaincy to Michael Clarke for the fifth Test. A new number 3 was brought in, too – Usman Khawaja, Australia's first player of Pakistan or Indian extraction (Dav Whatmore, who played in 1979–80, was Sri Lankan), more than a century after England's first (Ranji). Was this a sign of a new enlightenment?

A decade or so ago Australian domestic cricket was stuffed full of prolific run-makers who gorged themselves on state – or English county – bowling, but were often nowhere near the Australian team. (There were enough for two Australian sides in a quadrangular one-day tournament at home in 1994–5 and they contested the final.) There didn't seem to be any of those batsmen now. Just a glut of lively bits-and-pieces all-rounders who earned quite good money around the place. Rather like England in the 1990s.

Why might this be? Probably a bunch of the same reasons. The surfeit of one-day cricket, the loss of some school playing fields, the number of competing sports now available to young people. One teacher told me that in 1960 Aussie kids played four sports at school – cricket, Aussie rules, tennis and rugby. In 2010 some secondary schools offered up to 28 sports, including wakeboarding and kitesurfing. It was bound to dilute general sporting standards. Perhaps Australia's next great cricketer will be found on the beach. That, after all, is where Warne came from. Obesity was a growing problem. That's not meant to be funny. The Sydney Test was an embarrassment. Australia, led by Clarke – not the popular public choice as he didn't fit the gnarled, gimlet-eyed, gum-chewing, let's-stuff-'em stereotype – won the toss, but the team soon lost the plot. They seemed mesmerised by England's disciplined attack and only stumbled past 200 through a breezy 50 from Johnson.

In reply England batted for two days, rattling along at 3.6 an over. There were three centurions, Cook the rudder (again), Bell the propeller and Prior the turbo thrust. England racked up 644, their highest ever total in Australia. Then they bowled out Australia again for an unprecedented third victory by an innings in the series. Astonishing. It was 3-1 to England, but in the end the chasm between the teams felt wider. It is extraordinary how little momentum shifts can create such ultimate one-sidedness in sport. Of course, England still have a way to go in the overall stakes. Of the 326 Tests now played, Australia have won 133, England 102, with 91 draws.

Alastair Cook won the Compton-Miller medal as the outstanding player of the 2010–11 series. He had scored 766 runs, the second most by an Englishman in Ashes history, in his methodical, unhurried, way. He had occupied the crease for a total of 36 hours, 11 minutes. Many players won't have batted as long as that in their entire career. His lack of sweaty palms was vital to his team's cause in the field, too. His super-dry hands made him the ideal ball-polisher when England were seeking some reverse swing. They frequently found it. Cook was their facilitator.

And that's the funny thing. The killer line on the last Ashes series was that a second Cook had conquered Australia a little matter of 240 years after the first. Life is cyclical. We're back where we started. Uncanny isn't it? And, now Cook is chartering new waters as England captain, the story can begin all over again.

Excited?

SCORECARDS

Balls and minutes are listed only where they were recorded by the official scorers. Please note that some of this information is therefore not available and gaps appear in some of the scorecards.

1: AUSTRALIA IN BRITISH ISLES 1882 (ONLY TEST)

Venue:	Kennington Oval, Kennington on 28, 29 August 1882 (3-day match)
Balls per over:	4
Toss:	Australia won the toss and decided to bat
Result:	Australia won by 7 runs
Umpires:	L Greenwood, RA Thoms
Close of play day 1	England (1) 101 all out

Australia first innings		RUNS	BALLS	MINS	4S	6S
AC Bannerman	c Grace b Peate	9	86	70	–	–
HH Massie	b Ulyett	1	4	7	–	–
*WL Murdoch	b Peate	13	70	50	1	–
GJ Bonnor	b Barlow	1	6	5	–	–
TP Horan	b Barlow	3	18	20	–	–
G Giffen	b Peate	2	23	17	–	–
+JM Blackham	c Grace b Barlow	17	51	40	2	–
TW Garrett	c Read b Peate	10	34	25	–	–
HF Boyle	b Barlow	2	10	5	–	–
SP Jones	c Barnes b Barlow	0	14	12	–	–
FR Spofforth	not out	4	4	3	1	–
Extras	(1 b)	1				
Total	(all out, 80 overs)	63				

Fall of wickets: 1-6 (Massie), 2-21 (Murdoch), 3-22 (Bonnor), 4-26 (Bannerman), 5-30 (Horan), 6-30 (Giffen), 7-48 (Garrett), 8-53 (Boyle), 9-59 (Blackham), 10-63 (Jones, 80 ov)

England bowling	OVERS	MDNS	RUNS	WKTS	WIDES	NO-BALLS
Peate	38	24	31	4	–	–
Ulyett	9	5	11	1	–	–
Barlow	31	22	19	5	–	–
Steel	2	1	1	0	–	–

England first innings		RUNS	BALLS	MINS	4S	6S
RG Barlow	c Bannerman b Spofforth	11	35	30	–	–
WG Grace	b Spofforth	4	15	20	–	–
G Ulyett	st Blackham b Spofforth	26	64	55	1	–
AP Lucas	c Blackham b Boyle	9	64	65	1	–
+A Lyttelton	c Blackham b Spofforth	2	20	25	–	–
CT Studd	b Spofforth	0	3	2	–	–
England first innings (cont)		RUNS	BALLS	MINS	4S	6S
JM Read	not out	19	42	45	2	–
W Barnes	b Boyle	5	10	9	1	–
AG Steel	b Garrett	14	24	22	1	–
*AN Hornby	b Spofforth	2	9	5	–	–
E Peate	c Boyle b Spofforth	0	2	1	–	–
Extras	(6 b, 2 lb, 1 nb)	9				
Total	(all out, 71.3 overs)	101				

Fall of wickets: 1-13 (Grace), 2-18 (Barlow), 3-57 (Ulyett), 4-59 (Lucas), 5-60 (Studd), 6-63 (Lyttelton), 7-70 (Barnes), 8-96 (Steel), 9-101 (Hornby), 10-101 (Peate, 71.3 ov)

Australia bowling	OVERS	MDNS	RUNS	WKTS	WIDES	NO-BALLS
Spofforth	36.3	18	46	7	–	–
Garrett	16	7	22	1	–	–
Boyle	19	7	24	2	–	–

Australia second innings		RUNS	BALLS	MINS	4S	6S
AC Bannerman	c Studd b Barnes	13	61	70	–	–
HH Massie	b Steel	55	62	57	9	–
GJ Bonnor	b Ulyett	2	9	9	–	–
*WL Murdoch	run out	29	60	70	1	–
TP Horan	c Grace b Peate	2	6	10	–	–
G Giffen	c Grace b Peate	0	1	1	–	–
+JM Blackham	c Lyttelton b Peate	7	15	13	1	–
SP Jones	run out	6	29	30	1	–
FR Spofforth	b Peate	0	5	3	–	–
TW Garrett	not out	2	4	5	–	–
HF Boyle	b Steel	0	1	1	–	–
Extras	(6 b)	6				
Total	(all out, 63 overs)	122				

Fall of wickets: 1-66 (Massie), 2-70 (Bonnor), 3-70 (Bannerman), 4-79 (Horan), 5-79 (Giffen), 6-99 (Blackham), 7-114 (Jones), 8-117 (Spofforth), 9-122 (Murdoch), 10-122 (Boyle, 63 ov)

England bowling	OVERS	MDNS	RUNS	WKTS	WIDES	NO-BALLS
Barlow	13	5	27	0	–	–
Ulyett	6	2	10	1	–	–
Peate	21	9	40	4	–	–
Studd	4	1	9	0	–	–
Barnes	12	5	15	1	–	–
Steel	7	0	15	2	–	–

England second innings		RUNS	BALLS	MINS	4S	6S
WG Grace	c Bannerman b Boyle	32	52	55	2	–
*AN Hornby	b Spofforth	9	17	16	1	–
RG Barlow	b Spofforth	0	1	1	–	–
G Ulyett	c Blackham b Spofforth	11	28	32	1	–
AP Lucas	b Spofforth	5	55	65	1	–
+A Lyttelton	b Spofforth	12	54	50	1	–
AG Steel	c and b Spofforth	0	3	4	–	–
JM Read	b Spofforth	0	2	1	–	–
W Barnes	c Murdoch b Boyle	2	6	6	–	–
CT Studd	not out	0	2	5	–	–
E Peate	b Boyle	2	3	1	–	–
Extras	(3 b, 1 nb)	4				
Total	(all out, 55 overs)	77				

Fall of wickets: 1-15 (Hornby), 2-15 (Barlow), 3-51 (Ulyett), 4-53 (Grace), 5-66 (Lyttelton), 6-70 (Steel), 7-70 (Read), 8-75 (Lucas), 9-75 (Barnes), 10-77 (Peate, 55 ov)

Australia bowling	OVERS	MDNS	RUNS	WKTS	WIDES	NO-BALLS
Spofforth	28	15	44	7	–	–
Garrett	7	2	10	0	–	–
Boyle	20	11	19	3	–	–

2. AUSTRALIA IN BRITISH ISLES 1902 (4TH TEST)

Venue	Old Trafford, Manchester on 24, 25, 26 July 1902 (3-day match)
Balls per over	6
Toss	Australia won the toss and decided to bat
Result	Australia won by 3 runs
Umpires	J Moss, T Mycroft
Close of play day 1	England (1) 70–5 (Jackson 16*, Braund 13*)
Close of play day 2	Australia (2) 85–8 (Kelly 1*, Trumble 4*)

Australia first innings		RUNS	BALLS	MINS	4S	6S
VT Trumper	c Lilley b Rhodes	104		115	14	–
RA Duff	c Lilley b Lockwood	54		78	4	–
C Hill	c Rhodes b Lockwood	65		110	4	–
MA Noble	c and b Rhodes	2			–	–
SE Gregory	c Lilley b Rhodes	3			–	–
*J Darling	c MacLaren b Rhodes	51			5	2
AJY Hopkins	c Palairet b Lockwood	0			–	–
WW Armstrong	b Lockwood	5			–	–
+JJ Kelly	not out	4			1	–
H Trumble	c Tate b Lockwood	0			–	–
JV Saunders	b Lockwood	3			–	–
Extras	(5 b, 2 lb, 1 w)	8				
Total	(all out, 76.1 overs)	299				

Fall of wickets: 1-135 (Duff), 2-175 (Trumper), 3-179 (Noble), 4-183 (Gregory), 5-256 (Hill), 6-256 (Hopkins), 7-288 (Armstrong), 8-292 (Darling), 9-292 (Trumble), 10-299 (Saunders, 76.1 ov)

England bowling	OVERS	MDNS	RUNS	WKTS	WIDES	NO-BALLS
Rhodes	25	3	104	4	–	–
Jackson	11	0	58	0	–	–
Tate	11	1	44	0	–	–
Braund	9	0	37	0	–	–
Lockwood	20.1	5	48	6	–	–

England first innings		RUNS	BALLS	MINS	4S	6S
LCH Palairet	c Noble b Saunders	6			–	–
R Abel	c Armstrong b Saunders	6			1	–
JT Tyldesley	c Hopkins b Saunders	22			3	–
*AC MacLaren	b Trumble	1			–	–
KS Ranjitsinhji	lbw b Trumble	2			–	–
FS Jackson	c Duff b Trumble	128		255	16	–

England first innings (cont)		RUNS	BALLS	MINS	4S	6S
LC Braund	b Noble	65		165	9	-
+AFA Lilley	b Noble	7			1	-
WH Lockwood	run out	7			1	-
W Rhodes	c and b Trumble	5			1	-
FW Tate	not out	5			-	-
Extras	(6 b, 2 lb)	8				
Total	(all out, 114 overs)	262				

Fall of wickets: 1-12 (Abel), 2-13 (Palairet), 3-14 (MacLaren), 4-30 (Ranjitsinhji), 5-44 (Tyldesley), 6-185 (Braund), 7-203 (Lilley), 8-214 (Lockwood), 9-235 (Rhodes), 10-262 (Jackson, 114 ov)

Australia bowling	OVERS	MDNS	RUNS	WKTS	WIDES	NO-BALLS
Trumble	43	16	75	4	-	-
Saunders	34	5	104	3	-	-
Noble	24	8	47	2	-	-
Trumper	6	4	6	0	-	-
Armstrong	5	2	19	0	-	-
Hopkins	2	0	3	0	-	-

Australia second innings		RUNS	BALLS	MINS	4S	6S
VT Trumper	c Braund b Lockwood	4			1	-
RA Duff	b Lockwood	3			-	-
C Hill	b Lockwood	0			-	-
*J Darling	c Palairet b Rhodes	37			4	-
SE Gregory	lbw b Tate	24			2	-
MA Noble	c Lilley b Lockwood	4			1	-
AJY Hopkins	c Tate b Lockwood	2			-	-
WW Armstrong	b Rhodes	3			-	-
+JJ Kelly	not out	2			-	-
H Trumble	lbw b Tate	4			-	-
JV Saunders	c Tyldesley b Rhodes	0			-	-
Extras	(1 b, 1 lb, 1 nb)	3				
Total	(all out, 47.4 overs)	86				

Fall of wickets: 1-7 (Trumper), 2-9 (Hill), 3-10 (Duff), 4-64 (Gregory), 5-74 (Darling), 6-76 (Hopkins), 7-77 (Noble), 8-79 (Armstrong), 9-85 (Trumble), 10-86 (Saunders, 47.4 ov)

England bowling	OVERS	MDNS	RUNS	WKTS	WIDES	NO-BALLS
Lockwood	17	5	28	5	–	–
Braund	11	3	22	0	–	–
Rhodes	14.4	5	26	3	–	–
Tate	5	3	7	2	–	–

England second innings		RUNS	BALLS	MINS	4S	6S
LCH Palairet	b Saunders	17			1	–
★AC MacLaren	c Duff b Trumble	35		70	4	–
JT Tyldesley	c Armstrong b Saunders	16			3	–
KS Ranjitsinhji	lbw b Trumble	4			–	–
R Abel	b Trumble	21		25	3	–
FS Jackson	c Gregory b Saunders	7			–	–
LC Braund	st Kelly b Trumble	3			–	–
+AFA Lilley	c Hill b Trumble	4			–	–
WH Lockwood	b Trumble	0			–	–
W Rhodes	not out	4			1	–
FW Tate	b Saunders	4	4		1	–
Extras	(5 b)	5				
Total	(all out, 49.4 overs)	120				

Fall of wickets: 1-44 (Palairet), 2-68 (Tyldesley), 3-72 (MacLaren), 4-92 (Ranjitsinhji), 5-97 (Abel), 6-107 (Jackson), 7-109 (Braund), 8-109 (Lockwood), 9-116 (Lilley), 10-120 (Tate, 49.4 ov)

Australia bowling	OVERS	MDNS	RUNS	WKTS	WIDES	NO-BALLS
Trumble	25	9	53	6	–	–
Noble	5	3	10	0	–	–
Saunders	19.4	4	52	4	–	–

3. AUSTRALIA IN BRITISH ISLES 1926 (5TH TEST)

Venue	Kennington Oval, Kennington on 14, 16, 17, 18 August 1926 (timeless match)
Balls per over	6
Toss	England won the toss and decided to bat
Result	England won by 289 runs
Umpires	F Chester, HI Young
Close of play day 1	Australia (1) 60-4 (Woodfull 22★, Collins 1★)
Close of play day 2	England (2) 49–0 (Hobbs 28★, Sutcliffe 20★)
Close of play day 3	England (2) 375–6 (Rhodes 0★)

England first innings		RUNS	BALLS	MINS	4S	6S
JB Hobbs	b Mailey	37		55		–
H Sutcliffe	b Mailey	76		210	6	–
FE Woolley	b Mailey	18				
EH Hendren	b Gregory	8				
★APF Chapman	st Oldfield b Mailey	49		75		–
GTS Stevens	c Andrews b Mailey	17			2	1
W Rhodes	c Oldfield b Mailey	28		45		–
G Geary	run out	9				
MW Tate	b Grimmett	23		15		1
H Larwood	c Andrews b Grimmett	0				
+H Strudwick	not out	4			1	–
Extras	(6 b, 5 lb)	11				
Total	(all out, 95.5 overs)	280				

Fall of wickets: 1-53 (Hobbs), 2-91 (Woolley), 3-108 (Hendren), 4-189 (Chapman), 5-213 (Stevens), 6-214 (Sutcliffe), 7-231 (Geary), 8-266 (Tate), 9-266 (Larwood), 10-280 (Rhodes, 95.5 ov)

Australia bowling	OVERS	MDNS	RUNS	WKTS	WIDES	NO-BALLS
Gregory	15	4	31	1	–	–
Grimmett	33	12	74	2	–	–
Mailey	33.5	3	138	6	–	–
Macartney	7	4	16	0	–	–
Richardson	7	2	10	0	–	–

Australia first innings		RUNS	BALLS	MINS	4S	6S
WM Woodfull	b Rhodes	35		120		–
W Bardsley	c Strudwick b Larwood	2				
CG Macartney	b Stevens	25		30		–
WH Ponsford	run out	2				

Australia first innings (contd)

		RUNS	BALLS	MINS	4S	6S
TJE Andrews	b Larwood	3				
*HL Collins	c Stevens b Larwood	61		230	2	–
AJ Richardson	c Geary b Rhodes	16				
JM Gregory	c Stevens b Tate	73		100	10	–
+WAS Oldfield	not out	33				
CV Grimmett	b Tate	35		75		–
AA Mailey	c Strudwick b Tate	0				
Extras	(5 b, 12 lb)	17				
Total	(all out, 152.1 overs)	302				

Fall of wickets: 1-9 (Bardsley), 2-44 (Macartney), 3-51 (Ponsford), 4-59 (Andrews), 5-90 (Woodfull), 6-122 (Richardson), 7-229 (Gregory), 8-231 (Collins), 9-298 (Grimmett), 10-302 (Mailey, 152.1 ov)

England bowling

	OVERS	MDNS	RUNS	WKTS	WIDES	NO-BALLS
Tate	37.1	17	40	3	–	–
Larwood	34	11	82	3	–	–
Geary	27	8	43	0	–	–
Stevens	29	3	85	1	–	–
Rhodes	25	15	35	2	–	–

England second innings

		RUNS	BALLS	MINS	4S	6S
JB Hobbs	b Gregory	100		221	10	–
H Sutcliffe	b Mailey	161		428	16	–
FE Woolley	lbw b Richardson	27				
EH Hendren	c Oldfield b Grimmett	15				
*APF Chapman	b Richardson	19				
GTS Stevens	c Mailey b Grimmett	22				
W Rhodes	lbw b Grimmett	14				
G Geary	c Oldfield b Gregory	1				
MW Tate	not out	33		50		–
H Larwood	b Mailey	5		10		–
+H Strudwick	c Andrews b Mailey	2		5	–	–
Extras	(19 b, 18 lb)	37				
Total	(all out, 182.5 overs)	436				

Fall of wickets: 1-172 (Hobbs), 2-220 (Woolley), 3-277 (Hendren), 4-316 (Chapman), 5-373 (Stevens), 6-375 (Sutcliffe), 7-382 (Geary), 8-425 (Rhodes), 9-430 (Larwood), 10-436 (Strudwick, 182.5 ov)

Australia bowling	OVERS	MDNS	RUNS	WKTS	WIDES	NO-BALLS
Gregory	18	1	58	2	–	–
Grimmett	55	17	108	3	–	–
Mailey	42.5	6	128	3	–	–
Macartney	26	16	24	0	–	–
Richardson	41	21	81	2	–	–

Australia second innings		RUNS	BALLS	MINS	4S	6S
WM Woodfull	c Geary b Larwood	0				
WH Ponsford	c Larwood b Rhodes	12				
CG Macartney	c Geary b Larwood	16				
W Bardsley	c Woolley b Rhodes	21		65		–
*HL Collins	c Woolley b Rhodes	4				
TJE Andrews	c Tate b Larwood	15				
JM Gregory	c Sutcliffe b Tate	9				
AJ Richardson	b Rhodes	4				
+WAS Oldfield	b Stevens	23				
CV Grimmett	not out	8				
AA Mailey	b Geary	6				
Extras	(7 lb)	7				
Total	(all out, 52.3 overs)	125				

Fall of wickets: 1-1 (Woodfull), 2-31 (Macartney), 3-31 (Ponsford), 4-35 (Collins), 5-63 (Andrews), 6-83 (Bardsley), 7-83 (Gregory), 8-87 (Richardson), 9-114 (Oldfield), 10-125 (Mailey, 52.3 ov)

England bowling	OVERS	MDNS	RUNS	WKTS	WIDES	NO-BALLS
Larwood	14	3	34	3	–	–
Tate	9	4	12	1	–	–
Rhodes	20	9	44	4	–	–
Geary	6.3	2	15	1	–	–
Stevens	3	1	13	1	–	–

4. MARYLEBONE CRICKET CLUB IN AUSTRALIA AND NEW ZEALAND 1932–3 (3RD TEST)

Venue   Adelaide Oval, Adelaide on 13, 14, 16, 17, 18, 19 January 1933 (timeless match)

Balls per over   6

Toss   England won the toss and decided to bat

Result   England won by 338 runs

Umpires   GE Borwick, GA Hele

Close of play day 1   England (1) 236–7 (Paynter 25*, Verity 5*)

Close of play day 2   Australia (1) 109–4 (Ponsford 45*, Richardson 21*)

Close of play day 3   England (2) 85–1 (Jardine 24*, Wyatt 47*)

Close of play day 4   England (2) 296–6 (Ames 18*)

Close of play day 5   Australia (2) 120–4 (Woodfull 36*, Richardson 0*)

England first innings		RUNS	BALLS	MINS	4S	6S
H Sutcliffe	c Wall b O'Reilly	9	43	46	–	–
*DR Jardine	b Wall	3	18	20	–	–
WR Hammond	c Oldfield b Wall	2	15	15	–	–
+LEG Ames	b Ironmonger	3	38	39	–	–
M Leyland	b O'Reilly	83	190	180	13	–
RES Wyatt	c Richardson b Grimmett	78	176	164	3	3
E Paynter	c Fingleton b Wall	77	216	185	9	–
GOB Allen	lbw b Grimmett	15	30	37	2	–
H Verity	c Richardson b Wall	45	147	154	2	–
W Voce	b Wall	8	13	14	1	–
H Larwood	not out	3	4	3	–	–
Extras	(1 b, 7 lb, 7 nb)	15				
Total	(all out, 146.1 overs)	341				

Fall of wickets: 1-4 (Jardine), 2-16 (Hammond), 3-16 (Sutcliffe), 4-30 (Ames), 5-186 (Leyland), 6-196 (Wyatt), 7-228 (Allen), 8-324 (Paynter), 9-336 (Voce), 10-341 (Verity, 146.1 ov)

Australia bowling	OVERS	MDNS	RUNS	WKTS	WIDES	NO-BALLS
Wall	34.1	10	72	5	–	–
O'Reilly	50	19	82	2	–	–
Ironmonger	20	6	50	1	–	–
Grimmett	28	6	94	2	–	–
McCabe	14	3	28	0	–	–

Australia first innings

Australia first innings		RUNS	BALLS	MINS	4S	6S
JHW Fingleton	c Ames b Allen	0	8	5	-	-
*WM Woodfull	b Allen	22	65	89	-	-
DG Bradman	c Allen b Larwood	8	17	18	1	-
SJ McCabe	c Jardine b Larwood	8	25	21	1	-
WH Ponsford	b Voce	85	213	216	8	-
VY Richardson	b Allen	28	81	95	1	-
+WAS Oldfield	retired hurt	41	114	123	4	-
CV Grimmett	c Voce b Allen	10	24	29	1	-
TW Wall	b Hammond	6	19	22	-	-
WJ O'Reilly	b Larwood	0	9	8	-	-
H Ironmonger	not out	0	0	1	-	-
Extras	(2 b, 11 lb, 1 nb)	14				
Total	(all out, 95.4 overs)	222				

Fall of wickets: 1-1 (Fingleton), 2-18 (Bradman), 3-34 (McCabe), 4-51 (Woodfull), 5-131 (Richardson), 6-194 (Ponsford), 7-212 (Grimmett), 8-222 (O'Reilly), 9-222 (Wall, 95.4 ov)

England bowling

England bowling	OVERS	MDNS	RUNS	WKTS	WIDES	NO-BALLS
Larwood	25	6	55	3	-	-
Allen	23	4	71	4	-	-
Hammond	17.4	4	30	1	-	-
Voce	14	5	21	1	-	-
Verity	16	7	31	0	-	-

England second innings

England second innings		RUNS	BALLS	MINS	4S	6S
H Sutcliffe	c sub (LPJ O'Brien) b Wall	7	11	13	1	-
*DR Jardine	lbw b Ironmonger	56	266	254	2	-
RES Wyatt	c Wall b O'Reilly	49	138	133	4	-
GOB Allen	lbw b Grimmett	15	59	52	2	-
WR Hammond	b Bradman	85	247	221	8	-
M Leyland	c Wall b Ironmonger	42	93	108	5	-
+LEG Ames	b O'Reilly	69	173	169	6	-
H Verity	lbw b O'Reilly	40	131	115	2	-
H Larwood	c Bradman b Ironmonger	8	12	14	1	-
E Paynter	not out	1	15	17	-	-
W Voce	b O'Reilly	8	10	7	-	-
Extras	(17 b, 11 lb, 4 nb)	32				
Total	(all out, 191.3 overs)	412				

Fall of wickets: 1-7 (Sutcliffe), 2-91 (Wyatt), 3-123 (Allen), 4-154 (Jardine), 5-245 (Leyland), 6-296 (Hammond), 7-394 (Ames), 8-395 (Verity), 9-403 (Larwood), 10-412 (Voce, 191.3 ov)

Australia bowling	OVERS	MDNS	RUNS	WKTS	WIDES	NO-BALLS
Wall	29	6	75	1	–	–
O'Reilly	50.3	21	79	4	–	–
Ironmonger	57	21	87	3	–	–
Grimmett	35	9	74	1	–	–
McCabe	16	0	42	0	–	–
Bradman	4	0	23	1	–	–

Australia second innings		RUNS	BALLS	MINS	4S	6S
JHW Fingleton	b Larwood	0	14	8	–	–
*WM Woodfull	not out	73	208	235	2	–
WH Ponsford	c Jardine b Larwood	3	11	13	–	–
DG Bradman	c and b Verity	66	71	73	10	1
SJ McCabe	c Leyland b Allen	7	19	21	1	–
VY Richardson	c Allen b Larwood	21	76	83	3	–
CV Grimmett	b Allen	6	8	10	1	–
TW Wall	b Allen	0	4	1	–	–
WJ O'Reilly	b Larwood	5	10	3	1	–
H Ironmonger	b Allen	0	1	2	–	–
+WAS Oldfield	absent hurt					
Extras	(4 b, 2 lb, 5 nb, 1 w)	12				
Total	(all out, 69.2 overs)	193				

Fall of wickets: 1-3 (Fingleton), 2-12 (Ponsford), 3-100 (Bradman), 4-116
(McCabe), 5-171 (Richardson), 6-183 (Grimmett), 7-183 (Wall),
8-192 (O'Reilly), 9-193 (Ironmonger, 69.2 ov)

England bowling	OVERS	MDNS	RUNS	WKTS	WIDES	NO-BALLS
Larwood	19	3	71	4	–	–
Allen	17.2	5	50	4	–	–
Voce	4	1	7	0	–	–
Hammond	9	3	27	0	–	–
Verity	20	12	26	1	–	–

5. AUSTRALIA IN BRITISH ISLES 1948 (4TH TEST)

Venue	Headingley, Leeds on 22, 23, 24, 26, 27 July 1948 (5-day match)
Balls per over	6
Toss	England won the toss and decided to bat
Result	Australia won by 7 wickets
Umpires	HG Baldwin, F Chester
Close of play day 1	England (1) 268–2 (Edrich 41★, Bedser 0★)
Close of play day 2	Australia (1) 63–1 (Hassett 13★, Bradman 31★)
Close of play day 3	Australia (1) 457–9 (Lindwall 76★, Toshack 12★)
Close of play day 4	England (2) 362–8 (Evans 47★, Laker 14★)

England first innings		RUNS	BALLS	MINS	4S	6S
L Hutton	b Lindwall	81		187		–
C Washbrook	c Lindwall b Johnston	143		317	22	–
WJ Edrich	c Morris b Johnson	111		314	13	1
AV Bedser	c and b Johnson	79		177	8	2
DCS Compton	c Saggers b Lindwall	23		55		–
JF Crapp	b Toshack	5				
★NWD Yardley	b Miller	25				
K Cranston	b Loxton	10				
+TG Evans	c Hassett b Loxton	3				
JC Laker	c Saggers b Loxton	4				
R Pollard	not out	0				
Extras	(2 b, 8 lb, 1 nb, 1 w)	12				
Total	(all out, 192.1 overs)	496				

Fall of wickets: 1-168 (Hutton), 2-268 (Washbrook), 3-423 (Bedser), 4-426 (Edrich), 5-447 (Crapp), 6-473 (Compton), 7-486 (Cranston), 8-490 (Evans), 9-496 (Laker), 10-496 (Yardley, 192.1 ov)

Australia bowling	OVERS	MDNS	RUNS	WKTS	WIDES	NO-BALLS
Lindwall	38	10	79	2	–	–
Miller	17.1	2	43	1	–	–
Johnston	38	12	86	1	–	–
Toshack	35	6	112	1	–	–
Loxton	26	4	55	3	–	–
Johnson	33	9	89	2	–	–
Morris	5	0	20	0	–	–

Australia first innings		RUNS	BALLS	MINS	4S	6S
AR Morris	c Cranston b Bedser	6				
AL Hassett	c Crapp b Pollard	13				
*DG Bradman	b Pollard	33	56	59		–
KR Miller	c Edrich b Yardley	58				2
RN Harvey	b Laker	112		188	17	–
SJE Loxton	b Yardley	93		135	8	5
IWG Johnson	c Cranston b Laker	10				
RR Lindwall	c Crapp b Bedser	77				
+RA Saggers	st Evans b Laker	5				
WA Johnston	c Edrich b Bedser	13				
ERH Toshack	not out	12				
Extras	(9 b, 14 lb, 3 nb)	26				
Total	(all out, 136.2 overs)	458				

Fall of wickets: 1-13 (Morris), 2-65 (Hassett), 3-68 (Bradman), 4-189 (Miller), 5-294 (Harvey), 6-329 (Johnson), 7-344 (Loxton), 8-355 (Saggers), 9-403 (Johnston), 10-458 (Lindwall, 136.2 ov)

England bowling	OVERS	MDNS	RUNS	WKTS	WIDES	NO-BALLS
Bedser	31.2	4	92	3	–	–
Pollard	38	6	104	2	–	–
Cranston	14	1	51	0	–	–
Edrich	3	0	19	0	–	–
Laker	30	8	113	3	–	–
Yardley	17	6	38	2	–	–
Compton	3	0	15	0	–	–

England second innings		RUNS	BALLS	MINS	4S	6S
L Hutton	c Bradman b Johnson	57				1
C Washbrook	c Harvey b Johnston	65				1
WJ Edrich	lbw b Lindwall	54				1
DCS Compton	c Miller b Johnston	66				
JF Crapp	b Lindwall	18				
*NWD Yardley	c Harvey b Johnston	7				
K Cranston	c Saggers b Johnston	0	2		–	–
+TG Evans	not out	47				
AV Bedser	c Hassett b Miller	17			4	–
JC Laker	not out	15				
R Pollard	did not bat					
Extras	(4 b, 12 lb, 3 nb)	19				
Total	(8 wickets, declared, 107 overs)	365				

Fall of wickets: 1-129 (Washbrook), 2-129 (Hutton), 3-232 (Edrich), 4-260 (Crapp), 5-277 (Yardley), 6-278 (Cranston), 7-293 (Compton), 8-330 (Bedser)

Australia bowling	OVERS	MDNS	RUNS	WKTS	WIDES	NO-BALLS
Lindwall	26	6	84	2	–	–
Miller	21	5	53	1	–	–
Johnston	29	5	95	4	–	–
Loxton	10	2	29	0	–	–
Johnson	21	2	85	1	–	–

Australia second innings		RUNS	BALLS	MINS	4S	6S
AR Morris	c Pollard b Yardley	182		291	33	–
AL Hassett	c and b Compton	17		74	1	–
*DG Bradman	not out	173	292	255	29	–
KR Miller	lbw b Cranston	12		30	2	–
RN Harvey	not out	4			1	–
SJE Loxton	did not bat					
IWG Johnson	did not bat					
RR Lindwall	did not bat					
+RA Saggers	did not bat					
WA Johnston	did not bat					
ERH Toshack	did not bat					
Extras	(6 b, 9 lb, 1 nb)	16				
Total	(3 wickets, 114.1 overs)	404				

Fall of wickets: 1-57 (Hassett), 2-358 (Morris), 3-396 (Miller)

England bowling	OVERS	MDNS	RUNS	WKTS	WIDES	NO-BALLS
Bedser	21	2	56	0	–	–
Pollard	22	6	55	0	–	–
Laker	32	11	93	0	–	–
Compton	15	3	82	1	–	–
Hutton	4	1	30	0	–	–
Yardley	13	1	44	1	–	–
Cranston	7.1	0	28	1	–	–

6. AUSTRALIA IN BRITISH ISLES 1953 (5TH TEST)

Venue	Kennington Oval, Kennington on 15, 17, 18, 19 August 1953 (6-day match)					
Balls per over	6					
Toss	Australia won the toss and decided to bat					
Result	England won by 8 wickets					
Umpires	D Davies, FS Lee					
Close of play day 1	England (1) 1–0 (Hutton 0*, Edrich 1*)					
Close of play day 2	England (1) 235–7 (Bailey 35*, Lock 4*)					
Close of play day 3	England (2) 38–1 (Edrich 15*, May 6*)					

Australia first innings		RUNS	BALLS	MINS	4S	6S
*AL Hassett	c Evans b Bedser	53	99	135	4	–
AR Morris	lbw b Bedser	16	49	55	1	–
KR Miller	lbw b Bailey	1	6	4	–	–
RN Harvey	c Hutton b Trueman	36	60	77	3	–
GB Hole	c Evans b Trueman	37	47	64	2	–
JH de Courcy	c Evans b Trueman	5	6	9	1	–
RG Archer	c and b Bedser	10	48	54	–	–
AK Davidson	c Edrich b Laker	22	35	48	4	–
RR Lindwall	c Evans b Trueman	62	97	112	8	–
+GRA Langley	c Edrich b Lock	18	29	38	2	–
WA Johnston	not out	9	20	28	1	–
Extras	(4 b, 2 nb)	6				
Total	(all out, 81.3 overs)	275				

Fall of wickets: 1-38 (Morris), 2-41 (Miller), 3-107 (Hassett), 4-107 (Harvey), 5-118 (de Courcy), 6-160 (Hole), 7-160 (Archer), 8-207 (Davidson), 9-245 (Langley), 10-275 (Lindwall, 81.3 ov)

England bowling	OVERS	MDNS	RUNS	WKTS	WIDES	NO-BALLS
Bedser	29	3	88	3	–	–
Trueman	24.3	3	86	4	–	1
Bailey	14	3	42	1	–	1
Lock	9	2	19	1	–	–
Laker	5	0	34	1	–	–

England first innings		RUNS	BALLS	MINS	4S	6S
*L Hutton	b Johnston	82	185	218	8	–
WJ Edrich	lbw b Lindwall	21	33	38	3	–
PBH May	c Archer b Johnston	39	134	148	7	–
DCS Compton	c Langley b Lindwall	16	70	68	2	–

England first innings (cont)		RUNS	BALLS	MINS	4S	6S
TW Graveney	c Miller b Lindwall	4	36	46	–	–
TE Bailey	b Archer	64	222	228	6	–
+TG Evans	run out	28	34	45	4	–
JC Laker	c Langley b Miller	1	3	9	–	–
GAR Lock	c Davidson b Lindwall	4	43	52	–	–
FS Trueman	b Johnston	10	24	35	1	–
AV Bedser	not out	22	75	71	2	–
Extras	(9 b, 5 lb, 1 w)	15				
Total	(all out, 142.3 overs)	306				

Fall of wickets: 1-37 (Edrich), 2-137 (May), 3-154 (Hutton), 4-167 (Compton), 5-170 (Graveney), 6-210 (Evans), 7-225 (Laker), 8-237 (Lock), 9-262 (Trueman), 10-306 (Bailey, 142.3 ov)

Australia bowling	OVERS	MDNS	RUNS	WKTS	WIDES	NO-BALLS
Lindwall	32	7	70	4	–	–
Miller	34	12	65	1	–	–
Johnston	45	16	94	3	–	–
Davidson	10	1	26	0	1	–
Archer	10.3	2	25	1	–	–
Hole	11	6	11	0	–	–

Australia second innings		RUNS	BALLS	MINS	4S	6S
*AL Hassett	lbw b Laker	10	18	25	–	–
AR Morris	lbw b Lock	26	62	78	4	–
GB Hole	lbw b Laker	17	40	37	2	–
RN Harvey	b Lock	1	3	4	–	–
KR Miller	c Trueman b Laker	0	8	4	–	–
JH de Courcy	run out	4	8	16	1	–
RG Archer	c Edrich b Lock	49	65	60	7	1
AK Davidson	b Lock	21	44	40	1	1
RR Lindwall	c Compton b Laker	12	30	42	–	1
+GRA Langley	c Trueman b Lock	2	7	8	–	–
WA Johnston	not out	6	20	25	–	–
Extras	(11 b, 3 lb)	14				
Total	(all out, 50.5 overs)	162				

Fall of wickets: 1-23 (Hassett), 2-59 (Hole), 3-60 (Harvey), 4-61 (Miller), 5-61 (Morris), 6-85 (de Courcy), 7-135 (Davidson), 8-140 (Archer), 9-144 (Langley), 10-162 (Lindwall, 50.5 ov)

England bowling

	OVERS	MDNS	RUNS	WKTS	WIDES	NO-BALLS
Bedser	11	2	24	0	–	–
Trueman	2	1	4	0	–	–
Laker	16.5	2	75	4	–	–
Lock	21	9	45	5	–	–

England second innings

		RUNS	BALLS	MINS	4S	6S
*L Hutton	run out	17	30	33	2	–
WJ Edrich	not out	55	207	213	6	–
PBH May	c Davidson b Miller	37	89	113	5	–
DCS Compton	not out	22	57	63	1	–
TW Graveney	did not bat					
TE Bailey	did not bat					
+TG Evans	did not bat					
JC Laker	did not bat					
GAR Lock	did not bat					
FS Trueman	did not bat					
AV Bedser	did not bat					
Extras	(1 lb)	1				
Total	(2 wickets, 63.5 overs)	132				

Fall of wickets: 1-24 (Hutton), 2-88 (May)

Australia bowling

	OVERS	MDNS	RUNS	WKTS	WIDES	NO-BALLS
Lindwall	21	5	46	0	–	–
Miller	11	3	24	1	–	–
Johnston	29	14	52	0	–	–
Archer	1	1	0	0	–	–
Hassett	1	0	4	0	–	–
Morris	0.5	0	5	0	–	–

7. MARYLEBONE CRICKET CLUB IN AUSTRALIA AND NEW ZEALAND 1974–5 (1ST TEST)

Venue	Brisbane Cricket Ground, Woolloongabba, Brisbane on 29, 30 November, 1, 3, 4 December 1974 (5-day match)
Balls per over	8
Toss	Australia won the toss and decided to bat
Result	Australia won by 166 runs
Umpires	RC Bailhache, TF Brooks
Close of play day 1	Australia (1) 219–6 (Marsh 8★, Jenner 8★)
Close of play day 2	England (1) 114–4 (Edrich 40★, Greig 34★)
Close of play day 3	Australia (2) 51–2 (Redpath 24★, GS Chappell 7★)
Close of play day 4	England (2) 10–0 (Amiss 9★, Luckhurst 0★)

Australia first innings		RUNS	BALLS	MINS	4S	6S
IR Redpath	b Willis	5	20	23	–	–
WJ Edwards	c Amiss b Hendrick	4	15	19	–	–
★IM Chappell	c Greig b Willis	90	202	289	10	1
GS Chappell	c Fletcher b Underwood	58	132	155	5	–
R Edwards	c Knott b Underwood	32	120	147	2	–
KD Walters	c Lever b Willis	3	6	9	–	–
+RW Marsh	c Denness b Hendrick	14	56	67	–	–
TJ Jenner	c Lever b Willis	12	28	49	2	–
DK Lillee	c Knott b Greig	15	22	40	2	–
MHN Walker	not out	41	72	110	6	–
JR Thomson	run out	23	77	76	2	–
Extras	(4 lb, 8 nb)	12				
Total	(all out, 499 minutes, 92.5 overs)	309				

Fall of wickets: 1-7 (WJ Edwards), 2-10 (Redpath), 3-110 (GS Chappell), 4-197 (IM Chappell), 5-202 (Walters), 6-205 (R Edwards), 7-228 (Jenner), 8-229 (Marsh), 9-257 (Lillee), 10-309 (Thomson, 92.5 ov)

England bowling	OVERS	MDNS	RUNS	WKTS	WIDES	NO-BALLS
Willis	21.5	3	56	4	–	–
Lever	16	1	53	0	–	–
Hendrick	19	3	64	2	–	–
Greig	16	2	70	1	–	–
Underwood	20	6	54	2	–	–

APPENDIX 1

England first innings		RUNS	BALLS	MINS	4S	6S
DL Amiss	c Jenner b Thomson	7	31	42	1	–
BW Luckhurst	c Marsh b Thomson	1	27	30	–	–
JH Edrich	c IM Chappell b Thomson	48	147	209	4	–
*MH Denness	lbw b Walker	6	20	32	1	–
KWR Fletcher	b Lillee	17	40	31	2	–
AW Greig	c Marsh b Lillee	110	229	296	17	–
+APE Knott	c Jenner b Walker	12	39	53	2	–
P Lever	c IM Chappell b Walker	4	15	11	–	–
DL Underwood	c Redpath b Walters	25	53	75	3	–
RGD Willis	not out	13	35	47	2	–
M Hendrick	c Redpath b Walker	4	17	24	1	–
Extras	(5 b, 2 lb, 8 nb, 3 w)	18				
Total	(all out, 432 minutes, 80.5 overs)	265				

Fall of wickets: 1-9 (Luckhurst), 2-10 (Amiss), 3-33 (Denness), 4-57 (Fletcher), 5-130 (Edrich), 6-162 (Knott), 7-168 (Lever), 8-226 (Underwood), 9-248 (Greig), 10-265 (Hendrick, 80.5 ov)

Australia bowling	OVERS	MDNS	RUNS	WKTS	WIDES	NO-BALLS
Lillee	23	6	73	2	–	–
Thomson	21	5	59	3	–	–
Walker	24.5	2	73	4	–	–
Walters	6	1	18	1	–	–
Jenner	6	1	24	0	–	–

Australia second innings		RUNS	BALLS	MINS	4S	6S
IR Redpath	b Willis	25	125	163	2	–
WJ Edwards	c Knott b Willis	5	29	36	–	–
*IM Chappell	c Fletcher b Underwood	11	27	40	2	–
GS Chappell	b Underwood	71	202	255	7	–
R Edwards	c Knott b Willis	53	152	200	4	–
KD Walters	not out	62	96	126	9	–
+RW Marsh	not out	46	57	96	5	1
TJ Jenner	did not bat					
DK Lillee	did not bat					
MHN Walker	did not bat					
JR Thomson	did not bat					
Extras	(1 b, 7 lb, 6 nb, 1 w)	15				
Total	(5 wickets, declared, 463 minutes, 85 overs)	288				

Fall of wickets: 1-15 (WJ Edwards), 2-39 (IM Chappell), 3-59 (Redpath), 4-173 (GS Chappell), 5-190 (R Edwards)

England bowling	OVERS	MDNS	RUNS	WKTS	WIDES	NO-BALLS
Willis	15	3	45	3	–	–
Lever	18	4	58	0	–	–
Hendrick	13	2	47	0	–	–
Underwood	26	6	63	2	–	–
Greig	13	2	60	0	–	–

England second innings		RUNS	BALLS	MINS	4S	6S
DL Amiss	c Walters b Thomson	25	69	95	2	–
BW Luckhurst	c IM Chappell b Lillee	3	21	38	–	–
JH Edrich	b Thomson	6	28	43	1	–
*MH Denness	c Walters b Thomson	27	46	61	4	–
KWR Fletcher	c GS Chappell b Jenner	19	56	58	1	–
AW Greig	b Thomson	2	7	10	–	–
+APE Knott	b Thomson	19	94	119	3	–
P Lever	c Redpath b Lillee	14	32	39	2	–
DL Underwood	c Walker b Jenner	30	70	67	6	–
RGD Willis	not out	3	20	21	–	–
M Hendrick	b Thomson	0	16	15	–	–
Extras	(8 b, 3 lb, 5 nb, 2 w)	18				
Total	(all out, 291 minutes, 56.5 overs)	166				

Fall of wickets: 1-18 (Luckhurst), 2-40 (Edrich), 3-44 (Amiss), 4-92 (Denness), 5-94 (Fletcher), 6-94 (Greig), 7-115 (Lever), 8-162 (Underwood), 9-163 (Knott), 10-166 (Hendrick, 56.5 ov)

Australia bowling	OVERS	MDNS	RUNS	WKTS	WIDES	NO-BALLS
Lillee	12	2	25	2	–	–
Thomson	17.5	3	46	6	–	–
Walker	9	4	32	0	–	–
Jenner	16	5	45	2	–	–
Walters	2	2	0	0	–	–

APPENDIX 1

8. AUSTRALIA IN BRITISH ISLES 1981 (3RD TEST)

Venue	Headingley, Leeds on 16, 17, 18, 20, 21 July 1981 (5-day match)
Balls per over	6
Toss	Australia won the toss and decided to bat
Result	England won by 18 runs
Umpires	DGL Evans, BJ Meyer
Close of play day 1	Australia (1) 203–3 (Hughes 24★, Bright 1★)
Close of play day 2	England (1) 7–0 (Gooch 2★, Boycott 0★)
Close of play day 3	England (2) 6–1 (Boycott 0★, Brearley 4★)
Close of play day 4	England (2) 351–9 (Botham 145★, Willis 1★)
Man of the Match	IT Botham

Australia first innings		RUNS	BALLS	MINS	4S	6S
J Dyson	b Dilley	102	234	294	14	–
GM Wood	lbw b Botham	34	55	71	4	–
TM Chappell	c Taylor b Willey	27	135	161	2	–
★KJ Hughes	c and b Botham	89	208	270	8	–
RJ Bright	b Dilley	7	36	48	1	–
GN Yallop	c Taylor b Botham	58	167	208	5	–
AR Border	lbw b Botham	8	20	35	1	–
+RW Marsh	b Botham	28	50	65	5	–
GF Lawson	c Taylor b Botham	13	35	45	2	–
DK Lillee	not out	3	6	8	–	–
TM Alderman	not out	0	0	1	–	–
Extras	(4 b, 13 lb, 12 nb, 3 w)	32				
Total	(9 wickets, declared, 155.2 overs)	401				

Fall of wickets: 1-55 (Wood), 2-149 (Chappell), 3-196 (Dyson), 4-220 (Bright), 5-332 (Hughes), 6-354 (Border), 7-357 (Yallop), 8-396 (Lawson), 9-401 (Marsh)

England bowling	OVERS	MDNS	RUNS	WKTS	WIDES	NO-BALLS
Willis	30	8	72	0	–	–
Old	43	14	91	0	–	–
Dilley	27	4	78	2	–	–
Botham	39.2	11	95	6	–	–
Willey	13	2	31	1	–	–
Boycott	3	2	2	0	–	–

England first innings		RUNS	BALLS	MINS	4S	6S
GA Gooch	lbw b Alderman	2	7	17	–	–
G Boycott	b Lawson	12	58	89	–	–
*JM Brearley	c Marsh b Alderman	10	53	64	–	–
DI Gower	c Marsh b Lawson	24	50	58	3	–
MW Gatting	lbw b Lillee	15	29	58	2	–
P Willey	b Lawson	8	22	29	–	–
IT Botham	c Marsh b Lillee	50	54	80	8	–
+RW Taylor	c Marsh b Lillee	5	23	36	1	–
GR Dilley	c and b Lillee	13	17	30	2	–
CM Old	c Border b Alderman	0	4	4	–	–
RGD Willis	not out	1	4	5	–	–
Extras	(6 b, 11 lb, 11 nb, 6 w)	34				
Total	(all out, 50.5 overs)	174				

Fall of wickets: 1-12 (Gooch), 2-40 (Brearley), 3-42 (Boycott), 4-84 (Gower), 5-87 (Gatting), 6-112 (Willey), 7-148 (Taylor), 8-166 (Botham), 9-167 (Old), 10-174 (Dilley, 50.5 ov)

Australia bowling	OVERS	MDNS	RUNS	WKTS	WIDES	NO-BALLS
Lillee	18.5	7	49	4	–	–
Alderman	19	4	59	3	–	–
Lawson	13	3	32	3	–	–

England second innings (following on)		RUNS	BALLS	MINS	4S	6S
GA Gooch	c Alderman b Lillee	0	3	2	–	–
G Boycott	lbw b Alderman	46	141	215	1	–
*JM Brearley	c Alderman b Lillee	14	29	33	3	–
DI Gower	c Border b Alderman	9	22	36	1	–
MW Gatting	lbw b Alderman	1	10	10	–	–
P Willey	c Dyson b Lillee	33	56	84	6	–
IT Botham	not out	149	148	219	27	1
+RW Taylor	c Bright b Alderman	1	9	9	–	–
GR Dilley	b Alderman	56	75	80	9	–
CM Old	b Lawson	29	31	54	6	–
RGD Willis	c Border b Alderman	2	9	31	–	–
Extras	(5 b, 3 lb, 5 nb, 3 w)	16				
Total	(all out, 87.3 overs)	356				

Fall of wickets: 1-0 (Gooch), 2-18 (Brearley), 3-37 (Gower), 4-41 (Gatting), 5-105 (Willey), 6-133 (Boycott), 7-135 (Taylor), 8-252 (Dilley), 9-319 (Old), 10-356 (Willis, 87.3 ov)

Australia bowling	OVERS	MDNS	RUNS	WKTS	WIDES	NO-BALLS
Lillee	25	6	94	3	–	–
Alderman	35.3	6	135	6	–	–
Lawson	23	4	96	1	–	–
Bright	4	0	15	0	–	–

Australia second innings		RUNS	BALLS	MINS	4S	6S
GM Wood	c Taylor b Botham	10	10	9	2	–
J Dyson	c Taylor b Willis	34	83	119	3	–
TM Chappell	c Taylor b Willis	8	56	68	–	–
*KJ Hughes	c Botham b Willis	0	9	14	–	–
GN Yallop	c Gatting b Willis	0	3	2	–	–
AR Border	b Old	0	8	13	–	–
+RW Marsh	c Dilley b Willis	4	9	18	–	–
RJ Bright	b Willis	19	32	49	2	–
GF Lawson	c Taylor b Willis	1	2	2	–	–
DK Lillee	c Gatting b Willis	17	15	22	3	–
TM Alderman	not out	0	5	6	–	–
Extras	(3 lb, 14 nb, 1 w)	18				
Total	(all out, 36.1 overs)	111				

Fall of wickets: 1-13 (Wood), 2-56 (Chappell), 3-58 (Hughes), 4-58 (Yallop), 5-65 (Border), 6-68 (Dyson), 7-74 (Marsh), 8-75 (Lawson), 9-110 (Lillee), 10-111 (Bright, 36.1 ov)

England bowling	OVERS	MDNS	RUNS	WKTS	WIDES	NO-BALLS
Botham	7	3	14	1	–	–
Dilley	2	0	11	0	–	–
Willis	15.1	3	43	8	–	–
Old	9	1	21	1	–	–
Willey	3	1	4	0	–	–

9. AUSTRALIA IN BRITISH ISLES 2005 (2ND TEST)

Venue	Edgbaston, Birmingham on 4, 5, 6, 7 August 2005
	(5-day match)
Balls per over	6
Toss	Australia won the toss and decided to field
Result	England won by 2 runs
Umpires	BF Bowden, RE Koertzen
TV umpire	JW Lloyds
Referee	RS Madugalle
Reserve Umpire	AA Jones
Close of play day 1	England (1) 407 all out
Close of play day 2	England (2) 25–1 (Trescothick 19★, Hoggard 0★; 7 overs)
Close of play day 3	Australia (2) 175–8 (Warne 20★; 43.4 overs)
Man of the Match	A Flintoff

England first innings		RUNS	BALLS	MINS	4S	6S
ME Trescothick	c Gilchrist b Kasprowicz	90	102	143	15	2
AJ Strauss	b Warne	48	76	113	10	–
★MP Vaughan	c Lee b Gillespie	24	41	54	3	–
IR Bell	c Gilchrist b Kasprowicz	6	3	2	1	–
KP Pietersen	c Katich b Lee	71	76	152	10	1
A Flintoff	c Gilchrist b Gillespie	68	62	74	6	5
+GO Jones	c Gilchrist b Kasprowicz	1	15	14	–	–
AF Giles	lbw b Warne	23	30	34	4	–
MJ Hoggard	lbw b Warne	16	49	62	2	–
SJ Harmison	b Warne	17	11	16	2	1
SP Jones	not out	19	24	39	1	1
Extras	(9 lb, 14 nb, 1 w)	24				
Total	(all out, 356 minutes,					
	79.2 overs)	407				

Fall of wickets: 1-112 (Strauss, 25.3 ov), 2-164 (Trescothick, 32.3 ov), 3-170 (Bell, 32.6 ov), 4-187 (Vaughan, 36.6 ov), 5-290 (Flintoff, 54.3 ov), 6-293 (GO Jones, 57.4 ov), 7-342 (Giles, 65.1 ov), 8-348 (Pietersen, 66.3 ov), 9-375 (Harmison, 69.4 ov), 10-407 (Hoggard, 79.2 ov)

Australia bowling	OVERS	MDNS	RUNS	WKTS	WIDES	NO-BALLS
Lee	17	1	111	1	1	3
Gillespie	22	3	91	2	–	3
Kasprowicz	15	3	80	3	–	8
Warne	25.2	4	116	4	–	–

Australia first innings		RUNS	BALLS	MINS	4S	6S
JL Langer	lbw b SP Jones	82	154	276	7	-
ML Hayden	c Strauss b Hoggard	0	1	5	-	-
*RT Ponting	c Vaughan b Giles	61	76	87	12	-
DR Martyn	run out (Vaughan)	20	18	23	4	-
MJ Clarke	c GO Jones b Giles	40	68	85	7	-
SM Katich	c GO Jones b Flintoff	4	18	22	1	-
+AC Gilchrist	not out	49	69	120	4	-
SK Warne	b Giles	8	14	14	2	-
B Lee	c Flintoff b SP Jones	6	10	14	1	-
JN Gillespie	lbw b Flintoff	7	37	36	1	-
MS Kasprowicz	lbw b Flintoff	0	1	1	-	-
Extras	(13 b, 7 lb, 10 nb, 1 w)	31				
Total	(all out, 346 minutes, 76 overs)	308				

Fall of wickets: 1-0 (Hayden, 1.1 ov), 2-88 (Ponting, 19.5 ov), 3-118 (Martyn, 24.5 ov), 4-194 (Clarke, 44.2 ov), 5-208 (Katich, 49.4 ov), 6-262 (Langer, 61.3 ov), 7-273 (Warne, 64.5 ov), 8-282 (Lee, 67.1 ov), 9-308 (Gillespie, 75.5 ov), 10-308 (Kasprowicz, 76 ov)

England bowling	OVERS	MDNS	RUNS	WKTS	WIDES	NO-BALLS
Harmison	11	1	48	0	-	2
Hoggard	8	0	41	1	-	4
SP Jones	16	2	69	2	1	1
Flintoff	15	1	52	3	-	3
Giles	26	2	78	3	-	-

England second innings		RUNS	BALLS	MINS	4S	6S
ME Trescothick	c Gilchrist b Lee	21	38	51	4	-
AJ Strauss	b Warne	6	12	28	1	-
MJ Hoggard	c Hayden b Lee	1	27	35	-	-
*MP Vaughan	b Lee	1	2	2	-	-
IR Bell	c Gilchrist b Warne	21	43	69	2	-
KP Pietersen	c Gilchrist b Warne	20	35	50	-	2
A Flintoff	b Warne	73	86	133	6	4
+GO Jones	c Ponting b Lee	9	19	33	1	-
AF Giles	c Hayden b Warne	8	36	44	-	-
SJ Harmison	c Ponting b Warne	0	1	2	-	-
SP Jones	not out	12	23	42	3	-
Extras	(1 lb, 9 nb)	10				
Total	(all out, 249 minutes, 52.1 overs)	182				

Fall of wickets: 1-25 (Strauss, 6.2 ov), 2-27 (Trescothick, 11.2 ov), 3-29 (Vaughan, 11.5 ov), 4-31 (Hoggard, 13.5 ov), 5-72 (Pietersen, 24.6 ov), 6-75 (Bell, 26.5 ov), 7-101 (GO Jones, 33.6 ov), 8-131 (Giles, 44.3 ov), 9-131 (Harmison, 44.4 ov), 10-182 (Flintoff, 52.1 ov)

Australia bowling	OVERS	MDNS	RUNS	WKTS	WIDES	NO-BALLS
Lee	18	1	82	4	–	5
Gillespie	8	0	24	0	–	1
Kasprowicz	3	0	29	0	–	3
Warne	23.1	7	46	6	–	–

Australia second innings		RUNS	BALLS	MINS	4S	6S
JL Langer	b Flintoff	28	47	54	4	–
ML Hayden	c Trescothick b SP Jones	31	64	106	4	–
*RT Ponting	c GO Jones b Flintoff	0 5	4	–	–	–
DR Martyn	c Bell b Hoggard	28	36	64	5	–
MJ Clarke	b Harmison	30	57	101	5	–
SM Katich	c Trescothick b Giles	16	21	27	3	–
+AC Gilchrist	c Flintoff b Giles	1	4	8	–	–
JN Gillespie	lbw b Flintoff	0	2	4	–	–
SK Warne	hit wkt b Flintoff	42	59	79	4	2
B Lee	not out	43	75	99	5	–
MS Kasprowicz	c GO Jones b Harmison	20	31	60	3	–
Extras	(13 b, 8 lb, 18 nb, 1 w)	40				
Total	(all out, 301 minutes, 64.3 overs)	279				

Fall of wickets: 1-47 (Langer, 12.2 ov), 2-48 (Ponting, 12.6 ov), 3-82 (Hayden, 22.5 ov), 4-107 (Martyn, 26.1 ov), 5-134 (Katich, 31.6 ov), 6-136 (Gilchrist, 33.5 ov), 7-137 (Gillespie, 34.2 ov), 8-175 (Clarke, 43.4 ov), 9-220 (Warne, 52.1 ov), 10-279 (Kasprowicz, 64.3 ov)

England bowling	OVERS	MDNS	RUNS	WKTS	WIDES	NO-BALLS
Harmison	17.3	3	62	2	1	1
Hoggard	5	0	26	1	–	–
Giles	15	3	68	2	–	–
Flintoff	22	3	79	4	–	13
SP Jones	5	1	23	1	–	–

10. ENGLAND IN AUSTRALIA 2006–7 (2ND TEST)

Venue	Adelaide Oval, Adelaide on 1, 2, 3, 4, 5 December 2006 (5-day match)
Balls per over	6
Toss	England won the toss and decided to bat
Result	Australia won by 6 wickets
Umpires	SA Bucknor, RE Koertzen
TV umpire	SJ Davis
Referee	JJ Crowe
Reserve Umpire	AD Willoughby
Close of play day 1	England (1) 266–3 (Collingwood 98★, Pietersen 60★; 90 overs)
Close of play day 2	Australia (1) 28–1 (Hayden 12★, Ponting 11★; 9 overs)
Close of play day 3	Australia (1) 312–5 (Clarke 30★, Gilchrist 13★; 97 overs)
Close of play day 4	England (2) 59–1 (Strauss 31★, Bell 18★; 19 overs)
Man of the Match	RT Ponting

England first innings		RUNS	BALLS	MINS	4S	6S
AJ Strauss	c Martyn b Clark	14	44	63	–	–
AN Cook	c Gilchrist b Clark	27	57	90	2	–
IR Bell	c and b Lee	60	148	188	6	–
PD Collingwood	c Gilchrist b Clark	206	392	516	16	–
KP Pietersen	run out (Ponting)	158	257	379	15	1
★A Flintoff	not out	38	67	100	2	1
+GO Jones	c Martyn b Warne	1	7	10	–	–
AF Giles	not out	27	44	63	4	–
MJ Hoggard	did not bat					
SJ Harmison	did not bat					
JM Anderson	did not bat					
Extras	(10 lb, 8 nb, 2 w)	20				
Total	(6 wickets, declared, 707 minutes, 168 overs)	551				

Fall of wickets: 1-32 (Strauss, 14.3 ov), 2-45 (Cook, 20.5 ov), 3-158 (Bell, 61.4 ov), 4-468 (Collingwood, 145.5 ov), 5-489 (Pietersen, 151.6 ov), 6-491 (Jones, 154.2 ov)

Australia bowling	OVERS	MDNS	RUNS	WKTS	WIDES	NO-BALLS
Lee	34	1	139	1	1	8
McGrath	30	5	107	0	–	–
Clark	34	6	75	3	–	–
Warne	53	9	167	1	1	–
Clarke	17	2	53	0	–	–

Australia first innings

Australia first innings		RUNS	BALLS	MINS	4S	6S
JL Langer	c Pietersen b Flintoff	4	8	9	1	–
ML Hayden	c Jones b Hoggard	12	30	58	1	–
*RT Ponting	c Jones b Hoggard	142	245	353	12	–
DR Martyn	c Bell b Hoggard	11	33	42	1	–
MEK Hussey	b Hoggard	91	212	299	7	1
MJ Clarke	c Giles b Hoggard	124	224	319	10	–
+AC Gilchrist	c Bell b Giles	64	79	112	8	–
SK Warne	lbw b Hoggard	43	108	157	4	–
B Lee	not out	7	33	47	–	–
SR Clark	b Hoggard	0	7	9	–	–
GD McGrath	c Jones b Anderson	1	21	25	–	–
Extras	(4 b, 2 lb, 7 nb, 1 w)	14				
Total	(all out, 718 minutes, 165.3 overs)	513				

Fall of wickets: 1-8 (Langer, 1.6 ov), 2-35 (Hayden, 12.6 ov), 3-65 (Martyn, 22.2 ov), 4-257 (Ponting, 82.6 ov), 5-286 (Hussey, 90.4 ov), 6-384 (Gilchrist, 114.4 ov), 7-502 (Warne, 153.5 ov), 8-505 (Clarke, 157.1 ov), 9-507 (Clark, 159.2 ov), 10-513 (McGrath, 165.3 ov)

England bowling

England bowling	OVERS	MDNS	RUNS	WKTS	WIDES	NO-BALLS
Hoggard	42	6	109	7	–	–
Flintoff	26	5	82	1	–	5
Harmison	25	5	96	0	1	2
Anderson	21.3	3	85	1	–	–
Giles	42	7	103	1	–	–
Pietersen	9	0	32	0	–	–

England second innings

England second innings		RUNS	BALLS	MINS	4S	6S
AJ Strauss	c Hussey b Warne	34	79	124	3	–
AN Cook	c Gilchrist b Clark	9	35	47	1	–
IR Bell	run out (Clarke->Warne)	26	73	85	2	–
PD Collingwood	not out	22	119	198	2	–
KP Pietersen	b Warne	2	5	8	–	–
*A Flintoff	c Gilchrist b Lee	2	24	26	–	–
+GO Jones	c Hayden b Lee	10	24	42	1	–
AF Giles	c Hayden b Warne	0	8	14	–	–
MJ Hoggard	b Warne	4	24	26	–	–
SJ Harmison	lbw b McGrath	8	21	25	–	–
JM Anderson	lbw b McGrath	1	28	41	–	–
Extras	(3 b, 5 lb, 2 nb, 1 w)	11				
Total	(all out, 324 mins, 73 overs)	129				

Fall of wickets: 1-31 (Cook, 10.6 ov), 2-69 (Strauss, 29.6 ov), 3-70 (Bell, 31.6 ov), 4-73 (Pietersen, 33.1 ov), 5-77 (Flintoff, 38.6 ov), 6-94 (Jones, 48.4 ov), 7-97 (Giles, 51.6 ov), 8-105 (Hoggard, 57.5 ov), 9-119 (Harmison, 62.6 ov), 10-129 (Anderson, 73 ov)

Australia bowling	OVERS	MDNS	RUNS	WKTS	WIDES	NO-BALLS
Lee	18	3	35	2	–	2
McGrath	10	6	15	2	1	–
Warne	32	12	49	4	–	–
Clark	13	4	22	1	–	–

AUSTRALIA SECOND INNINGS		RUNS	BALLS	MINS	4S	6S
JL Langer	c Bell b Hoggard	7	8	13	1	–
ML Hayden	c Collingwood b Flintoff	18	17	32	2	–
*RT Ponting	c Strauss b Giles	49	65	95	5	–
MEK Hussey	not out	61	66	128	5	–
DR Martyn	c Strauss b Flintoff	5	4	4	1	–
MJ Clarke	not out	21	39	46	–	–
+AC Gilchrist	did not bat					
SK Warne	did not bat					
B Lee	did not bat					
SR Clark	did not bat					
GD McGrath	did not bat					
Extras	(2 b, 2 lb, 2 nb, 1 w)	7				
Total	(4 wickets, 161 minutes, 32.5 overs)	168				

Fall of wickets: 1-14 (Langer, 2.2 ov), 2-33 (Hayden, 5.4 ov), 3-116 (Ponting, 21.4 ov), 4-121 (Martyn, 22.2 ov)

England bowling	OVERS	MDNS	RUNS	WKTS	WIDES	NO-BALLS
Hoggard	4	0	29	1	–	–
Flintoff	9	0	44	2	–	2
Giles	10	0	46	1	–	–
Harmison	4	0	15	0	1	–
Anderson	3.5	0	23	0	–	–
Pietersen	2	0	7	0	–	–

ASHES TEST MATCH RESULTS

SEASON	HOST TEAM	AUSTRALIA WON	ENGLAND WON	DRAWS (INC. ABANS)	SERIES RESULT (A-E)	URN HOLDERS AFTER SERIES
1882–3	Australia	Melbourne 9w	Melbourne inns & 27r Sydney 69r		1-2	England
1884	England		Lord's inns & 5r	Old Trafford, The Oval	0-1	England
1884–5	Australia	Sydney 6r Sydney 8w	Adelaide 8w Melbourne 10w Melbourne inns & 98r		2-3	England
1886	England		Old Trafford 4w Lord's inns & 106 r The Oval inns & 217r		0-3	England
1886–7	Australia		Sydney 13r Sydney 71r		0-2	England
1887–8	Australia		Sydney 126r		0-1	England
1888	England	Lord's 61r	The Oval inns & 137r Old Trafford inns & 21r		1-2	England
1890	England		Lord's 7w The Oval 2w	Old Trafford (aban)	0-2	England
1891–2	Australia	Melbourne 54r Sydney 72r	Adelaide inns & 230 runs		2-1	Australia
1893	England		The Oval inns & 43r	Lord's, Old Trafford	0-1	England
1894–5	Australia	Adelaide 382r Sydney inns & 147 r	Sydney 10r Melbourne 94r Melbourne 6w		2-3	England
1896	England	Old Trafford 3w	Lord's 6w The Oval 66r		1-2	England
1897–8	Australia	Melbourne inns & 55r Adelaide inns & 13r Melbourne 8w Sydney 6w	Sydney 9w		4-1	Australia
1899	England	Lord's 10w		Trent Bridge, Headingley, Old Trafford, The Oval	1-0	Australia
1901–2	Australia	Melbourne 229r Adelaide 4w Sydney 7w Melbourne 32r	Sydney inns & 124r		4-1	Australia
1902	England	Sheffield 143r Old Trafford 3r	The Oval 1w	Edgbaston, Lord's	2-1	Australia
1903–4	Australia	Adelaide 216r Melbourne 218r	Sydney 5w Melbourne 185r Sydney 157r		2-3	England
1905	England		Trent Bridge 213r Old Trafford inns & 180r	Lord's, Headingley, The Oval	0-2	England

SEASON	HOST TEAM	AUSTRALIA WON	ENGLAND WON	DRAWS (INC. ABANS)	SERIES RESULT (A-E)	URN HOLDERS AFTER SERIES
1907–8	Australia	Sydney 2w Adelaide 245r Melbourne 308r Sydney 49r	Melbourne 1w		4-1	Australia
1909	England	Lord's 9w Headingley 126r	Edgbaston 10w	Old Trafford, The Oval	2-1	Australia
1911–12	Australia	Sydney 146r	Melbourne 8w Adelaide 7w Melbourne inns & 225 runs Sydney 70r		1-4	England
1912	England		The Oval 244r	Lord's, Old Trafford,	0-1	England
1920–21	Australia	Sydney 377r Melbourne inns & 91 runs Adelaide 119r Melbourne 8w Sydney 9w			5-0	Australia
1921	England	Trent Bridge 10w Lord's 8w Headingley 219r		Old Trafford, The Oval	3-0	Australia
1924–25	Australia	Sydney 193r Melbourne 81r Adelaide 11r Sydney 307r	Melbourne inns & 29r		4-1	Australia
1926	England		The Oval 289r	Trent Bridge, Lord's, Headingley, Old Trafford	0-1	England
1928–9	Australia	Melbourne 5w	Brisbane 675r Sydney 8w Melbourne 3w Adelaide 12r		1-4	England
1930	England	Lord's 7w The Oval inns & 39r	Trent Bridge 93r	Headingley, Old Trafford	2-1	Australia
1932–3	Australia	Melbourne 111r	Sydney 10w Adelaide 338r Brisbane 6w Sydney 8w		1-4	England
1934	England	Trent Bridge 238r The Oval 562r	Lord's inns & 38r	Old Trafford, Headingley,	2-1	Australia
1936–7	Australia	Melbourne 365r Adelaide 148r Melbourne inns & 200r	Brisbane 322r Sydney inns & 22r		3-2	Australia
1938	England	Headingley 5w	The Oval	Trent Bridge,	1-1	Australia

SEASON	HOST TEAM	AUSTRALIA WON	ENGLAND WON	DRAWS (INC. ABANS)	SERIES RESULT (A-E)	URN HOLDERS AFTER SERIES
			inns & 579r	Lord's, Old Trafford (aban)		
1946–7	Australia	Brisbane inns & 332r Sydney inns & 33r Sydney 5w		Melbourne, Adelaide	3-0	Australia
1948	England	Trent Bridge 8w Lord's 409r Headingley 7w The Oval inns & 149r		Old Trafford	4-0	Australia
1950–1	Australia	Brisbane 70r Melbourne 28r Sydney inns & 13r Adelaide 274r	Melbourne 8w		4-1	Australia
1953	England		The Oval 8w	Trent Bridge, Lord's, Old Trafford, Headingley	0-1	England
1954–5	Australia	Brisbane inns & 154r	Sydney 38r Melbourne 128r Adelaide 5w	Sydney	1-3	England
1956	England	Lord's 185r	Headingley inns & 42r Old Trafford inns & 170r	Trent Bridge, The Oval	1-2	England
1958–9	Australia	Brisbane 8w Melbourne 8w Adelaide 10w Melbourne 9w		Sydney	4-0	Australia
1961	England	Lord's 5w Old Trafford 54r	Headingley 8w	Edgbaston, The Oval	2-1	Australia
1962–3	Australia	Sydney 8w	Melbourne 7w	Brisbane, Adelaide, Sydney	1-1	Australia
1964	England	Headingley 7w		Trent Bridge, Lord's, Old Trafford, The Oval	1-0	Australia
1965–6	Australia	Adelaide inns & 9r	Sydney inns & 93r	Brisbane, Melbourne, Melbourne	1-1	Australia

SEASON	HOST TEAM	AUSTRALIA WON	ENGLAND WON	DRAWS (INC. ABANS)	SERIES RESULT (A-E)	URN HOLDERS AFTER SERIES
1968	England	Old Trafford 159r	The Oval 226r	Lord's, Edgbaston, Headingley	1-1	Australia
1970–1	Australia		Sydney 299r Sydney 62r	Brisbane, Perth, Melbourne(aban), Melbourne, Adelaide	0-2	England
1972	England	Lord's 8w The Oval 5w	Old Trafford 89r Headingley 9w	Trent Bridge	2-2	England
1974–5	Australia	Brisbane 166r Perth 9w Sydney 171r Adelaide 163r	Melbourne inns & 4r	Melbourne	4-1	Australia
1975	England	Edgbaston inns 85 r		Lord's, Headingley, The Oval	1-0	Australia
1977	England		Old Trafford 9w Trent Bridge 7w Headingley inns & 85r	Lord's, The Oval	0-3	England
1978–9	Australia	Melbourne 103r	Brisbane 7w Perth 166r Sydney 93r Adelaide 205r Sydney 9w		1-5	England
1981	England	Trent Bridge 4w	Headingley 18r Edgbaston 29r Old Trafford 103r	Lord's, The Oval	1-3	England
1982–3	Australia	Brisbane 7w Adelaide 8w	Melbourne 3r	Perth, Sydney	2-1	Australia
1985	England	Lord's 4w	Headingley 5w Edgbaston inns & 118r The Oval inns & 94r	Trent Bridge, Old Trafford	1-3	England
1986–7	Australia	Sydney 55r	Brisbane 7w Melbourne inns & 14r	Perth, Adelaide	1-2	England
1989	England	Headingley 210r Lord's 6w Old Trafford 9w Trent Bridge inns & 180r		Edgbaston, The Oval	4-0	Australia
1990–1	Australia	Brisbane 10w Melbourne 8w Perth 9w		Sydney, Adelaide	3-0	Australia
1993	England	Old Trafford 179r Lord's inns & 62r Headingley inns & 148r	The Oval 161r	Trent Bridge	4-1	Australia

SEASON	HOST TEAM	AUSTRALIA WON	ENGLAND WON	DRAWS (INC. ABANS)	SERIES RESULT (A-E)	URN HOLDERS AFTER SERIES
		Edgbaston 8w				
1994–5	Australia	Brisbane 184r Melbourne 295r Perth 329r	Adelaide 106r	Sydney	3-1	Australia
1997	England	Old Trafford 268r Headingley inns & 61r Trent Bridge 264r	Edgbaston 9w The Oval 19r	Lord's	3-2	Australia
1998–9	Australia	Perth 7w Adelaide 205r Sydney 98r	Melbourne 12r	Brisbane	3-1	Australia
2001	England	Edgbaston inns & 118r Lord's 8w Trent Bridge 7w The Oval inns & 25r	Headingley 6w		4-1	Australia
2002–3	Australia	Brisbane 384r Adelaide inns & 51r Perth inns & 48r Melbourne 5w	Sydney 225r		4-1	Australia
2005	England	Lord's 239r	Edgbaston 2r Trent Bridge 3w	Old Trafford, The Oval	1-2	England
2006–7	Australia	Brisbane 277r Adelaide 6w Perth 206r Melbourne inns & 99r Sydney 10w			5-0	Australia
2009	England	Headingley inns & 80r	Lord's 115r The Oval 197r	Cardiff, Edgbaston	1-2	England
2010–11	Australia	Perth 267r	Adelaide inns & 71r Melbourne inns & 157r Sydney inns & 83r	Brisbane	1-3	England

OVERALL		MATCHES	AUST WON	ENG WON	DRAW
Total		310	123	100	87

APPENDIX 3

ASHES STATISTICS AND RECORDS

TEAM RECORDS

Largest winning margin

Inns & 579 runs	by England	at The Oval, 1938
Inns & 332 runs	by Australia	at Brisbane, 1946–7
Inns & 230 runs	by England	at Adelaide, 1891–2
Inns & 225 runs	by England	at Melbourne, 1911–12
Inns & 217 runs	by England	at The Oval, 1886
Inns & 200 runs	by Australia	at Melbourne, 1936–7

Smallest winning margin

2 runs	by England	at Edgbaston, 2005
3 runs	by Australia	at Old Trafford, 1902
	by England	at Melbourne, 1982–3
6 runs	by Australia	at Sydney, 1884–5
10 runs	by England	at Sydney, 1894–5
11 runs	by Australia	at Adelaide, 1924–5

Highest team total

903/7d	by England	at The Oval, 1938
729/6d	by Australia	at Lord's, 1930
701	by Australia	at The Oval, 1934
695	by Australia	at The Oval, 1930
674/6d	by Australia	at Cardiff, 2009
659/8d	by Australia	at Sydney, 1946–7

Lowest team total

36	by Australia	at Edgbaston, 1902
42	by Australia	at Sydney, 1887–8
44	by Australia	at The Oval, 1896
45	by England	at Sydney, 1886–7
52	by England	at The Oval, 1948
53	by England	at Lord's, 1888
53	by Australia	at Lord's 1896

BATTING RECORDS

Highest individual innings in an Ashes Test

364	L Hutton, for England	at The Oval, 1938
334	DG Bradman, for Australia	at Headingley, 1930

311	RB Simpson, for Australia	at Old Trafford, 1964
307	RM Cowper, for Australia	at Melbourne, 1965–6
304	DG Bradman, for Australia	at Headingley, 1934
287	RE Foster, for England	at Sydney, 1902–3

Most hundreds in Ashes Tests

19	DG Bradman, for Australia
12	JB Hobbs, for England
10	SR Waugh, for Australia
9	WR Hammond, for England
	DI Gower, for England

Most runs in Ashes Tests

3222	AR Border, for Australia
3037	DI Gower, for England
3173	SR Waugh, for Australia
5028	DG Bradman, for Australia
3636	JB Hobbs, for England

Most runs in an Ashes series

974	DG Bradman, for Australia	1930
905	WR Hammond, for England	1928–29
839	MA Taylor, for Australia	1989
810	DG Bradman, for Australia	1936–37
766	AN Cook, for England	2010–11
758	DG Bradman, for Australia	1934

BOWLING RECORDS

Best bowling figures in an innings

JC Laker	51.2-23-53-10, for England	at Old Trafford, 1956
JC Laker	16.4-4-37-9, for England	at Old Trafford, 1956
AA Mailey	47.0-8-121-9, for Australia	at Melbourne, 1920–21
FJ Laver	18.2-7-31-8, for Australia	at Old Trafford, 1909
GA Lohmann	27.1-12-35-8, for England	at Sydney, 1886–7
GD McGrath	20.3-8-38-8, for Australia	at Lord's, 1997

Best bowling figures in a match

JC Laker	68-27-90-19, for England	at Old Trafford, 1956
RAL Massie	60.1-16-137-16, for Australia	at Lord's, 1972
H Verity	58.3-23-104-15, for England	at Lord's, 1934
W Rhodes	30.2-3-124-15, for England	at Melbourne, 1903–4
AV Bedser	55.5-23-99-14, for England	at Trent Bridge, 1953

Most wickets in Ashes Tests

195	SK Warne, for Australia	
157	GD McGrath, for Australia	
128	DK Lillee, for Australia	
128	IT Botham, for England	
123	RGD Willis, for England	
141	H Trumble, for Australia	

Most wickets in an Ashes series

46	JC Laker, for England	1956
42	TM Alderman, for Australia	1981
41	RM Hogg, for Australia	1978–9
	TM Alderman, for Australia	1989
40	SK Warne, for Australia	2005
39	AV Bedser, for England	1953
39	DK Lillee, for Australia	1981

FIELDING RECORDS

Most wicket-keeping dismissals in Ashes Tests

131	RW Marsh, for Australia
135	IA Healy, for Australia
101	APE Knott, for England
96	AC Gilchrist, for Australia
90	WAS Oldfield, for Australia
84	AFA Lilley, for England

Most wicket-keeping dismissals in an innings in an Ashes Test

6	RW Marsh, for Australia	at Brisbane, 1982–3
	RC Russell, for England	at Melbourne, 1990
	IA Healy, for Australia	at Edgbaston, 1997
	AJ Stewart, for England	at Old Trafford, 1997
	CMW Read, for England	at Melbourne, 2006–7
	CMW Read, for England	at Sydney, 2006–7
	MJ Prior, for England	at Melbourne, 2010–11

Most wicket-keeping dismissals in an Ashes Test

9	GRA Langley, for Australia	at Lord's, 1956
	RW Marsh, for Australia	at Brisbane, 1982–3
	IA Healy, for Australia	at Brisbane, 1994–5
	AC Gilchrist, for Australia	at Sydney, 2006–07

Most wicket-keeping dismissals in an Ashes series

28	RW Marsh, for Australia	1982–3
27	IA Healy, for Australia	1997
26	AC Gilchrist, for Australia	2001
	AC Gilchrist, for Australia	2006–7
	IA Healy, for Australia	1993
25	AC Gilchrist, for Australia	2002–3
25	IA Healy, for Australia	1994–5

Most catches in Ashes Tests

54	IT Botham, for England
51	AR Border, for Australia
48	GS Chappell, for Australia
46	MA Taylor, for Australia
45	H Trumble, for Australia
43	ME Waugh, for Australia
	WR Hammond, for England

Most catches in an Ashes series

15	JM Gregory, for Australia	1920–1
14	GS Chappell, for Australia	1974–5
12	WR Hammond, for England	1934
	LC Braund, for England	1901–2
	AR Border, for Australia	1981
	IT Botham, for England	1981
	AW Greig, for England	1974–5

Record partnerships for each wicket in Ashes Test

1st	329	Geoff Marsh and Mark Taylor for Australia at Trent Bridge, 1989
2nd	451	Bill Ponsford and Don Bradman for Australia at The Oval, 1934
3rd	276	Don Bradman and Lindsay Hassett for Australia at Brisbane, 1946-7
4th	388	Bill Ponsford and Don Bradman for Australia at Headingley, 1934
5th	405	Sid Barnes and Don Bradman for Australia at Sydney, 1946–7
6th	346	Jack Fingleton and Don Bradman for Australia at Melbourne, 1936–7
7th	165	Clem Hill and Hugh Trumble for Australia at Melbourne, 1897–8
8th	243	Roger Hartigan and Clem Hill for Australia at Adelaide, 1907–8
9th	154	Syd Gregory and Jack Blackham for Australia at Sydney, 1894–5
10th	130	Dick Foster and Wilfred Rhodes for England at Sydney, 1903–4

Fastest hundred in Ashes Tests (where recorded by balls faced)

FOR ENGLAND

76	Gilbert Jessop	The Oval	1902
87	Ian Botham	Headingly	1981
109	Matt Prior	Sydney	2010–11
121	Andrew Flintoff	Trent Bridge	2005

122	Ken Barrington	Melbourne	1965–6
124	David Gower	Perth	1986–7
	Kevin Pietersen	The Oval	2005

FOR AUSTRALIA

57	Adam Gilchrist	Perth	2006–7
94	Adam Gilchrist	Sydney	2002–3
113	Ricky Ponting	Headingley	2001
118	Adam Gilchrist	Edgbaston	2001
125	Damien Martyn	Headingley	2001
126	Matthew Hayden	Brisbane	2002–3

Most extras conceded in an innings in an Ashes Test

61	conceded by England	at Trent Bridge, 1989
55	conceded by England	at Lord's, 1981
54	conceded by England	at Headingley, 1973
52	conceded by Australia	at Brisbane, 1982–3
50	conceded by England	at The Oval, 1934
	conceded by Australia	at The Oval, 1985
	conceded by Australia	at The Oval, 1938

Most ducks in Ashes Tests

11	Syd Gregory (Australia)
10	Glenn McGrath (Australia)
	Shane Warne (Australia)
9	Darren Gough (England)
	Dick Lilley (England)
	Johnny Briggs (England)

Most runs conceded in an innings by a bowler in Ashes Tests

87-11-298-1	Chuck Fleetwood-Smith	for Australia	at The Oval, 1938
71-8-204-6	Ian Peebles	for England	at The Oval, 1930
64-14-191-2	Clarrie Grimmett	for Australia	at Sydney, 1928–9
59-9-189-7	Bill O'Reilly	for Australia	at Old Trafford, 1934
43.6-2-186-4	Arthur Mailey	for Australia	at Melbourne, 1924–5
45-4-183-3	John Price	for England	at Old Trafford, 1964

Most games as captain in an Ashes Test

28	Allan Border (Australia)
22	Archie MacLaren (England)
19	Don Bradman (Australia)
19	Ricky Ponting (Australia)
18	Joe Darling (Australia)
16	Ian Chappell (Australia)
16	Mark Taylor (Australia)

Most appearances by an umpire in an Ashes Test

27	Bob Crockett (Australia)
24	Jim Phillips (Australia)
15	George Borwick (Australia)
14	Dickie Bird (England)
14	Steve Bucknor (West Indies)
14	Frank Chester (England)

Most players used in a series

30	England in 1921 (5 Tests)
29	England in 1989 (6 Tests)
28	Australia in 1884–5 (5 Tests)
25	England in 1909 (5 Tests)
24	England in 1899 (5 Tests)
	England in 1993 (6 Tests)

Most runs in a day

475-2	Day 2 at The Oval, 1934
471-9	Day 3 at The Oval, 1921
458-3	Day 1 at Headingley, 1930
455-1	Day 1 at Headingley, 1934
436-7	Day 2 at The Oval, 1921
435-4	Day 1 at The Oval, 1899

Most wickets in a day

27	Day 2 at Lord's, 1888
25	Day 1 at Melbourne, 1902
24	Day 2 at The Oval, 1896
22	Day 1 at The Oval, 1890

Best bowling strike rates in Ashes Tests

38.1	William Bates (England)
42.2	John Ferris (Australia)
42.8	Billy Barnes (England)
42.9	George Lohmann (England)
43.3	Dean Headley (England)
45.6	Craig McDermott (Australia)

Longest innings in Ashes Tests

797 minutes	Len Hutton	364 for England at The Oval, 1938
762 minutes	Bobby Simpson	311 for Australia at Old Trafford, 1964
727 minutes	Bob Cowper	307 for Australia at Melbourne, 1966
683 minutes	Ken Barrington	256 for England at Old Trafford, 1964
649 minutes	Sid Barnes	234 for Australia at Sydney, 1946
629 minutes	Geoffrey Boycott	191 for England at Headingley, 1977

INDEX OF PEOPLE

ACKNOWLEDGEMENTS

I would like to thank all at Octopus Publishing Group for their diligent work on this book especially Trevor Davies and Joanne Wilson. Duncan Hamilton's biography of Harold Larwood and Simon Brigg's *Stiff Upper Lips* and *Baggy Green Caps* were especially useful in putting this book together and thanks also to Neil Robinson in the MCC Library for digging up so many fascinating books and reports. I would also like to commend Martin Williamson of Cricinfo for his amazing collection of historical articles.